The Art of War
in an Age of Peace

The Art of War
in an Age of Peace

U.S. Grand Strategy and
Resolute Restraint

MICHAEL O'HANLON

Yale UNIVERSITY PRESS/NEW HAVEN & LONDON

Published with assistance from the foundation established in
memory of Calvin Chapin of the Class of 1788, Yale College.

Yale University Press books may be purchased in quantity for
educational, business, or promotional use. For information,
please e-mail sales.press@yale.edu (U.S. office) or
sales@yaleup.co.uk (U.K. office).

Set in Minion type by Integrated Publishing Solutions.
Printed in the United States of America.

Library of Congress Control Number: 2020948369
ISBN 978-0-300-25677-2 (hardcover : alk. paper)

A catalogue record for this book is available from the
British Library.

This paper meets the requirements of ANSI/NISO Z39.48-1992
(Permanence of Paper).

10 9 8 7 6 5 4 3 2 1

For Bruce Jones, who convinced me to write this;
Suzanne Maloney, who followed Bruce in leading the Foreign Policy
program at Brookings while I wrote this in Covid-19 lockdown;
and Richard Bush, who retired in 2020 after a fantastic career during
which he taught me so much, as a scholar, role model, and friend.

Contents

Acknowledgments

M ore than anything else I've ever written, this book is the result of a lifetime of education and learning. So many have helped—parents, professors, students, policy makers, colleagues, friends, even the occasional foe (or at least sparring partner). With huge thanks to all. And particular thanks for reviewing the manuscript or otherwise helping me with key ideas and chapters to Madiha Afzal, Herb Allen, Herbert Allen, John Allen, Jeff Bader, Célia Belin, Alan Berube, Annika Betancourt, Steve Biddle, Sarah Binder, Bruce Blair, Bill Bradley, Hal Brands, Tom Brokaw, Duncan Brown, Thomas Burke, William Burke-White, William Burns, Richard Bush, Daniel Byman, Kurt Campbell, Victor Cha, Jaya Chatterjee, Tarun Chhabra, Amy Chua, Jim Cunningham, Jim Dobbins, David Dollar, Rush Doshi, Michael Doyle, Joseph Dunford, Chesley Dycus, Robert Einhorn, Fede Saini Fasanotti, Hal Feiveson, Vanda Felbab-Brown, Jeff Feltman, Michele Flournoy, Lindsey Ford, Jason Fritz, Bill Gale, Bill Galston, Jennifer Garner, David Gerken, James Goldgeier, David Gordon, Phil Gordon, Mike Green, Steve Hadley, Ron Haskins, Ryan Hass, Steve Heydemann, Fiona Hill, Martin Indyk, Robert Jervis, Bruce Jones, Bob Kagan, Fred Kagan, Kim Kagan, Marvin Kalb, Mara Karlin, Bob Kerrey, Jamie Kirchick, Bruce Klingner, Cheng Li, Ken Lieberthal, Maya MacGuineas, Tanvi Madan, Giovanna de Maio, Jim Mattis, Amy McGrath, H. R. Mc-

Master, Shelagh Meehan, Karim Mezran, Jim Miller, Mark Muro, Ron Neumann, Sam Nunn, Jung Pak, Bill Perry, David Petraeus, Steve Pifer, Jonathan Pollack, Kenneth Pollack, Richard Reeves, Eric Reid, Molly Reynolds, Bruce Riedel, Andrea Rice, Susan Rice, Alice Rivlin, Dave Robinson, Lori Robinson, Frank Rose, Natan Sachs, Belle Sawhill, Kori Schake, Chris Schroeder, Jeremy Shapiro, Mireya Solis, Tom Stefanick, Jim Steinberg, Constanze Stelzenmueller, Omer Taspinar, David Victor, Frank von Hippel, Fred Wehrey, Tamara Wittes, Jessica Worst, Tom Wright, Sean Zeigler, Dirk Ziff, and my family.

Preface

The Education of a Defense Analyst

I have now worked in Washington, D.C., for more than three decades. In that time, four earth-shattering geostrategic happenings have taken place: the fall of the Berlin Wall followed by the dissolution of the Warsaw Pact and the Soviet Union, the 9/11 attacks and aftermath, the financial crisis and great recession, and now the Covid-19 crisis. More gradually, but still fast by historical standards, China returned to a greatness it had not displayed in centuries, and Russia returned to rivalrous and dangerous geopolitics. All these events occurred as the digital revolution transpired. America also elected its first African American to the White House, followed by perhaps its most maverick president ever. The era was supposed to have been characterized by "the end of history," as Francis Fukuyama wrote in a 1989 article with that title. Instead, it has left many of us breathless at the pace of events.

On the above list of transformative developments since 1989, the coronavirus's place is not yet clear. My sense is that it may rank as even more important than the financial crisis and 9/11 attacks but perhaps slightly less tectonic in lasting significance than developments with Russia and China. It is far too soon to be sure. In any case, the book's main arguments, and its origins, do not derive from the recent, and ongoing, pandemic experience—though the world clearly has been substantially changed for the foreseeable future by that experience.

This book is an effort to wrestle with the question of U.S. grand strategy—the country's overall plan for ensuring its national safety and security—for the decade of 2020s. It does so even before the dust has begun to settle from that huge Covid-19 development as well as four years of President Donald J. Trump. But then again, in modern times at least, the dust never really settles before the next geopolitical transformation. Any U.S. grand strategy requires enough suppleness to adapt to the next big thing when it arrives—without losing sight of the significance of previous events and enduring conditions. Ideally, it will allow us to strengthen the nation's foundations while keeping powder dry to handle the next major crisis. My proposed grand strategy of "resolute restraint," as I describe it, is designed to do so. The emphasis is on both words in the title. Resoluteness is required to uphold firmly America's commitments to allies and its core interests like freedom of the seas. Restraint is just as important, however—in trying to avoid drawing first blood in any great power crisis, by generally avoiding further expansion of alliances even as we doggedly protect those that already exist and by seeking tough-minded yet realistic compromises on nuclear negotiations with North Korea and Iran. I also advocate complementing the Pentagon's current 4+1 threat framework (with its focus on Russia, China, North Korea, Iran, and transnational violent extremism or terrorism) with a second 4+1 list: biological, nuclear, climatic, digital, and domestic and economic dangers. This should be done without lessening our commitment to American military excellence and without substantial cuts to the defense budget. That is because these added threats do not now outrank, supersede, or diminish the others. In fact, they are likely to exacerbate and intensify them.

At a personal level, this book also reflects an attempt to start to piece together what I have learned in Washington since 1989—what LBJ's great aide and my old tennis buddy, Harry McPherson, might have called a political education, once my formal academic education was done. Over those three decades, two lessons stand out. I have on balance become even more wary of the use of force in international politics. And yet, pulling in a somewhat different direction, I have been reminded frequently of how easily the world can veer off course, threatening the amazing progress that humankind has achieved in recent decades. Usually, the origins of the security problems and crises occur between neighbors. Familiarity often breeds contempt, and proximity often whets countries' strategic appetites. Thus, a distant superpower—even a flawed one—can often be a more effective arbiter and foundation of stability than can regional powers or security relationships. Ultimately, these lessons make me a strong proponent of sustained American leadership and engagement globally but a skeptic on most specific possible uses of force. Hence the oxymoronic title of the book.

My first real Washington job was at a fantastic organization known as the Congressional Budget Office, created by Congress in the aftermath of Watergate and Vietnam and built by the formidable Alice Rivlin as well as her deputy (and later my boss there) Robert Reischauer. They are two of the most remarkable public servants I have ever met. After Saddam Hussein invaded Kuwait in August 1990, and President George H. W. Bush prepared a military response, a team of us at CBO was charged by Senator James Sasser of the Senate Budget Committee with estimating the cost of Operation Desert Storm *before* it occurred. Even though the United States had no treaty obligations to Kuwait, Bush courageously concluded that the aggression could not stand in the new world order that he was hoping to help build. But Congress had not yet decided how it felt about a conflict that some believed could resemble World War I—if not in scale or duration, then in style of combat, with trench lines and chemical weapons and intense close-quarters fighting. Our study for Sasser calculated that the cost to the United States might be some $28 billion to $86 billion, in the dollars of the day.[1]

My contribution to the effort, working with great analysts, including Lane Pierrot, Fran Lussier, and our immediate boss, Bob Hale, built on methods that outstanding professors Frank von Hippel, Hal Feiveson, Joshua Epstein, Aaron Friedberg, Richard Ullman, Barry Posen, and Steve Walt had just taught me in graduate school at Princeton. We followed a philosophy like that described by the famed defense analysts Alain Enthoven and K. Wayne Smith in their seminal book, *How Much Is Enough?*[2] Enthoven and Smith counseled that it is better, in defense analysis, to be "roughly right" rather than "precisely wrong." Given the uncertain nature of military matters, they argued, it is always better to make assumptions simple and clear and to use methodologies that are sufficiently straightforward that they can be understood and debated. They also insisted on framing all predictive calculations in defense analysis—for likely casualties in war or costs of weapons or many other things—with a range of values. There should be upper and lower bounds or optimistic and pessimistic estimates, not a single prognostication that implied false precision in the computation. The actual cost of Operation Desert Storm wound up almost exactly in the middle of that range (and was ultimately paid primarily by foreign governments).

The lesson? For that kind of limited war, some degree of credible prognostication is possible, with the right analytical tools and a strong dose of humility about how accurate one can aspire to be. The mission of Desert Storm seemed well defined, circumscribed, and eminently doable. It was not our job at CBO to support or oppose the war. But our ability to estimate credibly the cost of a major military campaign in advance, with "only" a threefold disparity between our lower and upper bounds, derived from the finite quality of the operation. By the standards of prognosticating outcomes in war, we did a good job—but that was possible only because the likely course of the war was fairly foreseeable and because we did not try to be *too* brilliant or precise.

That kind of war has proven the exception. More often, as Thucydides and Carl von Clausewitz and others wrote about wars in their earlier eras of history, war is highly unpredictable, often expanding well beyond immediate geographic constraints, involving types of fighting not widely anticipated, and lasting far longer than initially foreseen. That is still true today.

Sensing as much, Philip Gordon and I wrote a cautionary article late in 2001 in the *Washington Post* about the likely difficulties of any campaign to overthrow Saddam. Our op-ed provoked Ken Adelman's infamous response that the war would be a "cakewalk."[3] Tragically, Ken was wrong, though Phil and I took no joy in being proven right, as Gordon has discussed in a recent and excellent book of his own.[4] In 2002, I wrote an article predicting that an Iraq war could lead to three thousand U.S. fatalities during a five-year deployment of 150,000 GIs. Both predictions proved more accurate than I would have preferred (though I did not foresee the nature or scale of the insurgency and civil war that followed Saddam's overthrow). These concerns are what led me to argue in 2002 that, if we could confirm that Iraq had no weapons of mass destruction through inspections, war should be avoided. The risks of overthrowing the murderous Saddam Hussein were, as I saw it, greater than those of leaving him in power—however tragic that latter outcome would surely be for the people of his own country.[5]

But I should have been even *more* skeptical than I was of the case for the 2003 invasion of Iraq, a mission that eventually I begrudgingly supported when the weapons of mass destruction issue could not be definitively resolved through inspections. Certainly, in my writings, I should have pushed even harder for proper preparation for what the Pentagon calls a phase 4 operation to stabilize Iraq after Saddam was deposed (phases 1 and 2 are preparatory, and phase 3 involves major combat operations—at least for this particular type of war). Critics of the decision to go to war have largely been vindicated. That said, it is important to remember that virtually all major intelligence agencies on the globe believed that Saddam had weapons of mass destruction as well as nuclear ambitions and that the sanctions regime in place since Operation Desert Storm was eroding before our eyes.[6] German intelligence, for example, thought that Saddam might have a nuclear weapon within three years, at the time Washington's decision to unseat him was made.[7] Those who favored war may have been wrong, but they were generally not foolish (except in cases where they trivialized the likely difficulty of the operation).

I had also been wary about a much smaller operation, NATO's air war to save Kosovo, in 1999. I correctly warned in the *New York Times* that, on military and strategic grounds, the alliance's initial bombing plans were unlikely to cause Slobodan Milosevic to stand down from his ethnic cleansing campaign there and that things could get much worse before getting better.[8] Alas, even this limited war went badly for a time, until the United States and allies radically revamped their approach. Ultimately, NATO prevailed. But as Ivo Daalder and I argued in our book of the same title, this was a case of "Winning Ugly." We were also all lucky that when Milosevic conducted the mass waves of ethnic cleansing after the bombs started to fall, he generally did not have his henchmen kill many people—meaning that the initial damage from the war could later be largely undone. Usually in war one is not so fortunate.

The list of educational experiences goes on. While honored to have written with my colleague Ken Pollack, after our trip to Iraq in the summer of 2007, that the U.S.-led surge there was working, I wish I had anticipated how quickly Prime Minister Nouri al-Maliki could throw away much of the progress through misgoverning in the following years.[9] The surge did work, and brilliantly so, by most realistic measures—that is, it dramatically improved the security environment so as to give politics an opportunity to heal wounds and begin to bring the country together.[10] What General David Petraeus, Ambassador Ryan Crocker, General Raymond Odierno, General Lloyd Austin, and many other Americans as well as Iraqis themselves accomplished was remarkable. However, the surge did so only at very large costs in blood and treasure. Tragically, the opportunity for greater stability that it provided was later largely jettisoned by the way Maliki then governed. Whether Iraq can recover in a way that truly redeems, from a historical perspective, the sacrifices made, by Americans and Iraqis, in the surge remains to be seen.

The same goes for Afghanistan, a place I visited even more frequently than Iraq in my research—with gratitude to all the men and women of the U.S. armed forces, the diplomats and development specialists, and organizations like the International Republican Institute as well as the many Afghans who made my trips so informative. That war is not lost as of this writing, but my hopes for what might realistically be achieved there were too optimistic.

Again, this career trajectory has made me even more cognizant of the uncertainties of war—and more wary of its use as an instrument of American national security policy—than I had been before. It is amazing how long the Iraq and Afghanistan efforts have lasted. The Afghan conflict in some ways spans my entire adult life; I can remember watching President Jimmy Carter order us all to register for the draft, after the Soviet invasion of Afghanistan, when a sophomore at Hamilton College in 1980. The various Iraq wars and operations have spanned my entire thirty-plus years in Washington. Even by a conservative reckoning, these two missions together have incurred well over $3.5 trillion in costs to the United States, and taken roughly seven thousand American lives, with major sacrifices by a number of American allies as well. Meanwhile, hundreds of thousands of Iraqis and Afghans have died.

These recent experiences have profound lessons for today. If fighting in Iraq and Afghanistan has been remarkably slow and difficult, what would combat be like against Russia or China? The danger of any such lethal military engagements is even greater, I believe, than most realize. Our efforts to find ways short of war to oppose limited acts of aggression by either should be taken far more seriously than they have been to date.

Yet the United States cannot do so by pulling back from the world, given the absence of any other credible country or bloc or organization to play the same role of strategic backstop. It strikes me that humankind's potential for evil is as great today as ever before. When I first learned about the world wars, it was in history class in the 1970s. They seemed very distant to a young boy of that era. Now, they seem *closer* in time, not further away, than they did back then. I continue to be astounded that human beings as ruthless and evil as Hitler and Stalin could seize power, dominate and decimate their own countries, and launch massive wars of aggression that killed tens of millions of people . . . and do so *in the lifetimes of my parents*. It is all unimaginable. Yet it all happened. And not so long ago, in fact.

Of course, trouble did not end with the world wars. I was a Peace Corps volunteer in the former Zaire, now the Democratic Republic of the Congo, in the early 1980s. It was the experience of a lifetime. The Congolese are amazing people, fun-loving and kind to foreigners. Yet one of their own, Mobutu Sese Seko, oppressed them and stole blatantly from the state throughout his three decades in power. Genocides occurred shortly before and after my Peace Corps service in neighboring Rwanda, Burundi, and Uganda. Tragedies continue in various places today. France, Britain, and Germany seem to have permanently buried the hatchet, but not so Japan, Korea, and China, or Russia and its neighbors, or most countries in the broader Middle East and South Asia.

It is good that the incomparable Steven Pinker at Harvard University has written pathbreaking works reminding us of all the progress humanity has achieved over the centuries, as well as the generally favorable trajectory of civilization by almost any imaginable metric. We need that encouragement in a world of tragic wars, ongoing poverty and crime, opioid crises and other deaths of despair in our own land, heartbreaking pandemics, and other catastrophes. Yet there is still something slightly too deterministic about such optimism—given how close we still are in time to the world wars, which were not predestined to be won by the world's democracies; given the dangers of nuclear weapons and other advanced technologies in today's world; given the continued prevalence of poverty and suffering around the globe even today. Even if Pinker is right that humankind continues to "eke out victories against the forces that grind us down, not least the darker parts of our own nature," it is questionable whether we are doing so fast enough to overcome the dangers of a world headed toward holding ten billion humans who are competing for scarce resources, warming the planet, and wielding more lethal weapons than ever seen before in an era in which competitive geopolitics has returned.[11]

The world is becoming more dangerous again today. As I argue in this book, I believe it is in much better shape than during the Cold War or any previous time. Pinker is right about that. Yet the trendlines are moving in the wrong direction, and relations among the nuclear powers have again become dangerous. We do need to change the direction of the geostrategic tide—lest Pinker's positive prognosis ultimately be proven wrong, as it still could be.

For security specialists, it is always tempting to close an argument by genuflecting at the altar of the great Prussian military thinker Carl von Clausewitz, who famously said, "War is a continuation of politics by other means." But I would rather end by disagreeing on that point. Even if Clausewitz was right about the world he observed and described, things need to change given the dangers of the contemporary world. The great contemporary military historian John Keegan issued a blunt riposte to Clausewitz that, in the nuclear age, makes more sense for us today: "Politics must continue. War cannot."[12] The ultimately wiser advice comes from the ancient Chinese scholar Sun Tzu, who told us that winning *without war* was the pinnacle of strategic success. We do need to continue to master the art of war, and of military preparedness. But we also need to think hard about when and how *not* to fight in order to sustain and strengthen the twenty-first-century peace.

This book lays out an American grand strategy of resolute restraint. It is resolute in its commitment to defend the core territories, populations, polities, and economies of American allies, as well as the free and open skies and oceans on which the global economy depends. It emphasizes restraint in regard to any further alliance expansion or formation, in initiation of combat operations, and in diplomatic approaches for addressing matters like the North Korean nuclear program, where pragmatism and caution are needed. The strategy thus focuses much more on shoring up the core of the *rules-based* global order than on pursuing a more ambitious *liberal order* with a multitude of progressive goals across many issue areas, countries, and regions. That I might support many of those progressive ambitions does not mean that they should dictate or heavily influence U.S. grand strategy.

The strategy of resolute restraint is heavily informed by the three most important data points of global security in the twentieth century—the outbreak of World War I, the outbreak of World War II, and the non-outbreak of World War III. American disengagement preceded the first two; American commitment, in the form of clear alliances and forward-deployed military forces, contributed enormously to the last. These are not just three data points in a sea of information. They are by far the most consequential things we know about modern international relations.

The United States might not be exceptional in the ethics or wisdom of its individual people. But given its geography, its origins, its foundational documents and principles, and its form of government, it is still the only country that can undergird the most successful global order humans have yet devised. That is the correct interpretation of American exceptionalism. Yet this undergirding must be done economically, at a time when the American polity is under severe duress from within and in an era when American overreaction can be almost as dangerous as disengagement. And it must be done with an awareness of how excessive muscularity in international politics can worsen crises as easily as deter or solve them.

Maps

Country Abbreviations

ALB. - ALBANIA
AND. - ANDORRA
BELG. - BELGIUM
K. - KOSOVO
LI. - LICHTENSTEIN
LUX. - LUXEMBOURG
M. - MONTENEGRO
MAC - MACEDONIA
MON. - MONACO
NETH. - NETHERLANDS
SLOV. - SLOVENIA
S.M. - SAN MARINO
SWITZ. - SWITZERLAND

Map 1. Europe
Map drawn by Gerry Krieg

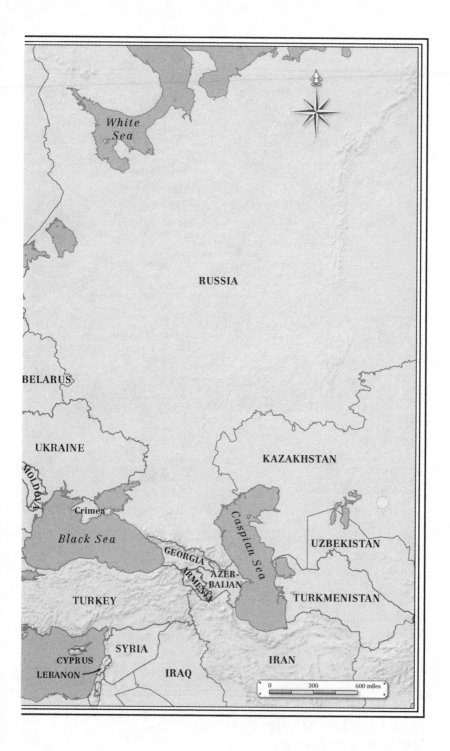

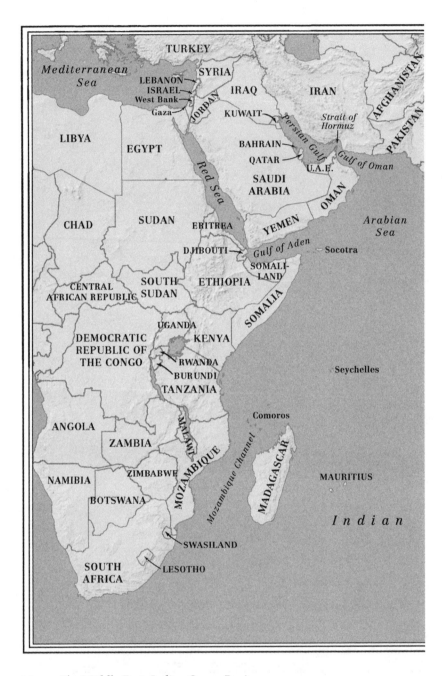

Map 2. The Middle East–Indian Ocean Region
Map drawn by Gerry Krieg

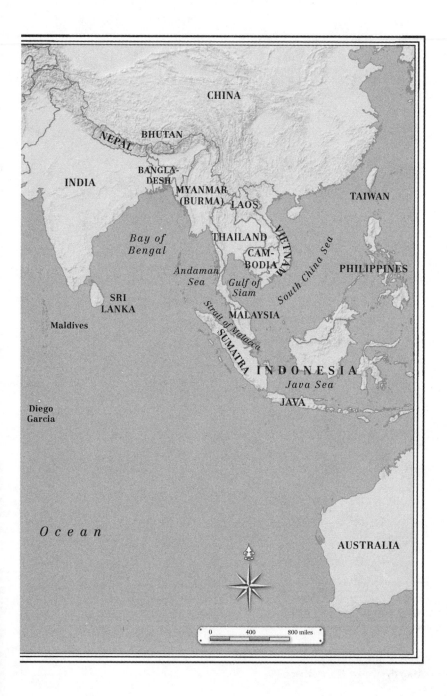

CHINA

NEPAL
BHUTAN

BANGLA-
DESH

INDIA
MYANMAR
(BURMA) LAOS
TAIWAN

THAILAND
VIETNAM

Bay of
Bengal
CAM-
BODIA

Andaman
Sea
Gulf of
Siam
PHILIPPINES

SRI
LANKA
South China Sea

Maldives
MALAYSIA

Strait of Malacca

SUMATRA
INDONESIA

Java Sea

JAVA

Diego
Garcia

Ocean

AUSTRALIA

0   400   800 miles

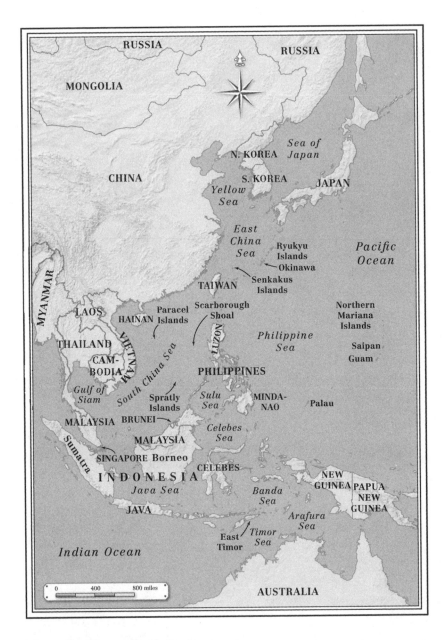

Map 3. The Western Pacific Region
Map drawn by Gerry Krieg

ONE

An Age of Fragile Peace
and an Unsure America

Winston Churchill is said to have remarked that Americans tend to come to the right answer after exhausting all the other possibilities.[1] There is often truth in this friendly critique of the United States and its foreign policy. We were unprepared for World War I, World War II, and the Korean War and had to build up military forces belatedly before retaking lost territory each time, at huge cost in blood and treasure. We fought the Korean, Vietnam, Iraq, and Afghanistan wars with many poor tactics; many Americans concluded that at least one or two of those conflicts should not have been fought at all. Our military leaders wanted to preempt against Soviet weapons (and troops) in the Cuban Missile Crisis; thankfully a young John F. Kennedy knew better and overruled the joint chiefs, likely preventing nuclear war. We were underprepared for the Covid-19 crisis as well, in terms of basic medical supplies as well as capacity for manufacturing and deploying tests—two decades after we failed to integrate intelligence in a way that might have prevented the 9/11 attacks.

Despite all these mistakes, the United States led an effort after World War II that created the most stable, prosperous, and democratic period in human history. The effort achieved a bloodless final chapter of the Cold War, as the Soviet Union effectively conceded defeat, so overwhelming was the verdict of history about which system and set of ideas should prevail. Thereafter, no major countries exited the U.S.-led Western alliance system, and many others sought to join it, especially through NATO, the North Atlantic Treaty Organization.

Even as the United States and allies struggled in the sands of the Middle East against violent extremism in the early years of the twenty-first century, the balance of power globally remained a remarkable imbalance in favor of the United States and allies. Such an enduring outcome was not necessarily predicted or expected by most prominent theorists of international relations.[2] Yet it happened. Beyond the formal alliances, the United States and India began a gradual and ongoing process of strengthening their relationship—an overdue, and highly significant, change between the world's oldest democracy and its most populous.

Great power war has not happened since World War II. There were close calls in the Cold War, but given the extremism, global ambitions, and violent mores of the Soviet Union, that is no great surprise. Civil conflict remains endemic in much of the world, especially the broader Middle East and the Sahel and central regions of Africa. Yet overall rates of violence on Earth are much lower than historical norms, as Steve Pinker and others have persuasively demonstrated, and on a per capita basis, global death rates from war are lower today than during virtually all of the Cold War.[3] For all the tragedy of Covid-19, it will not change this trendline—especially if we are smart enough to learn from it and prepare for the next pandemic. Any crisis creates opportunity for action, because it is easier to build political consensus in favor of difficult endeavors when the dangers of not doing so are palpable and visible to all.

Nuclear proliferation has continued, but slowly. John Kennedy once thought there could be twenty nuclear-weapons states by the mid-1960s and perhaps as many as twenty-five by the 1970s.[4] Two decades into the twenty-first century, there are only nine countries in possession of the bomb.

There is not a compelling case that the United States is in decline—indeed, that argument has been wrong each of the half dozen or more times it has gained traction going back at least to the 1950s.[5] Bruce Jones of the Brookings Institution and Michael Beckley of Tufts University re-

mind us of America's remarkable advantages even today: in higher education and innovation, in a strong legal underpinning for investment
and business, in geography and natural resources, through the prevalence of both the dollar and the English language in commerce around
the world, and in the way the country's melting-pot traditions give it a
strong demographic trajectory while also making it a natural magnet for
many of the world's most gifted immigrants.[6]

There are huge challenges to be sure. They include internal schisms
in the country, dramatized by the assault on the U.S. Capitol on January
6, 2021, a weakened sense of global leadership during the Trump presidency and a net reduction in favorable foreign views of America over
the past two decades typically ranging from 10 to 40 percentage points,
a floundering response to the novel coronavirus crisis that has weakened America's international legitimacy, and a fiscal situation that has
become even more foreboding due to Covid-19. The last could erode the
nation's long-term foundations of national power; it could also lead to
excessive cuts to the defense budget.[7] These concerns require substantial
attention, and they receive a good deal of it in this book. But the nation's
strengths remain remarkable.

Some would describe the U.S. international position as that of a
hegemon, invoking the ancient Greek concept and term.[8] That may be
true in one sense, if by that one means simply the country that is ahead
by most metrics in a competitive international environment. But what is
most striking about the overall U.S. position in the world is the system
of alliances it leads and the rules-based order it upholds, not American
power in some zero-sum sense. As such, I find the term "hegemon" more
wrong than right—or at least, more ripe for misunderstanding, given the
ultracompetitive type of state behavior to which terms like "hegemonic"
have classically been applied in the past. The "America first" tendencies
of the Trump administration smack more of classic hegemonic behavior, however, so it must be acknowledged that the current international
order could be threatened if such thinking continues in the future. It
should also be understood that Russia, China, and a few other American
rivals or adversaries probably *do* see the United States as hegemonic—a
perception that, whether right or wrong, we ignore at our peril.

Former President Trump, for all his flaws, did not dismantle most of what a dozen predecessors (six Democrat and six Republican) had built up since 1945. The core elements of the rules-based order are intact as of this writing in 2020. I mean that not as a compliment to Trump but rather as an observation on the resilience of some elements of the rules-based order—to date, at least.

The third wave of democracy expansion started with Spain and Portugal in the mid-1970s, then took off in Latin America, East Asia, and Eastern Europe in the 1980s.[9] But it did not stop then or there. About a third or so of African countries as well as many nations in South and Southeast Asia have by now also adopted democracy as their form of government.[10] Even during the slippage in global democracy in recent years, there have been positive trends in several important countries, including Indonesia and Pakistan. Statistically, a higher percentage of humanity now lives in countries deemed free or partly free by Freedom House than ever before.[11]

North America has remained a strategic bastion for the United States, providing a strong economic community and a safe haven from predatory neighbors. The hemisphere has serious problems, to be sure. But its main challenges in the realm of security and safety have to do with transnational crime rather than geopolitics.[12]

It is true that large parts of Asia and the broader Middle East are not converging toward liberal Western values, including in the realms of democracy as well as religious and political freedom. Nonetheless, there is widespread agreement globally about the virtues of *some degree* of trade, economic cooperation, and interdependence. This consensus has not been strong enough to supersede all centrifugal forces tearing at the seams of world order, to be sure. And on the economic front, we are now collectively in need of a new consensus that emphasizes fair trade at least as much as free trade and that ensures adequate domestic manufacturing capacity to keep the country resilient in the face of various possible threats. But the areas of accord do provide a strong centripetal force nonetheless. Despite the gradual return of history and great power competition of the past decade, the world is a far cry from the kind of truly dangerous place that characterized the leadups to the world wars last century.[13]

Despite the morasses of the Iraq and Afghanistan missions and ongoing radicalization of many individuals in the broader Middle East, al Qaeda and ISIS are much weaker than before—at least in terms of their leadership structure and their ability to plan and carry out complex attacks. The American homeland has not been hit hard again by terrorism since 9/11.[14] The world has now survived four years of maverick, intentionally disruptive leadership by POTUS 45 and a year of Covid-19 without any major trend toward anarchy or growing violence.

By 2019, according to Brookings scholar Homi Kharas, half the people on the planet reached a socioeconomic status of at least "middle class" in the respective countries of their citizenship. Coronavirus will likely set that number back somewhat for a time, with an economic downturn of about 5 percent globally estimated for 2020, including serious privation for certain populations and ripple effects for several years to follow.[15] But the antipoverty accomplishment is still remarkable and largely durable, and it will be restored. By contrast, just after World War II, only 10 percent of the world's citizens could make such a claim to relative prosperity.[16] Childhood mortality rates around the world have been cut fivefold since 1960, as one astounding indicator of improved basic health care practices and outcomes.[17] Nor has the progress slowed in more recent times. According to the Legatum Institute in London, considering 167 countries that together account for more than 99 percent of the world's population, social and economic indicators improved on balance in 148 of them between 2009 and 2019.[18]

Some are nostalgic for the Cold War, viewing it as a simpler geopolitical time. I am not of that school of thought. The Cold War was not simple or safe until perhaps the very end. It took strong U.S. leadership combined with effective deterrence to prevent superpower combat. The United States often erred badly in how it exercised that leadership, sometimes with brutal and tragic results, especially for the peoples and places where Cold War violence was most severe.[19] We should have a mixed view of the Cold War. It was an unsettled and dangerous time, considerably worse than today's world. Nonetheless, what Bob Kagan calls the "world America made" after World War II—in terms of basic security alliances, economic structures, and freedom of the seas and commerce—ultimately held firm against the communist juggernaut that sought to undercut it.

The late 1940s brought the descent of the Iron Curtain across Europe, the fall of China to communism, and the Soviet Union's acquisition of nuclear weapons—all within five years of the end of the most exhausting and deadly conflict in human history. The 1950s brought the Korean War, McCarthyism at home, huge nuclear buildups, and the revelation of how evil Stalin and his henchmen really were. If there was a Norman Rockwell moment with Ike's steady hand at the wheel of state that decade, it was brief. The 1960s and 1970s brought Vietnam and its aftermath, oil shocks and stagflation, together with the Soviet attainment of nuclear parity. They were capped off by the fall of the shah of Iran, the failed Iran hostage operation, the Soviet invasion of Afghanistan, and Jimmy Carter's declaration that any Soviet move toward the Persian Gulf would mean war. The early 1980s brought intensifying nuclear rivalry between the superpowers, aircraft downings, Beirut bombings, Central American civil wars, and a palpable sense of fear that the Cold War was becoming more rather than less dangerous. Even as the United States reached the pinnacle of geostrategic success in the late 1980s, with the Cold War winding down clearly in its favor, the great Yale historian Paul Kennedy wrote of "imperial overstretch" and the importance of managing what he saw as America's relative decline gracefully.[20] As troubled as the headlines of modern times may be, the world has in fact continued to move in generally positive directions not only since 1945 but since 1989. The Cold War wound up well, in terms of great power peace and the spread of democracy, but that outcome was not preordained and was not easily attained. Things have been better since. The U.S. leadership that emerged in World War II, became established during the Cold War, and has continued since the Berlin Wall fell has been undeniably beneficial for the planet as a whole.[21] Humankind has seen more democracy, great power peace, and prosperity than ever before in this period.

Yet the progress is at risk. In some places it has partially reversed itself, even without that possible U.S. retrenchment. And while Donald Trump has certainly not helped the situation, almost all concerning trends predated his election in November 2016. Democracy has receded from Turkey to the Philippines to Hungary and, most important, to Russia. The Arab Spring a decade ago generally fell flat, regressing into a democratic winter and civil warfare in much of the broader region.[22] For all the progress with growth, the global economy continued to suffer from serious problems of inequality, corruption, and criminal activity.[23] If half the world's population is middle class or above, half still is not. Some trends in basic human welfare are troubling, too. For example, while some 785 million people globally were considered undernourished in 2015, the number rose to 822 million by 2018.[24] And that was before Covid-19, which is setting back incomes in various places and also at least temporarily damaging democratic norms in some countries, as leaders with strongman tendencies use the coronavirus as an excuse to suspend or retract certain liberties.[25]

As the early decades of the twenty-first century unfolded, China did not continue to liberalize or gradually democratize as hoped. Thus, the bipartisan U.S. strategy dating back to Richard Nixon of trying to induce greater openness and cooperation from the People's Republic of China through engagement reached its limits.[26] We often downplay the significance of the enormous progress China has made in bettering the lives of its people. Alas, that very progress has now given it the capacity to compete with the United States and the West in a range of ways.

The vindictiveness and vitriol in U.S.-Russia relations that has been evident over the past decade would have been hard to predict during the heady days after the Berlin Wall fell. The degree and depth of animosity are quite surprising—and quite worrisome.

Moscow and Beijing are increasingly assertive in their near-abroad regions, including with their armed forces. Both also create dangerous close encounters with American military assets deployed in international airspace or waterways in the Western Pacific, eastern Europe, and the Middle East. Russia in particular is not even averse to rattling its nuclear saber from time to time. Together, those two nations, for all their differences with each other, now present something of a united front against the United States and the West on numerous issues.[27]

Pakistan and North Korea continued to expand their nuclear arsenals. Other threats from weapons of mass destruction exist, too. The United States wound up in dangerous nuclear brinkmanship with Kim Jong Un in 2017 that brought Northeast Asia closer to war than in decades. Any combat there could have quickly escalated to nuclear war in one of the most densely populated regions on the planet.

For these and other reasons, the erudite Bulletin of the Atomic Scientists in 2020 put its famous doomsday clock at one hundred seconds to midnight. That is the most foreboding reading ever.[28] I find that reading a major exaggeration. But it is hard to fault the bulletin for sounding the alarm about overall trends.

Even though interstate war is rare, there is still a good deal of violence in key parts of the world. The overall global progress toward peace seen in the early post–Cold War years has generally stalled since the 2010s.[29] There have been and continue to be more than thirty active conflicts at any given point during much of the twenty-first century.[30] More than ten have typically qualified as wars, using the standard threshold for such a designation of a thousand or more battle deaths a year. (By this methodology, there could be multiple wars in a given country, such as Syria.)[31] This remains a higher figure than in much of the twentieth century.[32] Estimated total fatalities in recent wars total in the many tens of thousands annually, according to the Peace Research Institute in Oslo and Uppsala University in Sweden.[33] Tolls are likely to worsen at least temporarily as Covid-19 runs its course in places where health care and basic sanitation resources are scarce.[34] (For sake of comparison, there have been more than four hundred thousand annual homicides worldwide in recent times—and more than a million fatalities from car accidents.)[35]

America's response to all of these difficulties has had its impressive features. Defense budgets remained strong throughout the Obama and Trump presidencies. NATO beefed up its defenses of eastern members, as well as overall levels of spending and burden sharing. No U.S. administration has wavered in its commitment to sustain America's access to the blue waters and shipping lanes of the South China Sea, even as Beijing has virtually claimed that body of water as the equivalent of a Chinese inland lake. President Trump has blustered, badgered, and threatened American allies and has scaled back U.S. military presence in Syria, with plans now to do the same in Germany. But as the Biden presidency begins, the U.S. military presence abroad will not have been dismantled in any of the major countries where it was found in 2017.

For all the justifiable criticism of the Trump administration's performance in response to Covid-19, the remarkable bipartisan cooperation among governors, mayors, and other national leaders has reminded us all what is best about America.[36] Individuals like Republicans Governor Larry Hogan of Maryland and Governor Mike DeWine of Ohio, as well as Democrats Governor Andrew Cuomo of New York and Governor Jay Inslee of Washington, experts like Dr. Anthony Fauci of the National Institute of Allergy and Infectious Diseases, and Americans volunteering and helping in their communities have shown the best of the country—and its ability to work together. Congress generally acted quickly on aid and relief packages, as did the Federal Reserve.

However, Americans are unsure and divided about the right grand strategic path going forward. If Covid-19 provides an opportunity for stitching up our wounds together, such a moment of national consensus also existed after 9/11—but it proved short-lived, and this one could as well. More broadly, Americans oscillate between wanting to be left alone and wanting to overdo it. Many hawks favor interventionism and assertiveness too instinctually. They might be inclined, for example, to forcibly evict Chinese soldiers who came ashore on an uninhabited Senkaku island, to shoot down North Korean missiles just after launch even in peacetime, to expand NATO to Ukraine and Georgia, and to preemptively destroy Iran's nuclear infrastructure with sustained airstrikes in the event of a further breakdown of the 2015 Iran nuclear deal. These are all ideas that have been voiced prominently and repeatedly in recent years. Depending on exact circumstances, I would tend to counsel against such ideas. Many hawks and military practitioners still emphasize traditional threats and types of combat, underestimating how much we will have to broaden our definition of national security threats in an era when nuclear, biological, digital, climate, and internal domestic threats have joined the conventional lists of American nemeses and enemies.

By contrast, many doves think that American military preeminence is so easily assured, or so unimportant to global stability, that the country could cut back dramatically on defense spending and overseas engagement without doing real damage. Yet others, like President Trump, support pulling back from some forward commitments to key overseas alliances in an effort to jar allies into greater military burden-sharing efforts of their own. Such temptations may be even stronger in the aftermath of Covid-19 and the nation's associated fiscal woes. Cutting the defense budget dramatically to pay for preparations against future types of threats like the novel coronavirus would, however, be a very risky idea, since the threats that have led to current defense spending levels have not yet diminished.

Polls like those of the highly reputable Chicago Council on Global Affairs generally suggest a solid core of supporters for U.S. alliances, strong American armed forces, international trade, and U.S. international leadership. Among those surveyed, 70 percent or more generally favor such instruments of national policy. But such polls may not always capture the intensity of how Americans feel when a real crisis or conflict threatens. Nor do they fully capture the willingness of those Americans who blame globalization and U.S. allies for their economic frustrations to support a much different kind of president than in the past (like Donald Trump, who campaigned in 2015 and 2016 with a disdain for alliances and for trade and then won the presidency with 46 percent of the popular vote).[37]

To be fair to hawks and doves, each group gets a lot right about American grand strategy. Hawks understand the ongoing relevance of power and the fact that there is no plausible alternative to U.S. leadership in the international security space. Doves understand that war is a last resort—and that we Americans, frankly, are often not that good at it as a nation (that is true even though the U.S. armed forces are outstanding in a technical sense). Many in both camps understand the importance of American renewal at home. If we can listen to each other's best arguments and allow our existing presumptions and biases to be challenged, there is much good grist to work with in the American strategic debate of today.

The nation needs a new consensus on U.S. grand strategy tailored to this unique moment, however—one that replaces the ragged residues of what is left from earlier periods.[38] Containment, then building a new world order, then promoting democracy and globalization, then taking on terror, then pushing back against Russia and China have all had their moments and their value. Some elements of those earlier grand strategies remain relevant today. Yet a new framing for the 2020s—the era after a return to great power rivalry, after Covid-19, after the racial tension and demonstrations of 2020, and after Trump—is now needed. It is particularly important to arrest the slide in American internationalism that, if unchecked, could erode the central foundations of global order that have prevailed since World War II.

As Jim Golby and Peter Feaver have shown, Americans still express high faith and trust in the U.S. military—by 75 percent or more. But the purposes to which that military is put are more contentious. Many Americans doubt its abilities, and even its truthfulness and trustworthiness, in regard to how the Afghanistan mission has unfolded, for example.[39] More generally, the United States today shows a type of self-doubt, or an uncertainty about its capacity to lead effectively, that may echo its outlook and behavior after World War I. Staying on this path could be tragic indeed.[40]

To be sure, grand strategy has its limits.[41] Even the containment doctrine of the Cold War had numerous competing interpretations and incarnations over the years. Although widely accepted at some level, it could not make difficult decisions for us about whether and how to fight in places such as Korea and Vietnam, how much nuclear superiority to seek against the Soviet Union, or how many simultaneous overseas war contingencies to assume in sizing and shaping the U.S. military.[42]

Grand strategy nonetheless helps American citizens understand what overall approach to the world they are being asked to support with their tax dollars and, sometimes, with the lives of their sons and daughters. It also helps us focus on those problems or potential dangers that could pose major risks to the safety and even survival of the nation along with its territory, people, and economy. Big ideas are also important because they help frame options, remind decision makers of constraints on U.S. action, direct attention and resources to some problems more than others, and seek to establish at least some connection between ends and means in a nation's foreign policy.[43] Doing so often works. For example, the Pentagon of the past five years has successfully refocused a good deal of time and money on problems related to the rise of Russia and China. Among other things, the new emphasis on great power competition led to an increase in the defense budget that might not have otherwise happened, as well as to much greater attention on the problem of rising rivals by top policy makers.[44] Thinking about grand strategy also helps highlight a nation's strengths and assets, and that exercise can improve the odds that they will be stewarded and reinforced.

A new grand strategy must sustain U.S. global leadership. That is not because the United States is so inherently virtuous. Its failings are palpable and ongoing. For all of America's mistakes, however, it is, as my remarkable colleague Bob Kagan argues, a country that is still sufficiently trustworthy, transparent in its motives, diverse in its population, democratic in its political system, and remote in its geography that it can play a relatively neutral and stabilizing role in key theaters abroad.[45] The nation's melting-pot origins, as well as the Declaration of Independence and the Constitution, reinforce the idea of a country built on ideals, not on some sense of ethnic or cultural homogeneity. Princeton professor Anne-Marie Slaughter refers to "The Idea That Is America."[46] Making such arguments is *not* the same thing as claiming that the United States is infallible or that Americans are innately exceptional or naturally peace-loving.[47] Rather, what is clear is that the nation's role is unique and, as Madeleine Albright said, indispensable.[48] The United States is large and powerful enough to be the world's superpower. We are remote enough from Eurasia not to be feared by others as overly interested in what happens there; we have no imperial designs in the vein of previous great powers in history. Yet since World War II, we have been interested enough, and present enough, to play a huge stabilizing role in many key parts of that huge landmass where most of humanity resides. The alliance system that has been created and sustained since then, while hardly without its flaws, is unprecedented both in U.S. history and in all of world history. It has also been unprecedentedly successful in dampening great power rivalry and keeping the peace.[49]

The United States champions universal values with an open, democratic system of government. Encouragingly, while American democracy makes lots of mistakes, it also usually recovers from them. That is partly because our democracy is so competitive, and combative, at times that we hold each other accountable for bad decisions and bad policy.[50] Checks and balances in different parts of the government help, too. So do election cycles that bring new blood to the White House fairly frequently. And even when we make mistakes in our foreign policy, it is generally not for reasons of imperial ambition. Other countries understand that, for the most part. While they often criticize America for its policies, they rarely fear the United States and prefer to ally with it than against it.

By comparison, the United Nations Security Council is far too divided on many tough issues, largely because China and Russia are feeling their oats and flexing their nationalistic muscles in various theaters. Europe (both the NATO and European Union versions) is too lacking in central decision-making authority and in raw military power—it has only about one-tenth the projectable military power as the United States, despite having a larger aggregate gross domestic product (GDP). It would be desirable that both the European Union and the U.N. Security Council become more effective—and Washington should promote such developments—yet it is not within America's power to ensure that will happen. Other possible geostrategic blocs are weak or nonexistent; as Brookings scholar Bruce Jones writes about one such group, made up of Brazil, Russia, India, China, and South Africa, "The BRICS have no mortar."[51] To be sure, American leadership only works if guided by moral principles, strong institutions in Washington and throughout the country, a supportive citizenry, and good judgment on the part of leaders. None of these things can or should be taken for granted. But our strengths have been enough to get us through tough times, even when leaders in Washington are seriously flawed. And there is no other candidate to play the global leadership role if the United States fails.

Some, including President Trump, complain that current arrangements lead to unequal burden sharing. The United States accounts for more than one-third of all global military spending. It currently spends more than 3 percent of gross domestic product on its military, while the typical U.S. ally averages about half that. But that 3 percent is less than Cold War norms, which averaged 5 to 10 percent—and is far less than the figures of 10 to 35 percent of GDP that typified U.S. defense spending during major wars of the twentieth century. Peace is still a bargain, even if the United States does a bit more than its fair share in ensuring it. And even though they don't tend to get as much out of their military expenditures as we do, America's allies do collectively account for almost as much defense spending as the United States. It is remarkable how large and sweeping the U.S.-led alliance system is in the post–Cold War

Table 1. Global GDP, 2019

Country	GDP (billion US$)	Global total (%)	Cumulative percentage
United States	21,440.0	25.8	25.8
NATO allies			
Canada	1,730.0	2.1	27.9
France	2,710.0	3.3	31.2
Germany	3,860.0	4.6	35.8
Italy	1,990.0	2.4	38.2
Spain	1,400.0	1.7	39.9
Turkey	774.0	0.9	40.8
United Kingdom	2,740.0	3.3	44.1
Rest of NATO[a]	4,378.6	5.3	49.4
Total NATO, excluding U.S.	19,582.6	23.4	
Total NATO	41,022.6	49.4	
Rio Pact[b]	3,805.2	4.6	54.0
Key Indo-Pacific allies			
Japan	5,150.0	6.2	60.2
South Korea	1,630.0	2.0	62.2
Australia	1,380.0	1.7	63.9
New Zealand	205.0	0.2	64.1
Thailand	529.0	0.6	64.7
Philippines	357.0	0.4	65.1
Total key Indo-Pacific allies	9,251.0	11.1	
Other security partners			
Israel	338.0	0.4	65.5
Egypt	302.0	0.4	65.9
Iraq	224.0	0.3	66.2
Pakistan	284.0	0.3	66.5
Gulf Cooperation Council[c*]	1,629.8	2.0	68.5
Jordan	44.2	0.1	68.6
Morocco	119.0	0.1	68.7
Mexico	1,270.0	1.5	70.2
Taiwan	5,860.0	0.7	70.9
India	2,940.0	3.5	74.4

Country	GDP (billion US$)	Global total (%)	Cumulative percentage
Singapore	363.0	0.4	74.8
Other nations			
Other Middle East and North Africa[d]*	338.9	0.4	75.2
Other Central and South Asia[e]*	745.7	0.9	76.1
Other East Asia and Pacific[f]	797.2	1.0	77.1
Other Caribbean and Latin America[g]*	32.4	0.0	77.1
Sub-Saharan Africa	1,755.0**	2.1	79.2
Iran	459.0	0.6	79.8
North Korea	40.0***	0.0	79.8
Venezuela	70.1	0.1	79.9
China	14,000.0	17.0	96.9
Russia	1,640.0	2.0	98.9
Indonesia	1,110.0	1.2	100.0
Other nations		25.2	
TOTAL	83,167.0	100.0	

Sources: International Institute for Strategic Studies, The Military Balance, 2020 *(New York: Routledge, 2020);* World Bank, GDP (current US$) *(Washington, D.C.: World Bank, 2020), available at https:// doi.org/10.1080/04597222.2020.1707977. These figures are not adjusted for purchasing power parity. They are based on market exchange rates. Figures may not add exactly due to rounding.*

Notes:

[a] Albania, Belgium, Bulgaria, Croatia, Czechia, Denmark, Estonia, Greece, Hungary, Iceland, Latvia, Lithuania, Luxembourg, Netherlands, Norway, Poland, Portugal, Romania, Slovakia, Slovenia

[b] Argentina, Bahamas, Bolivia, Brazil, Chile, Colombia, Costa Rica, Dominican Republic, Ecuador, El Salvador, Guatemala, Haiti, Honduras, Nicaragua, Panama, Paraguay, Peru, Trinidad and Tobago, Uruguay

[c] Bahrain, Kuwait, Oman, Qatar, Saudi Arabia, United Arab Emirates

[d] Algeria, Lebanon, Libya, Mauritania, Tunisia, Yemen

[e] Afghanistan, Bangladesh, Kazakhstan, Kyrgyzstan, Nepal, Sri Lanka, Tajikistan, Turkmenistan, Uzbekistan

[f] Brunei, Cambodia, Fiji, Laos, Malaysia, Mongolia, Myanmar, Papua New Guinea, Timor-Leste, Vietnam

[g] Antigua and Barbuda, Barbados, Belize, Guyana, Jamaica, Suriname

* At least a portion of the total cost cited here is from earlier years because 2019 data are not available

** World Bank, GDP (current US$), Sub-Saharan Africa, July 1, 2020, https://data.worldbank.org /indicator/NY.GDP.MKTP.CD?locations=ZG

*** Central Intelligence Agency, *The World Factbook, North Korea,* https://www.cia.gov/library /publications/the-world-factbook/geos/kn.html

Table 2. Global distribution of military spending, 2019

Country	Defense expenditure (billion US$)	Global total (%)	Cumulative percentage	National GDP (%)
United States	684.5	39.5	39.5	3.2
NATO allies				
Canada	18.7	1.0	40.5	1.1
France	52.2	3.0	43.5	1.9
Germany	48.5	2.7	46.2	1.2
Italy	27.1	1.5	47.7	1.3
Spain	12.9	0.7	48.4	0.9
Turkey	8.1	0.4	48.8	1.0
United Kingdom	54.7	3.1	51.9	2.0
Rest of NATO[a]	65.6	3.7	55.6	
Total NATO, excluding U.S.	287.8	16.1		
Total NATO	972.3	55.6		
Rio Pact[b]	54.5	3.1	58.7	
Key Indo-Pacific allies				
Japan	48.5	2.7	61.4	0.94
South Korea	39.7	2.2	63.6	2.44
Australia	25.4	1.4	65.0	1.8
New Zealand	2.7	0.1	65.1	1.3
Thailand	7.1	0.4	65.5	1.3
Philippines	3.4	0.2	65.7	0.9
Total key Indo-Pacific allies	126.8	7.0		
Other security partners				
Israel	19.2	1.1	66.8	5.8
Egypt	3.3	0.2	67.0	1.5
Iraq	20.4	1.2	68.2	9.1
Pakistan	10.3	0.6	68.8	3.6
Gulf Cooperation Council[c*]	95.2	5.5	74.3	
Jordan	1.6	0.1	74.4	4.6
Morocco	3.6	0.2	74.6	3.0
Mexico	5.0	0.2	74.8	0.4
Taiwan	10.9	0.6	75.4	1.8
India	60.5	3.4	78.8	2.0

Country	Defense expenditure (billion US$)	Global total (%)	Cumulative percentage	National GDP (%)
Singapore	11.2	0.6	79.4	3.1
Total	241.2	13.7		

Other nations

Non-NATO Europe	23.6	1.4	80.8	
Other Middle East and North Africa[d*]	13.4	0.8	82.0	
Other Central and South Asia[e*]	9.0	0.5	83.0	
Other East Asia and Pacific[f]	12.1	0.6	83.6	
Other Caribbean and Latin America[g*]	0.4	0.0	83.6	
Sub-Saharan Africa	17.0	1.0	84.6	
Iran	17.4	1.0	85.6	3.8
North Korea[h]	5.0	0.3	85.9	
Syria/Venezuela*	3.0	0.0	85.9	
China[i]	181.1	10.4	96.3	1.3
Russia	48.2	2.7	99.0	2.9
Indonesia	7.4	0.4	99.4	0.7
Other nations	337.55	20.0		
TOTAL	1,732.4		100.0	

Sources: International Institute for Strategic Studies, The Military Balance, 2020 (New York: Routledge, 2020), 529–534; World Bank, GDP (current US$) (Washington, D.C.: World Bank, 2020), available at https://doi.org/ 10.1080/04597222.2020.1707977. These figures are not adjusted for purchasing power parity. They are based on market exchange rates. Figures may not add exactly due to rounding.

Notes:

[a] Albania, Belgium, Bulgaria, Croatia, Czechia, Denmark, Estonia, Greece, Hungary, Iceland, Latvia, Lithuania, Luxembourg, Netherlands, Norway, Poland, Portugal, Romania, Slovakia, Slovenia

[b] Argentina, Bahamas, Bolivia, Brazil, Chile, Colombia, Costa Rica, Dominican Republic, Ecuador, El Salvador, Guatemala, Haiti, Honduras, Nicaragua, Panama, Paraguay, Peru, Trinidad and Tobago, Uruguay

[c] Bahrain, Kuwait, Oman, Qatar, Saudi Arabia, United Arab Emirates

[d] Algeria, Lebanon, Libya, Mauritania, Tunisia, Yemen

[e] Afghanistan, Bangladesh, Kazakhstan, Kyrgyzstan, Nepal, Sri Lanka, Tajikistan, Turkmenistan, Uzbekistan

[f] Brunei, Cambodia, Fiji, Laos, Malaysia, Mongolia, Myanmar, Papua New Guinea, Timor-Leste, Vietnam

[g] Antigua and Barbuda, Barbados, Belize, Guyana, Jamaica, Suriname

[h] North Korea value is an author estimate

[i] Some estimates for China are $30–$50 billion higher

* At least a portion of the total cost cited here is from earlier years because 2019 data are not available

world—accounting for roughly two-thirds of world GDP and total world military spending. Other countries have chosen, for the most part, not to balance against American power but to perceive that, because the United States was not a threat to them, they were better off joining its side than opposing it.[52]

Yet any grand strategy must bear in mind the stressed state of American politics that go well beyond Trump. Polling data over the decades show much less trust and belief in Washington's ability to rise to the occasion. Americans' trust in government was in the 75 to 80 percent range during the Eisenhower, Kennedy, and early Johnson years. The overall trend has been demonstrably downward ever since. Public faith in Washington bottomed out at the end of the Carter presidency at about 25 percent. Ronald Reagan restored it somewhat, to around 45 percent, and it got back to that level in the latter Bill Clinton and early George W. Bush years. However, over the past fifteen years, trust has been weaker than ever before in the modern era. The Iraq war, financial meltdown, polarization during the Barack Obama years, and now President Trump have driven Americans' faith in their government below 20 percent today.[53] And in economic terms, the working and middle classes in America have not generally uniformly benefited from the trends in globalization and automation of the last generation. Many now doubt the American dream.[54] Many also doubt how well Washington policy makers, including foreign policy experts, understand their concerns.[55] Numerous supporters of not only President Trump but Senator Bernie Sanders—who has led an almost equally improbable and powerful maverick political movement—feel this way. So do other Americans.

In summary, there is a strong case for resoluteness and engagement. That means a robust U.S. defense budget, vigilant military modernization, sustainment of existing alliances, continued small-scale military engagement in the broader Middle East against violent extremism and Iranian predation, and a strengthening of economic resiliency at home. It also means a greater focus on American leadership regarding the twenty-first-century threats that are becoming more and more evident with time, to encompass pandemic disease and climate change, among other things. But there is also a powerful argument for restraint—

especially in our national uses of force, with all the costs in blood and treasure they generally imply, further expansion of alliances, and American diplomatic goals.[56] Making that case in the abstract, though, is different than explaining how to achieve it in practice—and it is in that intersection of the theoretical with the practical where important decisions about U.S. national security policy will be made. Doing so requires concrete and specific policies and decisions about a given alliance, adversary, diplomatic challenge, or possible military intervention. Among other things, I argue for:

- A new approach to European security that would stop expanding NATO into former Soviet space;
- A pragmatic deal to cap verifiably rather than eliminate completely the North Korean nuclear arsenal in exchange for a partial lifting of sanctions;
- An approach to war-fighting that would seek to avoid drawing first blood in great power conflict even if Russia or China seizes (nonviolently) a small piece of allied territory; and
- A revamped nuclear deal with Iran that would do more than simply restore the 2015 Joint Comprehensive Plan of Action, instead indefinitely extending the limitations on Iranian nuclear activity that will soon expire under existing stipulations—but at the same time, without unrealistically expecting a complete change in all other aspects of Iranian behavior before lifting sanctions.

There is also a compelling need for renewal at home. America is divided and weakening at the foundations. The troubles on the home front are not unprecedented, but they are severe. In recent months, they have become much worse in notable ways. Covid-19 badly damaged the United States, its vulnerable populations, and its economy. Then, in the spring of 2020, domestic problems added insult to injury. The heinous killing of George Floyd in Minneapolis on May 25, and other tragic murders of African Americans, revealed and exacerbated problems in race relations, policing, and criminal justice.

As Richard Haass has rightly argued, foreign policy begins at home. Repairing the home front will take real resources and sacrifice, especially from those of us who have benefited so much from a globalized economy that has not treated all of our fellow Americans nearly so kindly. Before getting to such matters, however, I first lay out the broad logic for my proposed U.S. grand strategy of resolute restraint.

TWO

A Grand Strategy of Resolute Restraint

Thisplanet has never been a more peaceful or prosperous place for human beings to live. Yet globalization and shared prosperity are no guarantees of peace, especially when countries begin to doubt the future benefits of economic interdependence, as the outbreak of World War I should have proved for good.[1] Nuclear weapons make all-out war unthinkable—but that fact can encourage risk-taking behavior by adventurists who believe other nations will not have the nerve to stand up to them. The fact that democracies do not tend to fight each other is of great significance in a world composed mostly of democracies.[2] Unfortunately, democracies can regress. And America's main nemeses today—ISIS and al Qaeda, Iran, North Korea, China, even Russia—are not democracies in any event. China's rise is at once a hugely impressive phenomenon that has improved life for hundreds of millions in a way the United States should applaud (and take some credit for). Yet at the same time it is a potentially foreboding geopolitical development that is producing a second not altogether friendly superpower.

The territorial stakes over which great powers compete today are smaller than they were before World War I, in earlier eras of Nazi and Japanese aggression, or during the subsequent Soviet-led communist aspiration for global dominance.[3] Yet as Brookings scholar Tom Wright argues, the fact that Russia and China think in terms of strategic spheres of influence is dangerous, because large-scale security orders tend to break down in specific places over specific crises. In addition, ambitious great powers tend to increase their definitions of their own spheres of influence over time.[4] Even if to some extent relations with Russia and China may have partly settled into a new normal of tension from Ukraine to Syria to the East China Sea and South China Sea to cyberspace in recent years, with relatively fewer new areas of strategic contestation since the mid-2010s, that new normal is too unsettled and fraught for us to be comforted.

Against this backdrop, Americans need to remember, and improve on, the art of war in order to keep the peace.[5] But in doing so, we should also remember this *is,* at least by the standards of history, an age of great power peace. It is important not to overreact to problems and not to worry so much about short-term crises that we lose sight of broader trends, new types of security threats, and fundamental determinants of long-term national power. Part of the art of war is knowing when not to fight, instead employing the full range of instruments of statecraft, including the nation's fine diplomatic corps, so that violent uses of force can be limited in number and scale. Yet American strategic culture leans toward an overly assertive interpretation of the nation's role in the world as well as its security commitments. For example, mutual-defense obligations in some alliances, like article 5 of the Washington or NATO Treaty, are widely interpreted to mean that U.S. armed forces would have to respond quickly and violently to even the smallest incursion by an adversary. Concepts at the Pentagon, like weakening an aggressor during the contact and blunt phases of a future conflict, could lead to a situation in which predetermined war plans unnecessarily turn small-scale crises into all-out wars very quickly—echoing the outbreak of World War I more than that of World War II.

American grand strategy—the country's overall approach to ensuring its national security against physical threats—should reflect these competing realities.[6] Its central goal should be, of course, to protect the people, territory, polity, and economy of the United States against clear and present dangers as well as looming and often more insidious threats. But to do this, history strongly suggests that the United States should try to uphold a global order in which major wars are rare or nonexistent, most major powers are friendly toward the United States and certainly not aligned against it in military terms, weapons of mass destruction are in the fewest and safest hands possible, and vigilance is maintained against new kinds of dangers that could arise as well. Otherwise, trends in geopolitics could eventually put the United States at risk, even if in the short term it was not attacked or otherwise threatened.

To achieve such safety, the United States should be dogged in the defense of the central elements of the existing rules-based global order. These include the sovereignty and safety of allies, ensured access for all to the global commons, and control of the world's most dangerous technologies. These are the ways to ensure that major wars do not occur and hostile power blocs do not develop against the United States.

By contrast, the United States can and should be more patient in promoting values, or what some call a liberal order. It should generally not advance these goals with military force. Nor should it generally use the expansion of military alliances, and with them profound security obligations, to promote democracy or champion human rights in faraway countries of minor strategic importance.

The world is dangerous, yes. However, on balance, the United States is in a strong strategic position. It should be vigilant, and highly engaged internationally, with a very strong and constantly improving military. But it should also be patient and calm, knowing that most of the quieter forces of history are still gradually advancing many of the goals and values it champions.

The United States should also have greater self-awareness. It should understand that many of its strategic actions and aspirations are seen in a less charitable light, especially in Moscow and Beijing, than it intends.

The Big Idea

For today's world, the United States needs a grand strategy that might be called resolute restraint, with an equal emphasis on both words.

Washington should not retrench or pull back from the world in implementing such a strategy. Its best chance, and the world's best chance, for a sustained period of great power peace, continually increasing prosperity at home and abroad, and multilateral success in addressing new security threats is through an engaged and resolute foreign policy that displays strong American leadership—yet while also knowing when to be patient, avoid actions that could contribute to escalating crises, and play for the long game.

Restraint should characterize the nation's decisions on the use of force, including whether to go to war and whether to escalate once involved in combat. The United States should be wary about firing the first shot in any war, especially against nuclear-armed powers, and should rethink concepts of all-out victory to which it has become so accustomed ever since World War II. Generally, it should first look to every other tool of statecraft—including redeployments and reinforcements of military force, imposition of various types of economic sanctions, and diplomacy. If and when war against another nuclear-armed state occurs, conflict termination and deescalation will generally be higher priorities than outright victory.

A philosophy of restraint would also generally argue against any further expansion of America's alliances—especially in terms of membership but also in the functions those alliances are asked to play in support of the global security order. And it should counsel pragmatic compromise on contentious matters of international diplomacy, including nuclear negotiations with North Korea and Iran. On some of these matters, American allies often have considerable sophistication and good instincts on the approach to take. Washington should get better at listening to them—not always heeding their advice but consistently mulling it over thoughtfully. That is often true of South Korea with regard to North Korea, Australia and South Korea with regard to China, and Germany, France, and other European allies with regard to Russia and Iran, for example.

Resoluteness should define America's ongoing commitments to the core security interests of existing allies. For the most part, we are where we are with allies and alliances. Grand strategists sometimes inventory America's existing alliances, suggesting that we keep some and discard others. While theoretically useful at a certain level, this is generally not a practical exercise except in extreme circumstances. The credibility of deterrence and the essence of U.S. nuclear nonproliferation policy both necessitate a certain dependability and consistency in upholding treaty-undergirded alliance relationships when the core safety and security of alliance partners are put at risk. However, upholding obligations to allies does *not* necessarily mean using violence to come to their military defense at the first sign of trouble or even the first small probing attack by an aggressor. Nor does it mean being entrapped by an ally that has unwisely provoked a crisis with a neighbor and then subsequently expects Uncle Sam to come rescue its chestnuts from the fire.

Resoluteness should also characterize the country's commitment to a global rules-based order that promotes interdependence among nations while strongly opposing interstate conflict or the pursuit of territorial aggrandizement by other powers. We can be more patient, and accept incremental progress, on building a more *liberal* order (featuring more democracies and greater universal respect for human rights). The liberal or progressive agenda can and should be pursued, but largely through diplomatic and other soft-power instruments of statecraft.

The essence of the *rules-based* order is the prevention of interstate war and the protection of what Barry Posen calls the global commons—the sea lanes and other international space that make possible safe travel, global commerce, and the functioning of the world economy. The rules-based order must also include control of the world's most dangerous technologies. And, as we move deeply into the twenty-first century, it clearly must also include attention to worsening trends with pandemic disease, climate change, and other outgrowths of a rapidly growing, urbanizing, and globalizing human population.

The distinction in these two types of orders is crucial from the perspective of grand strategy. While progress toward a liberal order may have slowed or partly reversed in modern times, a rules-based order is still in fairly good shape. Today's international environment, with its nuclear weapons and memories of the world wars and shared prosperity—as well as the U.S. leadership that undergirds it all—is much different than previous eras in human history.[7]

A grand strategy of resolute restraint would seek to emulate many of the ideas of George F. Kennan, often called the father of Cold War containment doctrine. Kennan believed in a strong U.S. international role, to be sure. But his views were nuanced. His thinking included three often underappreciated ideas that should centrally inform American grand strategy today.[8]

First, some parts of the world are inherently more important strategically than others, and these should be prioritized in U.S. national security policy. Kennan emphasized western Europe, Japan, and Russia given the geopolitics of the day in which he wrote. Today, parts of East Asia and, to a certain extent, the Middle East might be logically added to the list. Kennan was not the first American to think this way, but he had the advantage of writing when his vision could help shape near-term decisions on creating the key edifices of post–World War II global order.[9]

Second, military alliances can be advantageous. But they should be used selectively and largely in defense of the key strategic regions. Since the United States has its most sacred and solemn alliance relationships in Europe and East Asia and its most important security partnerships throughout much of the broader Middle East, it would appear to be in fairly good standing in regard to these pillars of Kennan's strategic framework, adapted for the 2020s.

Third, economic instruments of statecraft are just as important as military tools in making national security policy. And strong economic foundations are essential to a nation's military prowess and long-term national security. Economic resilience against various shocks, natural or manmade, is crucial for both America and its allies.[10]

This grand strategy should not weaken the nation's commitment to military power. In some situations the United States would have no choice but to fight. And since it is far preferable to avoid fighting where possible, deterrence through military power will remain crucial for a number of problems. Defending NATO and East Asian allies tops the list.

In addition, ideally the United States would sustain enough military superiority over Russia and China to deny them the capacity to conquer the Baltic states and Taiwan, respectively—goals that, as Bridge Colby and Wes Mitchell rightly say, are worth pursuing.[11] Yet for the latter types of scenarios, we need other options, too. I am not as confident as Colby, Mitchell, or the Trump administration's National Defense Strategy that the United States will be able to establish, or reestablish, a clear capacity to predominate in the most demanding scenarios. Predicting outcomes in war is an inherently fraught business. Historically, outgunned militaries often win battles or wars against the odds. The precision of combat forecasting tools is, as discussed in the preface, not excellent.[12] That is because war is inherently a complex and highly uncertain human undertaking. It is far less amenable to prediction than, say, even major sporting events (where at least opposing sides have similar numbers of contestants and play by the same rules within well-defined physical spaces over limited periods of time). Prudent predictions of battle outcomes must allow for ranges of casualties, war duration, and other key variables that can vary by a factor of two, three, five, or even ten from lower to upper bounds. Being confident in advance of who will win and who will lose is generally not possible, except when initial capabilities are highly lopsided (and even then, insurgents or other underdogs may at times prevail against major powers).[13]

Modern technologies, such as the precision offensive weapons that leave fixed airfields and perhaps large naval combatants highly vulnerable given the current state of defense technologies, compound the problem seriously.[14] War games and computations suggest that U.S. military campaigns to defend the Baltics or Taiwan might fail today, at least short of all-out escalation. That will likely remain true given trends in precision-strike technology, as well as the economic and technological rise of China in particular. Russia has fewer economic strengths, but it still has dramatic geographic advantages for Baltic-state and several other scenarios.[15]

The National Defense Strategy of the Trump administration, like the Third Offset of the later Obama administration years, seeks to revitalize U.S. military superiority over Russia and China, especially in the conventional or nonnuclear military realm. That is all to the good. But what degree of success is realistic?

Today's American military establishment and national security community tend to hew to the belief that being able to defeat China or Russia in combat wherever an ally might be attacked is a credible goal. This prevalent opinion requires rethinking in light of fundamental technological trends and the military resources available to Russia and especially China. Secretary James Mattis was likely correct when he argued, in the Trump administration's National Defense Strategy in January 2018, that America's competitive edge vis-à-vis other great powers had been eroding in recent years. However, that does not mean that a 10 percent, or even 25 or 50 percent, increase in the U.S. defense budget, along with modest reallocations of current military priorities, can in and of itself change that fact—or change it enough to restore U.S. military preeminence in all regions next to Russian and Chinese territory. Primacy as we knew it in the 1990s and 2000s, or the late 1940s, is probably gone for good. Those earlier eras were unnatural in a sense, given the unusual weakness of many other powers—especially America's adversaries and neutral states—during those time periods. They cannot be reestablished.

Trends in technology, combined with Russian and Chinese strategic ambitions and geographic advantages, require a fuller reconceptualization of American grand strategy. Even some of the most creative ideas in defense thinking today, such as those emphasizing the need for more distributed, stealthy platforms involving mixes of manned and unmanned systems with improved weaponry and electronic warfare assets, seem more likely to mitigate the trends in warfare and technology than to reverse them.[16] Operating effectively near a major power's territory in wartime will remain very hard—much harder, for example, than was the case for the United States near China's coasts throughout the twentieth century. Make no mistake: the United States and allies can be competitive and quite likely superior, even in areas close to Russia and China, for many years to come if not indefinitely. But given the uncertainties of war, even a significant advantage need not translate into a guaranteed ability to prevail—and especially not at reasonable cost. We can certainly make these areas contested zones where no one can operate safely, as former John McCain aide Chris Brose has convincingly also argued. It is less clear that we can decisively defeat a superpower foe near Taiwan or the eastern Baltics.[17]

General U.S. military preeminence, as well as the ability to help ensure the core territorial sovereignty of key allies, is one thing. Being able to guarantee rapid victory anywhere, anytime is another. The former is attainable and important. The latter is not.

With a grand strategy that increased the emphasis on economic and other instruments of national power, Washington would in a sense just be catching up with Beijing and Moscow.[18] Russia has used economic punishment tactics against Ukraine in the energy and banking sectors, employed cyberattacks against a number of NATO countries, and interfered in Western elections through various methods of information war-fare. China has used economic coercion against a number of its neigh-bors. It banned shipments of rare earth metals to Japan for a time in 2010, froze imports of Norwegian salmon after the Chinese dissident Liu Xiaobo won the Nobel Peace Prize that same year, restricted imports and tourists from the Philippines over a dispute concerning the Scar-borough Shoal in the South China Sea in 2012, and punished South Korea economically after the deployment of a U.S. THAAD (terminal high altitude area defense) missile system to Seoul in 2016–17.[19] It has also stolen intellectual property from more advanced nations, not only to close the military-technological gap with the West but to advance its own economy. Its Belt and Road Initiative is in part a desirable effort to build up infrastructure from which many can benefit. But it is also a mercantilist means by which Beijing can maximize economic opportu-nities as well as strategic sway—making it harder for countries to chal-lenge China in future security crises or influence campaigns.[20] The United States should use transparency, information, and diplomacy—not mili-tary force or alliance formation—to oppose the more exploitative ele-ments of the initiative and help other countries hold China to a higher standard. It might create a database tracking major Belt and Road proj-ects and evaluating each one according to internationally established technical criteria for best practices—with a presumption that secret deals are not up to snuff.

But again, the larger point is that Russia and China clearly realize that economics is at the heart of national power and of national security policy. The United States itself has understood this same fact very well in the past, such as during the Cold War. Thus I am not proposing a radi-cally new theory so much as suggesting that we dust off, enhance, and expand old ideas for modern times.

This strategy would often emphasize deterrence by *punishment*, more than deterrence by *denial*, of an adversary's ambitions or objec-tives for certain small-scale aggressions. Deterrence by denial, though a popular concept in current Pentagon conversation, is simply not real-istic for all plausible and important scenarios in waters near China (or many regions near Russia). The advantages of geography, and possibility of using duplicity and stealth to create faits accomplis, render unrealistic a military strategy of denial. That is especially true in regard to small land formations like islands in the Western Pacific or small towns and enclaves near Russia in parts of central and eastern Europe.

Yet a strategy of deterrence by punishment can still work. It would seek to make the prospects of sanctions so severe that an adversary would not consider it worth undertaking even an aggression that it could likely get away with. With deterrence by punishment, ideally America's foes would suffer more than the U.S.-led coalition imposing the costs, even if they retaliated in kind. But it is actually not essential that they suffer more than America and allies, provided that the threat to apply such punishment is credible. The Western world is collectively so much stronger than Russia or even China—indeed, even the China of 2030 or 2040—that an effective sanctions-based policy need not literally hurt the other side more than it hurts oneself. What is important is that the punishment be significant, with the potential to be intensified, broadened, and sustained if need be.

The United States and allies have many types of economic tools—and they have generally gotten much better at applying them more surgically and effectively in the twenty-first century. As Cornell professor Jonathan Kirshner pointed out in an influential article two decades ago, sanctions can be categorized in various ways, to include:

- Economic aid (and the withdrawal of aid);
- Asset freezes or seizures;
- Finance (and withholding access to it, including through U.S. banks);
- Monetary policy (targeting a country's currency); and
- Trade in goods (finished or intermediate manufactures or commodities).[21]

Of course, sanctions can be overused and misused. The Trump administration's rather indiscriminate and widespread use of tariffs and other sanctions against friend, foe, and neutral alike was not sound.[22] With a more selective approach, however, Washington should be able to sustain a strong Western coalition conducting various forms of economic sanctions and indeed warfare—as has been the case, for example, in regard to Russia's aggressions since 2014, against North Korea especially since 2017, and against Iran until the 2015 Joint Comprehensive Plan of Action was negotiated.[23]

A strategy emphasizing indirect and asymmetric military tools as well as economic instruments of warfare could be gradually amplified and broadened if a crisis continued. For example, if Russia assaulted a town or small swath of a Baltic state (but with limited territorial implications, at least at first), an initial NATO and EU response should not be violent. It should have military elements, to be sure—reinforcements of NATO military positions in the Baltics, including with some forces near the initial Russian foray. But their size and character should be designed not to reverse the Russian land grab so much as to complicate and deter any further encroachment. The heart of the U.S., NATO, and EU response should curtail Russian oil and gas exports to Europe. Indeed, that punishment would be the most active, dynamic part of the strategy, with the capacity to be ratcheted up and down. If the situation were not resolved quickly, the cutback could turn into a complete ban on energy trade; Europe is now much better positioned to weather such economic warfare than it once was. Still later, if Russia tried to compensate by expanding energy exports, say to China, then secondary Western sanctions could be placed on the PRC. Such a two-front economic war would be challenging, to be sure—but it would be much more doable for the United States and allies than the possibility of a two-front *military* campaign. Imagine, for example, a case in which a U.S.-led coalition reacted to a Russian probing attack in the Baltics with a huge military effort that then left the United States ill-prepared to mount a comparable response on the other side of the world if Beijing then perceived a window of opportunity for aggression.

Yet for all the appeal of such strategies, and for all the dangers of relying too much on the sword for small-scale crises, U.S. military commands currently make little use of the economic instruments of statecraft. The U.S. government is mostly stovepiped when it comes to contingency planning.[24] Sanctions and related tools are generally seen as the policy domain of agencies such as the Treasury Department, the Office of the U.S. Trade Representative, and the Committee on Foreign Investment in the United States. They tend not to be viewed as instruments of warfare, or alternatives or complements to the application of military force in national security crises.

The new strategy of resolute restraint would embed economics experts from other home agencies within war-fighting commands and the Pentagon's joint staff. It would also consider the following changes in government structure or practice. First, it would create war-planning cells within nonmilitary agencies; although these cells will by necessity be small and focused more on big-picture ideas than on detailed development or implementation of policy, they can among other things function as helpful red teams to challenge Pentagon thinking. Second, it would emphasize economics much more in the curricula of war colleges. By economics, I do not mean macroeconomic or microeconomic theory the way economists tend to teach it, so much as understanding of the detailed workings of the modern global economy. Third, it would create new positions at the National Security Council (NSC) to focus on economics as a tool of security policy—and to focus on broader threats like those discussed below that go beyond the Pentagon's 4+1 list of Russia, China, North Korea, Iran, and violent extremism. Fourth, however, it would avoid overdependence on the NSC for such efforts, strengthening the State Department in particular as an agency of policy development and execution, as former secretary of defense Robert Gates has advocated.[25] Fifth, it would seek to pass legislation that would mandate a governmentwide review of war plans, as well as study by an independent commission, with an eye toward jumpstarting this overall agenda.

NATO is afflicted by similar limitations as the U.S. government. Almost assuredly, so are virtually all other American allies. The result is a situation aptly described by former State Department official Edward Fishman when he wrote in 2018 that "U.S. officials almost never design sanctions until crises are already under way."[26] Nor is it likely that U.S. officials sufficiently contemplate the question of the potential vulnerability of the U.S. economy to adversarial actions that might take place during protracted economic warfare. That should change, for the United States as well as NATO, in Washington as well as Brussels. Bilateral commands with countries like Japan should adopt these new approaches, too.

For some defense planners, it may seem inappropriate to think too much about economics. After all, what business do military experts have integrating economic matters into war plans? But the better question is how do we ensure that we have adequate options when crises occur? The question is especially important for crises that are small in scale, and in their immediate stakes, yet potentially quite fraught in their larger implications. In such cases, resolute response is essential, but firing the first shot in anger is generally unappealing. The U.S. government should not be in a position where its only strong recourse to an enemy aggression would be a military response that would run the high risk of leading to all-out war. War planners will do their country no favor if that is the result of their polite efforts to avoid thinking hard about instruments of national power that seem outside their bailiwick. As Robert Blackwill and Jennifer Harris rightly argue, "Despite having the most powerful economy on Earth, the United States too often reaches for the gun instead of the purse in its international conduct."[27] There may also be situations, such as the kinds of scenarios considered in this book, in which both the gun *and* the purse should be employed by the United States and allies—but the gun should not be fired in the first instance, only repositioned and prepared.

Sanctions do not always work, of course.[28] They do not always persuade adversaries to reverse promptly a given policy or to undo an aggression; some argue their track record has been quite poor, in fact, particularly through the twentieth century.[29] But the international community appears to have improved its use of sanctions, finding more surgical approaches to apply economic pain, while also lowering its expectations of what sanctions can accomplish in short order. The combination of improving methods with lowering expectations has had benefits. Certainly sanctions appear to have had some utility in regard to Iran and North Korea in modern times. It is possible that they have also helped persuade Vladimir Putin not to take more of Ukraine or attack a Baltic state—even if he has refused to return Crimea or end the separatist violence in the Donbas region of eastern Ukraine. In the right circumstances, and especially when combined with the credible deployment of military forces to deter further enemy encroachments, sanctions may still inflict enough punishment to signal resolve and deter more violence. For limited acts of war, that may be enough. Sanctions can and should punish bad actions. But just as much, they should signal that worse actions will be met with even stronger punishment. Deterrence is generally easier than compellence—and in the kinds of scenarios considered here, deterring further aggression is generally much more important than compelling a reversal of past offenses.[30] Pushing China quickly off one Senkaku island, for example, is much less important than deterring it from laying claim to large swaths of the East China Sea or the Ryukyu Islands, including Okinawa.

America's allies may not always be completely reassured by such policies. But it is not the job of Washington to be the geostrategic therapist for allies over each and every minor anxiety. In fact, blanket assurances could make some allies more prone to take risk or to remain inflexible in their diplomacy with other nations, knowing that Uncle Sam could defend them if things ever got serious. This is not the purpose of America's alliances. It is, rather, the job of the United States to have the backs of allies on matters of core importance and vital national security. Assurance on national survival is important.[31] Assurance on each and every dispute a country may have with neighbors is neither realistic nor desirable.

Indeed, in many cases, U.S. allies will prefer the kind of grand strategy proposed here because it reduces the risks of war. In this vein, the findings of a poll conducted by the Pew Charitable Trusts in 2015, shortly after the Russian attacks on Ukraine, are instructive. The survey revealed a deep ambivalence among many NATO citizens about whether a hypothetical Russian aggression against an eastern alliance member state should lead to a NATO military response. Indeed, clear majorities in a number of countries expressed opposition to any such action. As the alliance has expanded eastward, farther from original NATO nations and closer to the Russian heartland, many publics have clearly wondered if they want to send their own sons and daughters to defend faraway lands. This may be particularly true in response to possible aggressions that are limited in geographic scope, duration, and lethality. Yet the poll—and subsequent behavior by European governments—have demonstrated a clear allied willingness to inflict serious and sustained economic pain on a perpetrator of aggression.[32] Putin is no doubt unpleasantly surprised at just how well the EU and NATO have held together over the years on a long-term sanctions policy that punishes his aggression against Ukraine.

Basing a U.S. national security strategy on asymmetric response, without ensuring prompt liberation of any occupied allied territory, may seem defeatist to some. But that kind of approach effectively formed much of the basis of the containment strategy during the Cold War. Militarily, the West sought to prevent further Soviet conquests after a number of them had already occurred. That approach could not ensure the independence and sovereignty of much of Eastern Europe, which had to wait decades for its freedom. In broad foreign policy terms, however, it turned out to be an extremely successful long-term strategy for promoting democracy, prosperity, and peace. The military instruments provided a bulwark against further aggression well enough and long enough for the economic, diplomatic, political, and cultural instruments of America and its allies eventually to produce victory. So playing good defense with military policy is a time-tested philosophy that can allow the quieter tools of power and influence, including economics, to shape the world in favorable ways over time.[33] Sanctions-centered strategies also play to U.S. strengths, given America's role in the global economy as well as the roles of key rich and powerful allies like those in Europe and East Asia.[34]

Moreover, this strategy would not take more muscular options off the table. The United States should not telegraph in any detail which scenarios might ultimately lead to the use of military force—and, therefore, which scenarios might not. Most red lines should not be drawn too clearly—unless the core national security of key American allies, or other top-tier U.S. global interests like freedom of the seas, might be at risk. My proposed paradigm, which might also be described as asymmetric or integrated deterrence, is designed to increase available options, not foreclose existing ones. But it would tilt strongly against any presumption of a muscular kinetic response to a mild provocation or small crisis. The goal would generally be not to draw first blood in any crisis, especially one involving a nuclear-armed adversary. In this regard, the strategy, while not discounting the utility of the Trump Pentagon's concept of prevailing in the contact and blunt phases, early on in a crisis or conflict, would not rely exclusively on such an approach and would in fact favor indirect approaches that sought *not* to draw first blood and *not* to escalate.[35]

Some might worry that this approach would come across as American weakness, irresoluteness, or excessive casualty aversion—making an adversary think it could take even bigger risks in challenging U.S. interests down the road. It is true that Washington must take such concerns seriously in how it responds to any crisis. However, for a nation that has, just this century, used lethal force on multiple occasions in at least half a dozen countries around the world, its reputation for resoluteness may not be acutely at risk.

Last, with the grand strategy of resolute restraint, I would propose adding a second dimension of 4+1 threats to go along with the Pentagon's list of the original 4+1: Russia, China, North Korea, Iran, and transnational violent extremism or terrorism.[36] The new 4+1—nuclear, biological and pandemic, digital, climatic, and internal-societal dangers— would not be additional threats arrayed along the same dimension or axis. They are not hostile adversaries. Rather they are complicating, exacerbating, and/or accelerating aspects of the modern world that can make any other threat more dangerous. The last on the list is America's own social and economic and political cohesion. It is different in kind from the others—hence the use of the 4+1 framing (just as transnational violent extremism on the original list is different in kind from the other threats that can be clearly associated with specific nation-states). The new 4+1 threats are not primarily the province of the Department of Defense. But for broad allocation of national resources, as well as the attention and mindsight of policy makers, they should be viewed as constituting a second dimension in a matrix or a two-dimensional threat space.

Other Schools of Thought

An American grand strategy of resolute restraint, but not retrenchment, is different from most other ideas in today's debate.[37] Because grand strategy is often discussed in abstract terms, making it seem a bit tangential to actual foreign policy decision making, it is useful to clarify the implications of resolute restraint in contrast with other concepts.

First, consider the implications of my proposed strategy versus what might loosely be called the American strategic community's conventional wisdom. (I will compare them with some of the specific ideas of Presidents Obama and Trump below.) There are many similarities—

in the emphasis on strong U.S. military forces, in support for sustaining permanent U.S. military presence in East Asia, Europe, and parts of the Middle East, and in the willingness to go to war in defense of the core territorial interests and national survival of allies. In addition, while it generally would not see military force as the right tools to advance them, my strategy also shares a commitment to key values such as promotion of democracy and human rights, reduction of violence, and promotion of prosperity around the world. These values are not only important in their own right. They also give purpose and legitimacy to American alliance leadership.[38]

However, as will be detailed in subsequent chapters, my proposed strategy is wary of further expansion of alliances, disinclined to draw first blood in disputes over limited and relatively insignificant pieces of allied territory, unpersuaded about maximalist approaches to diplomacy such as are often attempted by the United States in regard to North Korea and Iran, and more focused on new threats as well as on the domestic underpinnings of long-term national power than is traditional military planning.[39]

I am also skeptical about elements of the Obama administration's Third Offset plan as well as the Trump administration's National Defense Strategy. Much of the thrust of these initiatives, with their focus on reaffirming and strengthening U.S. conventional military superiority, is welcome. However, it simply may not be realistic to achieve such levels of dominance that decisive war-winning capabilities can be relied on to deter the outset of conflict in the first place—or to prevail quickly in any war that does occur. Concepts like deterrence by denial and successful attacks on enemy assets in the contact and blunt phases of a future limited war may not be feasible or advisable.

My recommended strategy differs fundamentally with advocates of American "offshore balancing."[40] That strategy seeks to avoid most binding commitments to other countries' defense. Therefore, because America already has so many allies today, it would by necessity lead to the dismantling of existing U.S. alliances and security commitments. It would reduce the United States to the role of watching Eurasia, ready to step back into crises or conflicts there only if absolutely necessary—to avoid any hostile preponderance of power from forming in a way that could ultimately threaten the Western Hemisphere. It would in effect accept a multipolar world—rather than seeking to keep most chief elements of today's economic, strategic, and military power at least loosely aligned in a collective self-defense alliance system that possesses some two-thirds of aggregate world GDP and two-thirds of aggregate defense spending, as is currently the case. Because of this alliance network, while today's world might no longer be best described as unipolar, it is also far from multipolar. The United States with its many allies still constitute the economic and security backbone of today's world.

To my mind, the United States effectively attempted a strategy of offshore balancing before each world war, if not explicitly and consciously, then by default, due to the nation's inward focus at the time. Both times such a grand strategy failed catastrophically. Multipolar worlds and American disengagement have not kept the peace in the past. These are empirical, historical facts. In the first half of the twentieth century, the United States did not build peacetime alliances or deploy forces abroad to deter potential foes. Twice, global war erupted. For the three-quarters of a century since, we have maintained a system of alliances and forward military presence in key theaters abroad. No world war has resulted.

Relatedly, Barry Posen of MIT, one of the nation's top security experts and professors by any measure, advocates a U.S. grand strategy centered on the idea of restraint. He is compelling in much of what he argues. Avoiding war when possible in particular needs to be our lodestar. Posen, along with numerous other prominent academics, deserves credit for warning against the U.S.-led invasion of Iraq in 2003, which to my mind cannot currently be justified as worth the costs (perhaps someday that will change, but it is too soon to reach any such conclusion). His warning about the proclivities of current American grand strategy to overuse force is particularly compelling, as is his warning against further alliance expansion.

However, when advocacy for *restraint* becomes advocacy of U.S. *retrenchment*—and specifically, a weakening or dismantling of existing alliances—it is a much different argument. It is also, in my estimation, much less compelling. Posen calculates, carefully and convincingly, that such a grand strategy might reduce U.S. defense spending by 20 percent, reducing it from a bit more than 3 percent of GDP to about 2.5 percent. That is significant, to be sure, but in macroeconomic terms, it would not amount to a huge shift in resources or savings to the country. It could only be justified in cost-benefit terms if the ensuing strategy made war, or high-intensity great power arms racing, less likely than it is today. However, given the historical record—two world wars in the half century without a U.S. grand strategy of engagement but no great power war during the seventy-five years of American leadership—it is difficult to see how weakening or ending alliances would create a safer world for the United States.[41]

A policy of retrenchment has never been attempted before in world history on such a scale and would in fact therefore be revolutionary, not cautious. The closest parallel is probably the period after World War I, when the allied victors first sought to build a League of Nations to keep the peace, but then, led by Washington, they instead neutered that organization and dramatically downsized their military forces.[42] At the very best, implementation of any strategy of retrenchment would create a dangerous transition period, as the United States broke off alliances and pulled back from the world.[43]

Some advocates of American restraint argue that regional powers in various parts of the world should be left to find their own paths to peace with their neighbors. To be sure, on routine matters of diplomacy, that is sound advice. But when the chips are really down, the value of an outside superpower seen as relatively disinterested in the immediate stakes at hand, yet committed to the core security of its allies, can be enormously beneficial. As Asia expert Richard Bush warned in his excellent book by the same title, there are "Perils of Proximity."[44] Familiarity does not always breed better understanding in human affairs. Sometimes, it breeds contempt. Neighbors often have complex intertwined histories, ongoing grievances, and resulting mistrust. A faraway yet engaged superpower changes the dynamics in ways that can be quite beneficial.

The old adage about NATO, coined by its first secretary general, Lord Hastings Lionel Ismay, is that it was designed to keep "the Russians out, the Americans in, and the Germans down."[45] Keeping Germany down may not be necessary today. But the rest of the saying remains timely. Without credible U.S. power committed to the defense of NATO nations, the temptation for Russia to meddle, cajole, coerce, threaten, and perhaps even attack could be much greater than today, especially in nations that were once part either of the Soviet Union or of the Warsaw Pact. And once it established a degree of dominance in the near abroad, its ambitions might extend farther westward, in the kind of behavior European powers displayed for centuries until modern times. Would that likely lead to actual war in the event that the American security guarantee was withdrawn? It is hard to say. Perhaps not. But Moscow might be tempted gradually to up the ante in various showdowns with countries that had no inherent capacity to push back. And at some point, things could escalate, even if no one initially intended such an outcome. As the Australian historian Geoffrey Blainey argued, even if wars do not generally start by accident, they frequently begin when at least one side believes it can use a limited amount of military power in a controlled way for a quick and finite win. Quite often, such expectations prove wrong.[46]

One can debate whether such concerns should have precluded any expansion of NATO eastward after the Cold War ended in the first place. I was probably in the same place as many offshore balancers in regard to NATO expansion in the 1990s and 2000s, in fact. But what is done is done, and it is not easily undone. In any case, Moscow has no inherent right to dominate the space outlined by the Iron Curtain during the Cold War. It is one thing to acknowledge that NATO expansion to a place like Ukraine could be particularly concerning for Moscow, as I will argue in the next chapter, and quite another to concede predominance for Russia in a place like Poland or the Czech Republic. If our options for European security today are to keep NATO as it is, expand it, or dismantle it in whole or in part, I vote strongly for the first. At this juncture, expanding NATO further into the former Soviet space would likely provoke Moscow severely, and dismantling or dismembering it would likely make Russian hardliners feel vindicated—while whetting their appetites for more power and dominance in Europe.

The idea that neighbors do not necessarily get along on their own is valid elsewhere, too. For example, it is difficult to look at Northeast Asia today and believe that it would function in a more stable way without the U.S.-Japan and U.S.-Republic of Korea alliances. China, Japan, and the two Koreas do not consistently get along well on their own. (Russia may not get along that well with these players either—though it will be pragmatic enough to cooperate, or at least coordinate, with China in certain efforts to challenge American leadership and alliances in the years ahead.) Yet with American power engaged in the region, peace has prevailed, Japan has not remilitarized, and in fact, with the exception of North Korea, arms racing in general has been avoided.[47]

My proposed grand strategy may not be philosophically far from some of President Barack Obama's thinking. Obama wanted to avoid overreaction against the threat of terrorism as well as the return of Russia and rise of China. One of his closest aides, Derek Chollet, wrote an insightful book that sought to explore the forty-fourth president's outlook, entitled *The Long Game: How Obama Defied Washington and Redefined America's Role in the World.* According to Chollet, Obama was willing—and correct—to stave off calls for action from the pundits and policy makers who tend to want the United States to assert itself frequently in the world. Obama feared American overextension as much as inaction. That led to a number of policies and positions over the years, some of which stand up better in hindsight than others. Obama opposed the Iraq war, promised in 2009 to soon draw down U.S. forces in Afghanistan in the same speech that announced a temporary buildup, and tried to ensure that NATO allies would take the military lead in Libya in 2011. Starting that same year, he assumed that Bashar al-Assad in Syria would fall without America playing a significant role. He also held off providing lethal aid to Ukraine so as not to add tinder to the conflict with Russia from 2014 onward. He accepted an imperfect and temporary deal with Iran in 2015 rather than risk war over Iran's nuclear program. To Chollet, and others, this was all admirable restraint. As Obama himself put it, there was great wisdom in the mantra "Don't do stupid [stuff]" and in trying to hit singles and doubles rather than home runs most of the time—and in playing the long game.

But Obama had the misfortune of having too many unfortunate things happen on his watch. Some were his fault. Syria and Libya must rank high on this list, where there was a constant mismatch between ends and means and a long-standing lack of clear strategy.[48] However, most of the undesirable events that occurred during his presidency had larger and longer-term causes. In any event, after a period of increasing Russian and Chinese adventurism, a failed Arab Spring combined with an increasingly assertive Iran in the Middle East, the rise of ISIS, a continually nuclearizing North Korea, and other crises, most Republicans and even some Democrats concluded that Obama's foreign policy smacked of a certain irresoluteness rather than restraint. Ironically, for someone so eloquent, he also generally failed to explain the logic behind his caution, a point his last secretary of defense, Ashton Carter, has acknowledged.[49] In fairness to Obama, the critiques sometimes went too far. Obama did keep forces in Afghanistan throughout his presidency, conducted far more drone strikes against al Qaeda than his predecessor, authorized the raid that killed Osama bin Laden, began a rebalancing toward the Asia-Pacific region, sustained military budgets in excess of $600 billion a year (well above the Cold War inflation-adjusted average) even in the face of Tea Party Republicans who called for deep cuts in spending, initiated NATO's military buildup in eastern Europe after Russia's 2014 attacks on Ukraine, and sent U.S. Navy ships through the South China Sea to shore up America's claims to free passage in those waters. But these actions often seemed a penny short and a day late to critics. As such, his foreign policy vision is not likely to cohere into what historians will see as a clear doctrine or paradigm. Former deputy secretary of state Bill Burns frames America's strategic choices going forward as retrenchment, restoration, or reinvention (and strongly counsels in favor of the last option). Alas, employing this framework, many likely saw Obama's approach as more akin to retrenchment.[50] Yet I think there was, philosophically at least, a useful element in restraint in his thinking that should in fact inform more American foreign policy debates.

How does a Kennanesque grand strategy of resolute restraint compare with President Trump's approach to the world? Any grand strategy of sustained, values-based American leadership is inherently much different than Trump's view of the world. Nonetheless, I find at least four interesting points of agreement between President Trump's approach to U.S. foreign policy and my own. First, I believe that Trump was rightly skeptical about many possible uses of American military force. Second, he was bold and creative in his dealings with Kim Jong Un, though he later failed to follow through on his instincts for "the art of the deal" and squandered the chance for a compromise accord to curtail North Korea's nuclear weapons program. Third, he was rightly uninterested in any further expansion of NATO into the former Soviet space. And fourth, however flawed his tactics, Trump understood that the United States had great potential leverage through economic and financial tools of statecraft. Often such tools are preferable to those of the Department of Defense, even when dealing with security challenges.

How does my grand strategy of resolute restraint stack up against well-known frameworks for guiding American decision makers on the use of force? The president of the Council on Foreign Relations, Richard Haass, wrote a powerful book advocating that the United States avoid "wars of choice" and fight only "wars of necessity."[51] That distinction is pithy and useful. However, it does not easily tell us which types of war are which, absent analysis and judgment (many of Haass's other excellent works often provide such broader analysis). I try to create a framework here that can help in such decisions. Former secretary of defense Caspar Weinberger articulated several rules about intervention in the 1980s that gained the mantra of the Weinberger doctrine. They include the idea that the United States should only fight wars when other ways of resolving a crisis have failed, when vital national interests are at stake, when there is strong consensus in favor of an operation, and when the country can map out a clear path to victory before initiating combat operations. Again, there is wisdom in these ideas. But they do not account for the unpredictability of war; they imply that it is a technical undertaking with largely controllable results. Nor do they resolve the question of what is, in fact, a vital interest of the United States.[52] And finally, the Powell doctrine, named after retired general Colin Powell, places less dogmatic emphasis on determining when a vital American interest is at stake than Weinberger. Instead, it underscores the importance of anticipating pitfalls in the use of force and of ensuring success in any operations that are undertaken.[53] It does share a healthy skepticism about the use of force with the Weinberger doctrine. It, too, is thoughtful. But it is more a list of warnings and conditions about the use of force than a grand strategy that would prioritize interests and focus on deterrence at least as much as on combat. It is that issue of deterrence to which I turn next.

Why Deterrence Is Doable

Perhaps, if deterrence were extremely hard, and if alliance commitments therefore made it likely that the United States would wind up entangled in foreign wars of little immediate bearing to its own security, a grand strategy of offshore balancing would be compelling. But in fact, the history of recent decades should make us much more optimistic than that. The key is to figure out what interests are worth fighting for and consistently demonstrate a national will and capability to defend them—while also having other, nonkinetic and nonlethal tools available for complex, murky, and gray-zone cases where it is unrealistic or undesirable to draw a clear red line in advance of any possible crisis.

Deterrence often does fail when rhetorical commitments are not backed up by real military power, formal alliance commitments, and demonstrated resolve.[54] For example, the Berlin crises of the early Cold War years occurred when Soviet leaders likely doubted America's will to respond—with the Kremlin also safe in the knowledge that it had local conventional superiority and thus that the United States lacked the capability to prevent the construction of the wall absent major preparation or escalation.[55] The Soviet suppression of the 1956 Hungarian uprising occurred even farther from the locations of any major American military forces. Kim Il Sung and Saddam Hussein doubted America's will to respond to their aggressions against South Korea and Kuwait in 1950 and 1990, respectively, after unfortunate comments by Secretary of State Dean Acheson and U.S. Ambassador to Iraq April Glaspie, among others (indeed, it is difficult to classify these cases as deterrence failure, since the United States had no formal commitments to the security of these countries and signaled that it was *not* interested in defending them).[56] The Soviet Union had no reason to think that the United States would consider military intervention in opposition to its 1979 invasion of Afghanistan.[57] More recently, Russia's forays into Georgia, Ukraine, and Syria over the past eleven years also occurred when Moscow doubted Washington's will to respond—there were no U.S. alliance commitments and no nearby American combat forces.[58]

Former secretary of defense Bob Gates was fond of saying that the United States has a perfect record in modern times of predicting when and where future outbreaks of war will occur—we always get it wrong.[59] That is another way of saying we do not always successfully deter. There is considerable truth to that statement. But the obverse is also true—we have a nearly perfect record of preventing further large-scale aggression in places where we really put our mind, national will, resources, and forward-deployed military forces to the task. When we can predict accurately the possibility of a future war, the United States would appear to be fairly good at preventing it. When we are clear about our interests, commitments, and capabilities, for example in Japan, western Europe, and later Korea in the early postwar years, deterrence has generally worked—or, to be more precise (since we cannot know the counterfactual), deterrence has not failed in these places. Countries will usually not risk war against the United States when they see that Washington is resolute—and especially when it has permanently stationed some of the world's best military forces in places where they would quickly be implicated in most possible conflicts. President Donald Trump inadvertently conducted a stress test of sorts on the strength of U.S. deterrence commitments, suggesting especially in the first months of 2017 that his willingness to defend NATO and East Asian allies was very much conditional, at best. Yet no one attacked U.S. allies in this period, and we have no evidence that any adversaries even seriously considered doing so.[60] The fact that Trump's musings about the questionable value of alliances did not lead to any major redeployments of American combat forces or abrogations of treaties is probably a major part of the reason why.

None of this means that deterrence is easy, of course. It requires serious will and capability. The capability involves retaining by far the best armed forces in the world. And as for the serious will, for a country that has been waging multiple military campaigns during virtually all of the twenty-first century and that has been, in Bob Kagan's memorable phrase, a "dangerous nation" since its inception, demonstrating a will to fight in defense of core allies is probably a less brittle commodity than American strategists sometimes tend to think.[61]

This sense of U.S. readiness to fight has not always been equally robust. Osama bin Laden said the following to ABC News correspondent John Miller back in 1998: "We have seen in the last decade the decline of the American Government and the weakness of the American soldier who is ready to wage cold wars and unprepared to fight long wars. This was proven in Beirut when the Marines fled after two explosions. It also proves they can run in less than 24 hours, and this was also repeated in Somalia. . . . After a few blows, they ran in defeat and America forgot about all the hoopla and media propaganda . . . about being the world leader, and the leader of the new world order."[62] But bin Laden himself found out the hard way the willingness of the United States to defend itself against terrorism once a certain threshold of American casualties was crossed. Other would-be adversaries likely took note. The willingness of the United States to risk war in defense of core interests is probably not doubted by most potential adversaries and aggressors around the world today.

There is more good news about deterrence, too. The United States generally need not fight just to protect its reputation for toughness or resoluteness, as scholars including Dartmouth professor Daryl Press and University of Washington professor Jonathan Mercer have persuasively argued by examining cases like the Berlin and Cuban Missile crises. What matters most for creating credibility in the minds of adversaries is deployable power, combined with a clear commitment beyond the merely rhetorical to the country or interest at issue. In today's world, when dealing with nuclear-armed nemeses, that U.S. military power probably requires conventional forces backed up by a nuclear deterrent.

What is *not* essential, for maintaining deterrence in key theaters, is sustaining some vague notion of airtight general global credibility across all interests and regions.[63] This is not an argument to ignore humanitarian horrors in Syria or shut our eyes to Vladimir Putin's transgressions in Ukraine or forget the plight of Venezuelans and the Rohingya in Myanmar and those nations in central and Sahel Africa so victimized by civil war today. However, would-be aggressors are unlikely to doubt America's commitment to key allies just because the United States may not be fully committed to a crisis of secondary strategic importance elsewhere. Kim Jong Un would not, and did not, see a window of opportunity to attack South Korea just because Barack Obama failed somehow to uphold a red line over chemical weapons in Syria in 2013, for example. The United States is fallible enough that we know it will make numerous mistakes in addressing crises or conflicts of secondary or tertiary importance to the country. Fortunately, deterring threats to top-tier U.S. national security interests is unlikely to suffer as a result, especially when forward-deployed American combat forces are in position.

Alas, even when deterring all-out attack is successful, dissuading smaller challenges to allies' interests and the existing order is more difficult, as Alexander George and Richard Smoke documented in their landmark study on early Cold War deterrence.[64] Such types of crises and conflicts are less inherently dangerous in one sense. But in another sense, they always run the risk of creating escalation dynamics. Think of North Korea's various acts of violence against South Korea and against American military personnel in the 1960s, 1970s, and 1980s, the Soviet Union's use of military advisers in the Middle East in the Cold War, China's supporting roles in the Vietnam War, Soviet decisions to obstruct U.S. access to Berlin and ultimately build the Berlin Wall, or China's attempts to take Quemoy and Matsu during the 1950s. As Fred Ikle noted about the dangers of escalation, "Fighting sharpens feelings of hostility. . . . More is expected of a settlement because both the government and the people will feel that the outcome of the war ought to justify the sacrifices incurred. In addition, various institutional forces will compound the difficulties of making peace."[65] Once war begins, and people start dying, it is hard to stop. The key is not to rely primarily on the threat of the early and lethal use of military power to deter small-scale or gray-zone aggression. In the next four chapters I therefore focus on improving nonlethal tools for the most probable major direct threats to American security today.[66]

But . . . the Dangers of Overdoing It

If deterrence of core interests and allies should be achievable for the United States going forward, that does not mean that each and every American foreign policy ambition is achievable. Nor is each one necessarily even desirable or prudent. Foreign policy specialists, when writing books like this, usually lament Americans' disinterest in global affairs and their unwillingness to resource and otherwise support an adequately robust U.S. foreign policy. But there is an equal and opposite danger as well. We often overdo it.

Our enemies today do not look like Hitler, Tojo, or Stalin, and therefore the United States and allies should not address future challenges the way we faced the Nazis or Soviets or wartime Japanese. Future conflict could begin more like the outbreak of World War I—when a small crisis escalated due to great power rivalry and mistrust—than of World War II, when fundamentally evil regimes sought to conquer large swaths of the world.[67] Indeed, a future conflagration could also resemble World War I in its ethical complexity. In that conflict, the United States declared war against Germany only in April 1917 and Austria-Hungary in December of that year. Previously, President Woodrow Wilson and others had had reservations about the aggressive and imperialistic ways of Britain and France, and they favored "peace without victory" rather than the outright defeat of any side.[68] The war had not been a simple black-and-white case of democracy against autocracy, of peaceful nations against aggressive ones. In the eyes of many, at least, a future war pitting, say, the United States and allies against China might not be so morally unambiguous, either, depending of course on specifics.

Because the United States spent much of the last century countering terrible foes with unlimited aims, it developed what Columbia professor Stephen Sestanovich calls "maximalist" tendencies. Former deputy secretary of state Jim Steinberg and I make a related argument in our 2014 book on China. These instinctual proclivities have their advantages. But they can also be dangerous in a more complex world with more shades of gray than Hitler or Stalin presented.[69]

One dangerous and prevalent American way of strategic thought is to believe that alliances, and NATO in particular, should expand as the natural course of events. I am most concerned about NATO's potential further expansion into the former Soviet space (though the alliance expansion issue could also arise in regard to, say, Vietnam or other countries in South, Southeast, and East Asia in the future). This is not a matter of mistaken motives on the part of Western policy makers. I am firmly convinced, after watching the debates of the post–Cold War world, that the vast preponderance of American advocates of NATO expansion did so for the worthy reasons of consolidating a zone of peace and democracy in Europe. The goal was not to embarrass or threaten Russia. At most, some advocates of NATO expansion feared a Russian resurgence someday and wanted to offer security guarantees to countries in eastern Europe before they were threatened. The goal was not to weaken, not to humiliate, and certainly not to attack Russia. Yet humans being who they are, and Russians having the political culture and history that they possess as a proud people who have been through much, a strong counterreaction was not only possible but probable. This is not an argument for offering any apology to Russia now. What's done is done—and again, Americans and other Western advocates of growing the NATO alliance did so with perfectly reasonable motives. We cannot risk suggesting that some members of NATO today are somehow undeserving—or unworthy of our protection should they be attacked. There could be no better way to increase the risks of deterrence failure. But the idea of bringing Ukraine and Georgia into NATO, as the alliance has promised to do someday going back to 2008, is a different matter. As discussed more in chapter 3, we need to rethink that policy—not just put the idea on the back burner. (Vladimir Putin most assuredly does not take great comfort in seeing it on the back burner.)

The United States can also overdo things in terms of our definition of victory—both in war and in diplomacy. Strangely, for a country that has waged several wars of inconclusive or unsatisfying outcome since World War II, the United States still tends to expect outright wins on most big national security issues—perhaps because of how World War II and then the Cold War both ended. Those outcomes foster the myth that, if we really try, we can achieve whatever we want. In present times, this attitude is producing very ambitious goals in our dealings with Iran and North Korea in regard to their nuclear programs. The American motivation here is not foolish. A world with more nuclear weapons states, some of them run by extremist dictators or autocracies, is much more dangerous than a world with fewer. Political scientists who assume that any nuclear-armed nation would be deterred from ever taking decisions that could lead to war, or nuclear war, assume too much rationality and predictability in a world of imperfect humans, imperfect decision-making processes, and vulnerable command and control systems.[70]

But it is almost certainly unrealistic to persuade Pyongyang to give up all of its several dozen nuclear weapons in one fell swoop, as I discuss more in later chapters. Attempting to achieve that goal likely increases the risks of nuclear war rather than reducing them. And although the 2015 Iran nuclear deal was flawed, especially for its short time horizons, we should not aim for de facto regime change as the alternative objective. It is very unlikely to be attainable.

In addition to alliances, and to diplomatic strategies with the likes of North Korea and Iran, there is the American way of war—when we decide to fight and what aims we tend to pursue once engaged in combat. Here, again, Americans are prone to overconfidence and to maximal ambitions. We do not have the ability to control crises as much as we might think, even if in possession of superior power. Thus, the United States should be very wary to enter into kinetic contests with nuclear-armed opponents. Governments can still make major mistakes in such scenarios, especially in situations characterized by sycophantic aides, groupthink, or narcissistic leaders. (Some of these conditions can even arise in the United States.)[71]

Technical problems can happen, too. For example, early in any conventional war, reconnaissance and communications assets that are also important to a country's nuclear forces could be put at risk or destroyed. That could render leaders and subordinates largely blind about their circumstances, and perhaps prone to overreaction, in a problem my former Brookings colleague Bruce Blair and others discussed decades ago. It remains a real danger today. Even if the United States has fixed some of the earlier problems, other nuclear powers may not have taken adequate steps themselves. Also, standard U.S. practices like trying to destroy preemptively the nuclear-armed submarines of an adversary even in a conventional conflict could blur the line between conventional and nuclear war-fighting, as professors Barry Posen and Caitlin Talmadge have convincingly argued.[72] Cyber, space, and undersea fiber-optic cable vulnerabilities introduce a whole new dimension of risk for everyone.[73] Simple accidents or organizational miscommunications and failures can create crises as well.[74] There have been several such incidents in the nuclear age, all harrowing to varying degrees in retrospect. If new cases were to occur during a shooting war, preventing escalation could prove very difficult.

McGeorge Bundy, Kennedy's national security adviser, looked back on the Cuban Missile Crisis and thought the risks to be not so great. But that is because he focused on the calm and sobriety of the key leaders, especially Kennedy. Bundy focused less on how the fog of war, and the passions incurred once violence begins, could have led to a very different outcome, especially if other leaders had been in charge. For all of Kennedy's flaws, he handled that crisis with steadiness, aplomb, and an excellent sense of priorities; there is little reason to think all leaders in similar circumstances would do as well.[75]

America has had a penchant, since World War II, of thinking that it must use military power to signal engagement and to demonstrate resoluteness, even in peacetime and in small crises. That way of thinking was useful in the Cold War, when we waged a global competition against nations with an expansionist communist ideology. It still has a certain purpose. But it can also get us into trouble—if we do not demonstrate a consistent element of restraint and reassurance in our foreign policy as well. One sees this tendency in policies like the Pentagon's inclination to write war plans that might treat minor assaults (however concerning) as tantamount to major attacks on allies and Strategic Command's inclination to favor plans for massive nuclear attacks in the event that the nuclear threshold is crossed.[76]

Excessive hawkishness can make it more likely that small crises will escalate. How should the United States respond, for example, if China seizes one or more of the eight uninhabited Senkaku Islands, in the East China Sea, that Japan and China both claim? The United States has no view as to whose islands these should rightly be. Yet we have publicly committed to help Japan defend its claims if they are threatened. Thus, disputes over small and basically worthless rocks could literally provoke direct conflict between the United States and China. What if Vladimir Putin expands his aggression against Ukraine or attempts a probing attack on nonaligned but Western-leaning Finland or Sweden or undertakes a limited form of covert aggression against a NATO member like Estonia, Latvia, or Lithuania?

Many Americans would see rapid and robust military response as our only acceptable option in such situations. That may be especially true if they see the world as highly dangerous—since if it already teeters near the brink of war, any further deterioration of strategic conditions could push us right up to or over the edge, and thus be unacceptable.[77] Without wanting to dismiss a prompt and strong military response option altogether, or lower our military preparations in any way, I worry that taking a kinetic approach could amount to destroying a village in order to save it. Indeed, once war between nuclear-armed superpowers begins, it is not clear where it ends.[78]

In fact, the United States would have multiple choices even in these kinds of crises. Article 5 commitments within NATO and the U.S.-Japan alliance are typically interpreted as absolute and inflexible, especially within American defense and national security circles. They are not.

Article 5, which commits all allies to action if any one of them is attacked, is the essence of NATO's mutual defense pledge. A somewhat different but similar article 5 is also the backbone of the U.S.-Japan Security Treaty, and a related stipulation is found in article 4 of the U.S.-Philippines military and defense accord. Specifically, NATO's article 5 reads as follows: "The Parties agree that an armed attack against one or more of them in Europe or North America shall be considered an attack against them all and consequently they agree that, if such an armed attack occurs, each of them, in exercise of the right of individual or collective self-defence recognised by Article 51 of the Charter of the United Nations, will assist the Party or Parties so attacked by taking forthwith, individually and in concert with the other Parties, such action as it deems necessary, including the use of armed force, to restore and maintain the security of the North Atlantic area."[79] The language in the Treaty of Mutual Cooperation and Security between Japan and the United States from 1960 reads: "Each Party recognizes that an armed attack against either Party in the territories under the administration of Japan would be dangerous to its own peace and safety and declares that it would act to meet the common danger in accordance with its constitutional provisions and processes."[80] The 1951 Mutual Defense Treaty between the United States and the Republic of the Philippines states: "Each Party recognizes that an armed attack in the Pacific Area on either of the Parties would be dangerous to its own peace and safety and declares that it would act to meet the common dangers in accordance with its constitutional processes."[81] Any incursion onto any part of an ally's territory is to be treated as a fundamental threat to that country's security and to alliance credibility.

But none of these treaty provisions automatically commits the

United States to a specific type of counterattack. We have every right, and reason, to be creative, smart, indirect, and asymmetric. As Secretary Mattis underscored in the 2018 National Defense Strategy, the United States should "be strategically predictable, but operationally unpredictable" in its national security policy.[82] Another useful Mattisism is that we should "expand the competitive space."[83] That admonition can be interpreted in geographic terms. But it can also be interpreted in broader strategic terms. Not all security crises or competitions need to be contested on the military playing field.

The flexibility of article 5 is also crucial to preserve the Congress's constitutional power to declare war—however outdated such a concept may now seem. And it reduces the risks of entrapment—of a U.S. ally going to war and then effectively dragging the United States into the conflict through some automatic provision in a treaty accord. In fact, Washington has already chosen *not* to back up allies that might be responsible for the outbreak of a conflict. This happened, for example, with Pakistan in its 1965 and 1971 wars against India, when the United States was formally a security partner of Islamabad through the Southeast Asia Treaty Organization and Central Treaty Organization yet did not rally to Pakistan's military side. (Admittedly, that treaty is worded slightly differently than the NATO or U.S.-Japan treaties, but the broader point remains valid.) And in 1964, Lyndon Johnson wrote a letter to Ankara indicating that if Turkey attacked Cyprus as part of an ongoing rivalry with Greece over that island, and the Soviet Union responded by attacking Turkey, the United States would not feel bound by article 5 of the NATO Treaty to come to Turkey's defense. Even with formal treaty allies, the United States has established the precedent of not letting other countries automatically drag it into war through mistakes of their own making.[84]

Spelling Out the Grand Strategy

Most of the rest of this book is organized to address the Pentagon's five threats of greatest concern: Russia, China, North Korea, Iran, and transnational violent extremism (read, terrorism with global reach). The Pentagon's list is sensible for several reasons. It includes the world's other established nuclear superpower and other major industrial-military powers (besides the United States). It includes the rogue or extremist regime with the world's largest nuclear arsenal (North Korea) as well as the non-nuclear extremist country with perhaps the greatest nuclear ambitions (Iran). And it includes the broader region from which most terrorism has emanated in modern times. The Middle East also remains very important to the world oil economy. It also still contains several countries that have sought, and may again seek, nuclear weapons.

The preponderance of the world's industrial capabilities, military power, and key raw materials are found in these countries together with the American allies and partners contiguous to them. They thus define a reasonable spectrum of top-tier potential dangers to the nation. Moreover, even if certain other kinds of threats were to emerge, these five should define a reasonable range of plausible conflicts that would likely help prepare the American military for combat across a much wider range of plausible possibilities than did the "two major regional war" or two major regional contingency paradigm of the 1990s and 2000s.[85]

This list places a lower U.S. military priority on South America, Africa, and a large swath of Central, South, and Southeast Asia. I do not mean to suggest that these places are categorically unimportant, of course. At some point in the twenty-first century, they will collectively hold more than half the world's population. There are military scenarios that could emerge in them that might require American participation in some way—in a massive reconstruction and relief effort after a nuclear accident or nuclear war in South Asia, for example, or the outbreak of a contagious disease that the world sought to contain within a given geographic zone. But because these regions do not contain the world's major industrial powers, large military organizations, or nuclear-armed adversaries of the United States, they are not as important to U.S. national security as the Big 5 countries or threats arguably are. At least, they do not hold individual countries with as much capacity to shape broader world events—and to seriously damage the United States. Again, Kennan's method for establishing strategic priorities is helpful in understanding the importance of these countries to core U.S. national security.

Yet there are new threats, as well, and a number of them should not be relegated to lower overall national security priority than the 4+1 of

Russia, China, North Korea, Iran, and transnational violent extremism or terrorism. Weapons of mass destruction or pandemics can kill many millions; climate change can displace hundreds of millions, with major consequences for international politics; cyber vulnerabilities can bring down militaries, national infrastructure, or democratic voting processes; America's fraying polity can lose its willingness to lead globally, with potentially very serious consequences for global order. Therefore, as noted above, I argue that the United States should complement the Pentagon's list of classic threats with a parallel 4+1 framework of other dangers: nuclear weapons, biological weapons and pandemic disease, cyber and digital threats, climate change, and a weakening of America's internal strength. Thus, in addition to addressing the Pentagon's existing 4+1 threat framework, the book includes chapters on this second dimension of 4+1 dangers. A final main chapter focuses on the future of the American armed forces.[86]

Grand strategy is not only about addressing threats. It is also about preserving and reinforcing strengths that contribute to a nation's security. For the United States, these include the nation's broad alliance system, the democratic-market model of governance and economics that has helped so many people in the world in modern times while legitimating American leadership in the eyes of the majority of the world's nations and peoples, and the country's own internal strengths in everything from science and engineering to manufacturing and services to information technology and other manifestations of innovation. These matters, too, are addressed here, even if threats get the greater part of the attention for their ability to disrupt quickly and catastrophically what is otherwise a generally favorable set of trends in the world today.

America's allies can be particularly useful in reinforcing these strengths of the existing global order. To be sure, they can and must help with the instruments of hard power, including greater military burden sharing—and many are already very good in how they think about the application of economic sanctions toward countries like Russia, North Korea, and Iran. However, they may have particularly valuable contributions in regard to the second dimension of 4+1 dangers that I elucidate here. South Korea, Australia, New Zealand, and partners like Singapore and Taiwan have been impressive in their handling of Covid-19; they can do much to improve strategy toward biological threats, including future pandemics. Most European countries and Japan are more effective in limiting carbon emissions, and protecting the environment, than is the United States. Many East Asian allies as well as Germany and certain other allies have demonstrated more consistent commitment to strong infrastructure, effective education for all, and a sense of shared national economic and political purpose than has the United States of late.

Just how to implement a strategy of resolute restraint region by region and subject by subject—with its echoes of George Kennan's thinking about the selective and careful use of alliances, as well as the patient and confident use of economics and diplomacy in U.S. foreign policy—is the question to which the rest of this book now turns.

THREE

Europe and Russia

An image of Europe that sticks in my mind comes from a
2017 trip to Ukraine, a beautiful country with a proud history. It is also a country to which the United States owes a
debt of gratitude. After the Soviet Union dissolved in the
early 1990s, Ukraine agreed to give up its considerable share
of the Soviet nuclear weapons then on its territory. That
decision served a fundamental American national security
interest in stemming nuclear proliferation. To ease along
Ukraine's decision, Washington, with London and Moscow,
promised to help Ukraine with its security as a result. Unfortunately, Moscow later violated that promise when it
attacked Ukraine in 2014. But in traveling to Kiev in a cold
stretch of February weather, so far from the United States
or even western Europe yet so close to Russia, I wondered
again why the United States felt that it should commit the
lives of its own sons and daughters to protect Ukraine by
bringing that country into the NATO alliance. NATO has a
mutual-defense clause known as article 5: an attack on one
is an attack on all. We are somewhat inured to the significance of that concept since it has been around so long
in modern times. But it is a striking and even unnatural

commitment—to treat another country's territory as one's
own in solemnly swearing to defend it. In 2008, President
George W. Bush convinced other NATO states to promise
Ukraine eventual membership (yet with no date certain for
that outcome and no interim security guarantee either).
That had always seemed a bridge too far to me. Militarily,
getting enough U.S. and other NATO forces to Ukraine to
help protect it would be daunting. Strategically and psycho-
logically, Ukraine just seems too distant as well. Certainly,
Russia deserves no veto over Ukrainian decision making.
But should the West really offer this snowy land, deep in the
steppes of Eurasia, membership in a security organization
that had originally been set up among North Atlantic–
bordering countries to counter a Soviet Union that no longer
even exists? Russian reactions to the eastward spread of
NATO, however nasty and petulant, are far from surprising
and should be expected, in the past, present, and future.

My other instructive recent image comes from Lithuania, a small but beautiful Baltic state that is now part of
NATO. It was forcibly annexed into the Soviet Union during
World War II but freed when the Soviet bloc broke up, and
it joined the NATO alliance in 2004. I was privileged to visit
in 2019 (this time in the late spring, thankfully!) as part of a
delegation kindly organized by the Atlantic Council in Washington. During our trip, we took a ride into the choppy
Baltic Sea aboard a Lithuanian coast guard vessel, surveying
the murky waters. Looking around, it was easy to sympa-
thize with the Balts. Collectively, they have Russia on two
sides of them, southwest (in the Kaliningrad region of
Russia) and northeast. But tilt the map of Europe on its side
and look at the whole thing from Russia's perspective. The
city of St. Petersburg is at one far corner of the Baltic Sea,
accessed only through a narrow strait. Looking out from
there, one sees only NATO countries and close NATO
friends—the Baltic states, Poland, Germany, Denmark,
Norway, plus the neutral but western-leaning countries of

Sweden and Finland. The Baltic Sea seems practically to be a NATO lake. None of those countries intends to attack Russia, of course. And the Russians are reckless to harass NATO ships and shorelines in the region, as they sometimes do. But psychology is an important part of the human condition and of international relations. For Russians looking out, it is easy to feel bottled in. There are good reasons to have the Baltics in NATO and to sustain favorable rapport with Sweden and Finland. But there are also good reasons to think that expansion has gone far enough.

Europe has had a horrible dozen-plus years in so many ways. Starting with the 2008 financial crisis and ensuing great recession, which endured much longer in Europe than in the United States, and then continuing through the failed Arab Spring, resulting refugee flows into Europe, ISIS attacks in major European cities, Russian military assaults on Ukraine, cyber and disinformation campaigns on a number of other countries, the Brexit saga, and the 2020 coronavirus outbreak, the continent has endured a remarkable string of setbacks.

Yet Europe is still Europe. It contains many of the world's great civilizations, most of the world's strong economies, most of the world's best-functioning democracies—and arguably, still, the best quality of life on the planet. As one indication, recent happiness measures that ask people to score their own lives against a realistic range of plausible possibilities are higher in Europe than anywhere in the world.[1] Although European levels of GDP per capita are generally less than in the United States, a more comprehensive gauge of quality of life that accounts for leisure, work-life balance, and community involvement puts Europe near or at the top as well.[2]

Despite the setbacks, in the broad brush of history, Europe has made enormous strides toward building a community of prosperous and democratic nations.[3] The transatlantic community between North America and western Europe is crucial for global order—accounting for some 40 percent of world GDP, more than 50 percent of world military spending, and the greatest collection of like-minded democracies in history. The North Atlantic Treaty Organization remains a very smart and rea-

sonably economical investment in this relationship, as well as an insurance policy against any who would attack its members. As Henry Kissinger
notes, even if it was designed against a Soviet threat that no longer exists, its core strategic logic for the United States remains compelling—
to prevent the possible development of a bloc of nations in Eurasia that
could over time dominate the planet and threaten the United States.[4]

I also believe that the Western alliance, for all the transatlantic and
intra-European discord of late, is reasonably resilient. This is not a call
for complacency—or for the kind of rhetoric that President Trump often
employed at the expense of allies. But I do not anticipate Europe somehow going its own way, as Chancellor Angela Merkel of Germany said
it might in a piqued response to a Trump provocation in the early years
of his presidency. Europe as an entity unto itself is an economic power
but not a top-tier global strategic power. Notably, it is not capable of
addressing the Russian threat on its own. Unless and until an American president does far more than insult allies the way Trump has done
and actually drags them into a war or other catastrophic event that the
United States is widely believed to have started, the alliance will likely
remain intact and strong for many years to come. And despite the regres-
sion in democracy, especially in Hungary, the overall state of the internal
politics among the alliance's European members is relatively impressive.
Yes, Turkey has suffered setbacks under the autocratic rule of President
Recep Tayyip Erdogan. But the idea of "throwing Turkey out of NATO,"
sometimes bandied about by various pundits, would seem to forget just
how many strengths Turkey still has as an ally—and how much it has
suffered due to the Syrian civil war, a conflict exacerbated by American
mistakes and inattention.[5]

Some worry that the European Union's ambitions over the years to
create a stronger continental defense capability could lead to a weakening of the transatlantic bond. But bear in mind that European members
of NATO and/or the European Union, two largely overlapping groups
of countries, together spend some $300 billion annually for their armed
forces, in contrast to America's $700 billion-plus. European countries do
not have an interest in doubling or tripling their own defense expenditures just for the privilege of being able to say they can defend their
collective territory without American help (recall that the Baltic states

as well as Finland and Sweden are all EU members—and they are difficult to defend, as discussed further below). Yet they do have an interest in making decisions about their own foreign policy, as they should. And where they disagree with the United States, there are often good reasons for the disagreements that can lead to better policy outcomes if the two sides listen to each other.[6]

The various initiatives that the EU sometimes undertakes in an attempt to beef up its own capacity, however worthwhile, are generally most notable for their small scale—not for constituting any plausible path toward strategic autonomy. Most EU (and NATO) common military expenditures, for new headquarters or shared assets or the like, are measured in the millions or at most the low billions of dollars a year.[7] The European Defense Fund, designed to spur collaborative technology development, was initially funded in 2018 at about $2 billion a year but has since been cut in half after the onset of the Covid-19 crisis.[8] Almost all military capacity in Europe and North America is planned, budgeted, and controlled by individual nation states, not Brussels or any other supranational being. The latest headline-grabbing initiative, Europe's Permanent Structured Cooperation (PESCO), has by now mostly been forgotten except by specialists—precisely because, however useful, its ambitions are necessarily modest.[9] It is an extension of previous efforts by European countries, most of them small or midsized at best, to make their defense procurement more efficient and thus their military forces more capable per euro expended. Americans, frequently critical of Europeans for inadequate military burden sharing and inadequate investment in new weaponry, should be applauding any such efforts, not worrying about them. Indeed, a number of important European countries have important ongoing defense cooperation relationships with U.S. companies and the Department of Defense, so the potential for such intra-European collaboration is limited for several reasons.[10]

Yet even if the West is fairly strong, and unified, serious threats do remain. The Middle East and North Africa present serious concerns. I address those in a subsequent chapter focused on that broader region. My central concern here is with Russia—and how it can endanger all of Europe as well as the United States.

It is remarkable how badly relations have soured between Russia, on the one hand, and the United States as well as much of Europe on the other. After the Cold War ended, the future seemed very promising. The most serious threat from Russia in those days appeared to be the potential for loose nukes in a country that had tens of thousands of nuclear warheads and tens of thousands of top-tier scientists in a destitute nation whose services might conceivably be purchased by extremist nation-states in the Middle East or elsewhere. The return of great power competition in more recent times must therefore be seen, in one sense, as a great disappointment and great failure of policy.

Yet in other ways, and particularly since the mid-2010s, I would argue that Western policy toward Russia is in reasonably good shape on a number of fronts. The simple continued existence and cohesion of the NATO alliance provides much of the good news. So do its recent moves to boost military spending and increase forward presence in Poland and the Baltic states. The Obama administration's Third Offset strategy, and the Trump-McMaster-Mattis National Security Strategy and National Defense Strategy, rightfully reemphasized military competition with Russia as well as China. They collectively sent a powerful message of resolve. The West's ability to impose and sustain strong sanctions is also heartening. And its ability to identify and counter Russian disinformation, while still in need of work, is improving.

But in another sense, recalling just how far things have fallen since the heady days of the 1990s, U.S. and European policy toward Russia cannot be considered fully successful or adequate. There must be a greater effort made to understand, in broad historical and strategic terms, how we got here and to try to defuse the state of confrontation. It is not enough simply to deter specific possible encroachments or attacks. The state of U.S.-Russia and NATO-Russia relations is unnecessarily and dangerously bad. Most of the problem is Putin's, and Russia's, doing, meaning that patience as we await new and better Russian leadership needs to be a central plank of longer-term policy. But that could take fifteen years—or more. Meanwhile, there is one big thing that the United States as well as Canadian and European partners should do themselves. We must rethink NATO's standing desire to push the alliance farther east—a policy virtually guaranteed to continue to produce a higher state of tension and greater risk of war than would otherwise characterize the West's relationship with Russia.

NATO was not created, and should not now be used, in an attempt to solve every European security problem. Nor was its original intent to expand. It started with just twelve members. It added only four in the next forty years—Germany, Turkey, Greece, and Spain. The goal was never growth for growth's sake. In fact, since NATO makes decisions by consensus at the North Atlantic Council in Brussels, there were clear advantages in keeping membership modest—and the scope of its main activities clearly focused on mutual self-defense, together with a few central related activities such as promotion of nuclear nonproliferation. Most of all, visionaries like George Kennan, together with NATO leaders, saw the purpose of a unified West as ensuring that the core industrial, economic, and military regions of the world not fall under the sway of a hostile power.

Ukraine, Georgia, and other former Soviet republics do not meet those criteria. They are wonderful, proud, sovereign countries. They are not, with all due respect, key parts of the world's core strategic zones in terms of scientific, industrial, or economic prowess. Beyond that, the practical effect of attempting to enlarge NATO into these countries has arguably been to set back Russian relations with the West enormously. To be sure, the main fault is with Russia's behavior, and in any event, NATO expansion has not been the only contributing Western policy. But it is the main policy that the West can and should rethink, given the very nature of alliances and the inevitable way they tend to be seen by countries that are not part of them. Indeed, it has arguably had a great effect not only on Western relations with Russia but on Russian democracy itself—just as Mikhail Gorbachev and George Kennan foresaw. Perhaps today's thirty NATO members—nearly double the sixteen that together won the Cold War—is enough.

Getting at Putin's Mindset and Russia's Ambitions

To evaluate our options going forward, we need as clear a sense as possible of what motivates Vladimir Putin and other Russians today. In addition, we must bear in mind the recent effects of economic sanctions, Russian demographics, and the Covid-19 crisis, especially for an economy that has already been stagnant for a decade, averaging perhaps 1 percent growth since 2009.[11]

A solid starting point is the observation that Russia is not the Soviet Union of old, with a fervent ideology and grand ambitions of global conquest. Putin is not a nice guy, but neither is he Stalin. He wants to restore Russia as one of the world's major strategic powers, often in objectionable ways. Yet he also partially cooperates with the West on numerous issues, such as Afghanistan, Iran, and North Korea in recent years, as well as on such matters as nuclear nonproliferation.[12] Deciphering which elements of Russian policy we can work with, which we can at least live with, and which could be dangerous unless firmly opposed is crucial for Western policy makers. Hedging against the possibility that Russia may be even more ambitious and aggressive than the above analysis would suggest is important, too. Yet the hedging should try to avoid creating a self-fulfilling prophecy—and with it a security dilemma that spirals into worsening rivalry.

As Fiona Hill and Clifford Gaddy have elegantly described, Putin is best understood as part nationalist, part romantic about Russian history and culture, part former KGB operative with deep mistrust of others and penchant for covert activities. He sees U.S. and allied actions since the Cold War—the expansion of NATO, use of military force without proper U.N. authorization in Kosovo and Iraq, support for the color revolutions in former Soviet republics to include Ukraine and Georgia in the 2000s—as overuses of American hegemonic power. He perhaps resents above all the efforts of the United States to promote political pluralism in Russia, including in the run-up to his election for a third presidential term in 2012 (it is probably then that he developed his disdain for Hillary Clinton, helping to explain his opposition to her in 2016).[13] The release of the so-called Panama Papers by investigative journalists in 2016 implicated Putin and his associates in a number of corrupt economic activities; the Russian strongman also likely resented these disclosures deeply.[14]

Yet Putin is smart, or at least calculating. He believes in Russian greatness but seems to appreciate his country's limits, too. With 140 million people, Russia has about one-fifth the population of NATO, one-twentieth the military budget, and one-twenty-fifth the GDP. And while we in the West often feel that Europe is unraveling before our eyes these days, the overall strength of our position is striking—as Russians surely appreciate. Major NATO nations are bending, but they are generally not breaking or becoming autocracies either. The United Kingdom may have left the European Union. But it is not leaving Europe or NATO or the close economic interlinkages it will retain with countries in the OECD (Organisation for Economic Co-Operation and Development). Right-wing parties in France and Germany are stronger than before, but hardly carrying the day in their nations' politics. Putin surely appreciates that NATO with its thirty members, twenty-eight of them in Europe, accounts for *more than half* of all world military spending and 40 percent of world GDP. Putin wants to push back against this conglomeration of military and economic power in the hands of leaders and countries who, in his mind, act unilaterally on the world stage in advance of their own narrow national interests—and who would challenge his very right to lead Russia if they could.

There is nothing noble about Putin's worldview or his foreign policy. Yet in terms of when and where he chooses to flex Russian muscle, he would seem more of a counterpuncher, and opportunist, than an imperialistic global conqueror. As Georgetown professor Angela Stent notes, his geopolitics resembles judo, in keeping with his preferred sport, more than Machiavellian three-dimensional global chess.[15] He waits for opportunities, seeking to exploit others' mistakes and security vacuums to maximize Russian influence where possible at reasonable cost and risk. He clearly relishes using limited amounts of Russia's military power in carefully chosen operations—to seize Crimea with little green men in 2014, to sneak into Syria with a few thousand troops the next year after correctly concluding that the Obama administration did not care enough about the issue to oppose him, letting the mercenary Wagner Group support a strongman in Libya in a way that could extend Russian influence. So far at least, there are no brazen invasions of huge landmasses. Going back to the deterrence framework I employ in chapter 2, he seems (like most foreign leaders) relatively easy to deter from attacking the core territories or sovereign existence of U.S. allies but quite hard to deter where our own interests are less clearly and consistently established. The way to handle such a situation is not to pretend that we care more about certain places, like Crimea or Syria, than we really do—and start drawing noncredible red lines all over the map. Rather, we need tools that are commensurate with the risks and stakes at hand.

Putin is just one person, of course. But he is representative of a good deal of Russian thinking, judging by opinion polls and the worldviews of even many of his critics. He may well stay in office until 2036. Even if he does not, and even if democracy makes a comeback of sorts in Russia, an equally hardline Russian nationalist may wind up replacing him.[16]

The way in which a proud, but also sometimes petulant and vindictive, strand of Russian nationalism could quickly sour on the West was predicted by many Russia and Europe experts and historians even before Putin's rise to power in 1999–2000 or his turn to vindictiveness around 2006–8. Tony Judt wrote of the politics of "aggrieved memory" by many Russian nationalists who, after the Cold War ended, expected more gratitude from the countries that the Soviet Union had helped save from Hitler. They were through with communism but not with the idea of Russian power and greatness—or Russian spheres of influence. They resented the West's introduction of economic shock therapy in Russia, the expansion of NATO, and Western displays of military power in the Balkans and Middle East.[17]

Richard Betts of Columbia University wrote perceptively that "in traditional strategic terms NATO expansion was a threat to Russia, but the West's leaders considered traditional strategic terms passé, antiquated concerns of outmoded realpolitik. Americans tend to assume that their benign intentions are obvious to all and that their right to shape world order in a virtuous direction should be unobjectionable."[18] Not so, however, to most Russians.

As Thomas Graham wrote about Russia and the United States, "The two countries espouse profoundly different concepts of world order. . . . A new Russia strategy must dispense with the magical thinking of previous administrations and instead seek incremental gains that advance long-term U.S. interests. Rather than trying to persuade Moscow to understand its own interests differently, Washington must demonstrate that those interests can be more safely pursued through both considered competition and cooperation with the United States."[19]

Without kowtowing to the objectionable, indeed often arrogant and self-serving aspects of the Russian national security narrative, the West needs to make future policy in full awareness of what reactions it will likely engender within the world's other nuclear superpower. This assessment suggests several elements for future U.S. and Western policy toward Russia.

The Need for a Resolute NATO Capability

The Russia threat, in a plausible worst-case situation, has the potential to lead to all-out war. This prospect is not likely, but it cannot be dismissed. Hence, the Russia component of any U.S. grand strategy needs a strong military component.

Russia's shenanigans in Europe (and elsewhere) are likely far from over. Low-level probing and harassing attacks, or minor events that then take on a life of their own, can lead to miscalculation and escalation. Cyberweapons, hypersonic missiles, and other new technologies complicate the technical task of maintaining stability and preventing escalation, potentially blurring perceptions of the line between conventional and nuclear war in some scenarios.[20] Nuclear weapons raise the stakes dramatically. Russia's willingness to threaten the Baltics in particular, even with an invasion and annexation, cannot be safely dismissed as somehow obsolescent or impossible. Even with Russia's economic challenges of late, its ability to sustain a military of roughly the current size and capability, with pockets of modernization and excellence as well as a large nuclear force, is hard to doubt.[21]

There are multiple possible paths to war. Russia could choose to threaten one or more of the Baltic states in numerous ways, from cyberattacks to quick maneuvers by little green men like those used in the stealthy invasion of Crimea in 2014 to some type of partial naval blockade against shipping.[22] The most stressful case for U.S. force planning purposes would probably be a classic invasion to seize one of the small countries outright. Indeed, Russia may have hoped to conjure up fears of such a capability with its summer 2017 exercise in Belarus, which involved many tens of thousands of troops.[23] Moscow might hope that it could somehow create a fait accompli with a conventional invasion and then threaten nuclear attacks to dissuade NATO from liberating the conquered territory.[24]

In such scenarios, geography would work against NATO. The region presents relatively open terrain for the movement of large armies.[25] Russia is well positioned to act quickly with large forces in this area. NATO is not.

According to recent RAND war games, just to have a partially viable defense in the Baltic states, NATO might require some seven brigades— meaning perhaps fifty thousand total uniformed personnel, after adding support and airpower capabilities.[26] Counting Baltic state armed forces and NATO forces prepositioned in the Baltics today, the alliance has only about half of that in place.

To be confident of success in a major counteroffensive operation, NATO would likely need to deploy a multidivisional force of several hundred thousand troops. NATO would need not only the combat punch to defeat Russian forces, including possible reinforcements, but also the capacity to establish and protect bases and supply lines in the theater.[27] Achieving such a deployment would be no mean feat. NATO is poorly prepared to meet such standards today. At its Wales summit in September 2014, NATO proposed creating a rapid reaction force of four thousand.[28] Such a force, however useful for trip-wire deterrence, would have a meager combat capability against plausible Russian threats.[29] Within about a month, Britain, France, and Germany might each be able to deploy a brigade, putting their combined contributions at somewhat more than ten thousand—still only a modest fraction of what would surely be required even for robust defense.[30]

Fortunately, although NATO has certainly not stationed a robust forward-defense capability in eastern Europe, it has by now established a rather unambiguous and clear trip wire. My guess is that this will be adequate, since Putin would almost certainly not choose war with NATO even if he thought he could win the opening battles. Through what the United States has called the European Reassurance or Deterrence Initiative and what NATO has called Operation Atlantic Resolve, some twenty

NATO nations now continuously rotate some five thousand troops in the Baltic states—an enhanced Forward Presence, or eFP, capability. The United States has a comparable number of American GIs in Poland right next door.[31] It also has a prepositioned stock of another brigade's worth of heavy equipment in eastern Europe, strewn across some nine nations.[32] A 2018 NATO proposal would back these initial forces up with thirty thousand ground troops plus thirty supporting ships and thirty aircraft squadrons, to be deployable within thirty days.[33] This is the worthy Four 30s initiative, subsequently released as a formal NATO declaration after the July 2018 Brussels summit.[34] Things are moving in the right direction, albeit slowly.

The eFP capability is a rather impressive trip wire, inevitably and quickly implicating as it would most of NATO's members and all of its major powers in any large-scale Russian aggression against the Baltic states. And the 30/30/30/30 initiative, if implemented, will show that NATO is watching carefully, and planning carefully, for scenarios in its eastern regions. These policies together reduce the risks of an all-out Russian attack to seize and annex the Baltics, perhaps with an operation that attempted to close off NATO's land paths to reinforce the Baltics by moving forces from Belarus toward Kaliningrad through the Suwalki corridor in Poland. Further measures, such as establishing standing headquarters and predeploying logistical enabler units, would also be desirable. They would expedite the potential of NATO to reinforce these eastern positions, clarifying that the NATO commitment to the Baltics is not purely a trip wire.[35] So would improving and harmonizing European rail lines, creating European civil reserve air fleets for military use in crisis, building more airfields, hardening some infrastructure, and creating more capacity for European military mobility in general—as argued in an excellent April 2020 Atlantic Council report.[36] But the basic policy is sound.

Yet even if Russian invasion and annexation of the Baltics seems an unlikely prospect that is becoming even less likely with time, due to various NATO policies, we should not yet rest content. There are still considerable dangers that lurk, especially in regard to smaller-scale and/or gray-zone aggressions that would not have the character of a classic war of conquest or in regard to countries such as Ukraine that are not part of NATO.

Moscow might, for example, conduct a limited operation designed to protect native Russian speakers, particularly in Latvia or Estonia, where they number some 25 percent of the population. Russia's goal here could be less to reestablish full Russian control of the Baltics—at least in the short term—than to reveal NATO to be a paper tiger in its commitment to honor its article 5 obligations—perhaps creating an existential crisis for the alliance that could lead to its overall weakening and even dissolution.[37] After all, the NATO Treaty's article 5 mutual-defense pledge is not a predesignated plan for a military response; it requires interpretation in any given situation. Again, it reads as follows: "The Parties agree that an armed attack against one or more of them in Europe or North America shall be considered an attack against them all and consequently they agree that, if such an armed attack occurs, each of them, in exercise of the right of individual or collective self-defense recognized by Article 51 of the Charter of the United Nations, will assist the Party or Parties so attacked by taking forthwith, individually and in concert with the other Parties, such action as it deems necessary, including the use of armed force, to restore and maintain the security of the North Atlantic area."[38] The phrase "*including the use of armed force*" would seem to suggest an inevitable military response, but the preceding words, "*as it deems necessary,*" convey considerable ambiguity. Some allies might invoke this ambiguity to opt out of a military response and even to disapprove of a formal NATO decision to send force.

Weakening, neutering, or even ending the NATO alliance would for Putin surely count as a major strategic victory. He might also come to believe that he could get away with such a limited invasion if he created a partially believable pretext (using disinformation campaigns and other tools) that Russian speakers in the area of interest were somehow under threat. His government's recent claims of a right to protect Russian speakers (or any others considering themselves "Russian people") anywhere in the world could provide a strategic predicate for such an aggression.[39] That such Russian strategic ambitions could extend to areas that were once part of the Soviet Union, especially regions inhabited by large numbers of Russian speakers, seems particularly plausible. New military concepts emerging from Russia of late, including *maskirovka* (or masked, camouflaged warfare), hybrid warfare, and escalate to de-escalate (threatening to employ nuclear weapons to persuade an adversary to back down), suggest active thinking in Russia's strategic and military communities about exactly these kinds of scenarios.[40] The blatant military element of the attack would be but one element in a broader strategy.

Why might some NATO allies choose not to fight, even when their sworn obligations to each other would seem to require it? Beyond the semantic ambiguity inherent in the language of article 5, there are deeper strategic reasons. Some allies might believe there was little plausible threat to them, even if the initial aggression was allowed to stand, since Russia's current military posture presents little plausible capacity to conduct a deeper penetration of NATO territories.[41] By contrast, other allies might fear provoking Russia into a larger war. Russia does have some capacity to bring in reinforcements over time, a result of improvements to its land forces west of the Urals in recent years.[42] And, of course, it has nuclear weapons. Against this backdrop, some NATO states might prefer not to risk further arousing the Russian bear, even if it had already committed an initial limited act of aggression. If Russia carried out the aggression in a way that maintained a semblance of deniability, with little green men instead of regular troops, few would really be fooled even for a short time. But some NATO countries looking to avoid confrontation might invoke Moscow's excuse as a reason to delay any military response and give diplomacy a chance to reverse the aggression.

To counter such thinking, the West needs options that do not all rely on the immediate deployment of counteroffensive capability to liberate the seized swath of land or retaliate for the harassment. We should *not* depend exclusively on plans that would have NATO fire the first shot in anger in response to a Russian act of aggression. Nor should we depend centrally on escalating any war that begins. The West needs to be able to engage in a more integrated form of warfare that depends less on the early use of military force and more on an integrated, asymmetric, indirect approach. This approach might take many years to liberate a village or small swath of land in the Baltics that Russia might have seized. But at least it would not destroy that proverbial village—and perhaps even risk nuclear war—in order to save it.

The active elements of such a strategy would center on economic warfare. The tools of economic warfare would include punitive sanctions against specific targets that could be expanded over time; sectoral sanctions designed to affect a larger part of an adversary's economy and the basic trajectory of its GDP; asset seizures designed to be proportionate in some sense to the consequences of the original transgression; limits on access to the American or global financial system; and export controls designed to limit an adversary's technological advancement over a longer time period. Just as central would be various measures to improve the economic resilience of the United States and its allies so that they could outlast Russia in what could easily become a reciprocal economic war. These measures should include expanding strategic stockpiles of key materials and ensuring adequate access to alternative energy sources (even if more expensive) for countries in Europe. They should be undertaken now, as a matter of prudence and a means of buttressing deterrence.

At this point in time, most of western Europe has so integrated its energy markets and its pipeline systems that it could find ways to replace Russian hydrocarbons through such means as increased imports of liquefied natural gas. Yes, additional annual costs could be greater than today—as much as several tens of billions of dollars a year, in fact.[43] But Europe's sizable wealth compared with Russia's should allow western Europe to tolerate an interruption of this trade much more easily than Russia could, and compared with the costs of war, which could of course very easily reach into the tens of trillions of dollars or more, these costs would be a bargain. To strengthen Europe's resilience even further, NATO infrastructure funds could be used now to help create more terminals at the continent's ports for liquefied natural gas.

Some claim that sanctions to date have not been very effective and cannot form the basis for any future strategy. I disagree. The sanctions imposed against Russia to date hurt the country's economy. Putin's popularity has suffered considerably, and many young Russians now say they wish to leave the country.[44] The sanctions could be expanded further if Russian aggression expanded—and Putin surely knows it.

Sanctions have not persuaded Moscow to return Crimea to Ukraine or relent in its support for Ukrainian separatists in the east of the country. However, they have punished elites, restricted access to Western banks and Western visas, and limited Russia's access to certain forms of high technology, among other effects. It is striking that Russia has not expanded the geographic scope of its aggression. We can only speculate why. But perhaps Vladimir Putin and cronies have deduced that if the West would be so resolute, over such a long time, in punishing him for his earlier aggressions, an even more ambitious use of Russian military force would be foolish.[45] It would likely result in additional sanctions that would drive the Russian economy into prolonged recession (already, it has enjoyed little net growth this past half decade due largely to sanctions imposed to date). From a U.S. grand strategy perspective, preventing attacks on NATO member states is far more important than having our way on every relatively minor territorial issue in distant Eurasia. In terms of what really counts for U.S. security, it strikes me that these sanctions should hardly be deemed a failure.

Beyond NATO: Creating a New
Security Order in Eastern Europe

While most of what the United States and European nations themselves are doing to promote security on the continent is sound, one major change merits serious consideration: an end to NATO expansion, if that can be achieved as part of a broader understanding with Moscow that promotes the security of nations in eastern Europe.

NATO expansion policy has gotten stuck. Since the spring of 2008, the United States and the rest of NATO have promised publicly to bring Ukraine, as well as the smaller and even more remote country of Georgia, into the North Atlantic Treaty Organization. However, this policy aspiration that dates back to the Freedom Agenda of the George W. Bush administration has now been in a sort of deep freeze for more than a decade. President Obama did not promote it enthusiastically, either before or after Russia attacked Ukraine in 2014. President Trump was even warier than President Obama about the NATO expansion concept.

Yet no one has taken further NATO enlargement off the table— and Putin has undoubtedly noticed that fact. And on a trip to Georgia in 2017, Vice President Mike Pence publicly repeated to his hosts the pledge of eventual alliance membership. Whether anyone in the United States or other NATO countries really took Pence's words seriously at this point, many in both Tbilisi and Moscow probably did. The concept of NATO expansion, which dates to the Clinton administration, has incensed Russian nationalists like Putin—just as everyone from Soviet leader Mikhail Gorbachev to George Kennan to former senator Sam Nunn of Georgia to former secretary of defense William Perry thought it would. It has also likely set back Russia's own democracy by empowering chauvinistic nationalists who used the issue to paint an image of supposed Western conspiracy against their nation.[46]

One need not concede Russia a sphere of influence to appreciate that geography matters in alliance formation. NATO knocking on the doorstep of Russia was hardly likely to engender a positive response from proud nationalists in that country. From the perspective of many Russians, it was the United States that was trying to expand its own already-large sphere of influence—and to do so deeply into the Eurasian heartland.

In fairness to President Bill Clinton, it was one thing when NATO expansion encompassed Poland, Hungary, and the Czech Republic in the late 1990s.[47] And in fairness to what President George W. Bush did in his first term, when NATO grew by seven more members including Estonia, Latvia, and Lithuania, Washington had never recognized those Baltic states to be part of the Soviet Union even after Moscow annexed them in 1940. But it is something else altogether to bring into NATO a former core part of the Soviet Union whose history is so closely intertwined with Russia's own.

Worse, NATO promised eventual membership to Ukraine and Georgia but with no timetable for how that might happen—and with no interim security guarantee. Completing the package of perverse incentives, NATO also maintains that, to be eligible for alliance membership, a country must have resolved territorial disputes with neighbors, no matter whose fault those disputes might be. Taken together, this set of pronouncements has provided Russia a clear rationale to continue to stoke unrest and conflict within both Ukraine and Georgia—and to seize chunks of each country, as it did in 2008 in Georgia and since 2014 in Ukraine.

Admittedly, the prospect of NATO expansion was probably not the spark that created the 2014 Russian annexation of Crimea and support for separatist forces in eastern Ukraine, as my colleague the esteemed ambassador Steven Pifer has persuasively underscored.[48] Ukraine's interest in closer association with the European Union was the immediate catalyst to crisis, perhaps partly because it could have threatened the crony capitalism and corrupt economic networks of Putin and associates. But NATO expansion did generate angst and anger in Russia over the years. It created the general backdrop against which specific incidents like the Maydan crisis in Ukraine in 2013–14 took place—ladening them with a much greater rivalrous zero-sum aspect in Moscow's eyes. It left Ukraine exposed to Russian retribution in a way that Bill Clinton had anticipated it might, back in the 1990s.[49]

Alliances like NATO are different from other types of organizations. They are inherently exclusionary by nature. They also concern matters of war and peace, which elicit a different type of human passion than other endeavors. The ancient Greek scholar Thucydides might or might not have liked Vladimir Putin. But my sense is that he would have understood him. Thucydides wrote that nations go to war for three reasons: honor, fear, and interest.[50] With Putin and many Russians, it is all about honor—or, to be more precise perhaps, wounded pride. In Russian eyes, NATO is exploiting a Cold War victory and piling on, bringing its influence as well as its military bases deep into the Eurasian heartland in a way that is offensive to Russia.

Some say that we must honor an open-door policy of NATO that is codified in article 10 of the treaty. But if alliance aspirants have rights, then so do Americans and other existing members of the alliance. That includes, for the United States, the right to decide which countries we are willing to promise to protect with the lives of our citizens. For all of NATO's strengths, it still depends overwhelmingly on the U.S. military backstop.[51] Of course, article 10 does not, and could not, *require* admitting aspirants to the alliance. In fact, it counsels doing so only if their membership would "contribute to the security of the North Atlantic area."[52] Judgment is therefore required as to which types of NATO expansion would be net plusses for the region's security—versus which might be net negatives.

Putin was of course wrong when he asserted that Ukraine is not even a real country. It is indeed true that Ukrainian and Russian history are intertwined going back centuries—more so than Russian and Baltic state history, for example. Thus, the Russian sensitivities on Ukraine are hardly surprising. Yet, as Steven Pifer points out, nothing has unified Ukrainians more in their history, or given them a clearer sense of identity distinct from association with Russia, than Putin's long-standing assault on their independence and sovereignty.[53] Putin has no grounds for denying Ukraine any of its innate rights on matters such as eventual European Union association or membership. The country needs such economic relationships badly. At the end of the Cold War, Ukraine and Poland, countries with similar size populations, had about the same gross domestic product. Now, Poland's dwarfs Ukraine's by more than a factor of four, given the sorry state of Kyiv's economic policies ever since.

Of course, Moscow has no right to dictate events near its borders at the expense of its neighbors. There should be no Yalta II whereby the great powers would in effect divvy up Europe into respective spheres of influence as happened in World War II and its aftermath. The countries of eastern Europe are fully sovereign and deserve every right to make their own domestic *and* foreign policy decisions. We in the West also owe a debt to Ukraine, which aided in global nonproliferation efforts when it gave up its nearly two thousand nuclear warheads after the breakup of the Soviet Union in the early 1990s and to which we joined then in offering a multilateral security guarantee, the Budapest Memorandum of 1994.[54] Russia has violated that memorandum and should not be allowed to get away with doing so. More broadly, Putin's machinations constitute a broader assault on democracy, the rule of law, freedom and free speech, economic openness, and basic human decency.[55] And it is hard even to view the current situation as much of a win for Russia, which has been mired in mediocre economic growth and political ostracization for years now.[56]

The United States, with NATO allies and the EU, has been right to push back against Russia. Putin's war against Ukraine has caused some fifteen thousand deaths since 2014 in the country's eastern Donbas region, where Russia has stoked and armed a separatist movement. The United States has been right to help Ukraine, first with nonlethal military assistance and training and more recently with such weaponry as antitank missiles. Russia's aggression is unacceptable, and the security aid has apparently helped Ukraine fight the separatists to a standstill—perhaps thereby helping deter further Russian ambitions in more of Ukraine.[57]

That said, we are not in a good place today. A situation in which the United States provides lethal aid to forces fighting Russian soldiers—however justifiable that may be—increases the odds of Russian retribution in a place like Afghanistan or Syria. Moreover, the aid Ukraine really needs is economic reform and development, once Kyiv makes the tough decisions necessary to make such assistance useful. The Trump administration's Ukraine policy has failed to address this matter. Rather than try to help the country overcome its internal problems of corruption and economic mismanagement and its external problem of improving relations with Russia, Trump attempted to bully Ukraine for personal political gain.

It is time to rethink strategy toward Ukraine and Russia. A centerpiece of that strategy should be a new security architecture for eastern Europe. We should do so in a way that would improve the well-being and future prospects of countries like Ukraine and Georgia relative to the uncertain path they are on now—perpetually in Russia's crosshairs yet offered no near-term path to alliance membership or protection by NATO.

The core concept should be one of permanent neutrality for countries of eastern Europe. The countries in question collectively make a broken-up arc from Europe's far north to its south: Finland and Sweden, Ukraine and Moldova and Belarus, Georgia and Armenia and Azerbaijan, and finally Cyprus plus Serbia, as well as possibly other Balkan states. The most important countries for this purpose are the former Soviet republics (to my mind, it would be undesirable but much less concerning if Sweden or Finland were to join NATO, for example). Under such a new construct, these nonaligned countries' existing security affiliations with NATO and/or Russia could be continued, but formal security commitments would not be extended or expanded by Brussels or Moscow.

This idea should not be imposed on any nation and should not be done in Yalta style, with the superpowers determining the fate of smaller countries absent their participation. In fact, the consultation process should begin within NATO and then quickly include the neutral countries. But it is time to be honest with ourselves and with them—recognizing that even under existing policy, no more former Soviet republics are likely to receive membership action plans (MAPs) to prepare to join NATO soon, if ever, in any event. Once we reach a greater recognition of reality, and agreement on a better path forward, with these countries, formal negotiations would then—and only then—take place with Russia. A Track 1.5 dialogue process involving scholars together with policy makers acting in informal capacity could be used to flesh out, and sound out, the idea before NATO leaders formally propose it.

The new security architecture would require that Russia, like NATO, commit to help uphold the security of Ukraine, Georgia, Moldova, and other states in the region. (Crimea, however, might need to be finessed, and autonomy arrangements would need to be developed for parts of eastern Ukraine and northern Georgia.)[58] Russia would have to withdraw its troops from those countries in a verifiable manner. After that occurred, and conflict subsided, corresponding sanctions on the Russian Federation imposed after the assaults on Georgia and Ukraine would be lifted.

In pursuing such a diplomatic solution, no apology should be made for NATO's growth, which was in fact not done with any hostile intent. That Russia has acted predictably in its anger about NATO expansion (and EU expansion) to date does not mean that Russia was justified in its anger—or use of violence and other tactics—against the idea. The possibility that enlargement was always an idea of dubious wisdom does not mean that it was sinister or imperialistic. And now that they are in, new members cannot be seen as second-class citizens of the alliance. To convey contrition for NATO's past actions would only embolden Russia and make it unwilling to offer compromises of its own in pursuit of a new security order. To convey any sense that some alliance members are more important than others would jeopardize NATO's deterrence in those very places where Moscow is most likely to test it—especially if the negotiations ultimately prove unsuccessful. NATO leaders should avoid comments like President Donald Trump's, after the July 2018 Helsinki summit, when he raised doubts about U.S. willingness to defend a NATO ally like Montenegro.[59]

Ideally, this architecture might be codified in treaty form and ratified by key legislative bodies, including, in the case of the United States, the Senate. But we need not get hung up on this excessively. Even some accords that are successfully formalized as treaties are later fairly quickly jettisoned by presidents, without a major role for Congress, such as the Anti-Ballistic Missile Treaty; even some informal accords, or treaties that are never ratified, wind up guiding action for years to come, like the Comprehensive Nuclear Test Ban Treaty.

The new security paradigm should be couched as of indefinite duration. If, someday, the world were to evolve to where a new security order also including Russia were possible, or if Russian politics and strategic culture evolved to the point where Moscow no longer objected, NATO (or a new organization) might expand further—but only after mutual agreement had been reached.

As part of the broader understanding, Russia would acknowledge the prerogative of those countries not yet in the European Union to join it someday, should that someday be of interest to them as well as current EU members. The security-related provisions of the European Union could be finessed as part of the understanding, so that they did not appear to carry the same weight as article 5 of the NATO Treaty.

Putin could still brag to his people that he had stopped encroachments toward Russia's borders by a competitor, and he could improve Russia's prospects for a return to sustained economic growth of the type that helped make him a popular leader in the first place in the 2000s. As such, the odds are good that he would be interested in such an idea.

This kind of new architecture would not turn Putin into a nice guy or the West's relationship with Russia into a friendly one. But it would likely produce a very substantial lowering of tensions and risk of war. That is the greatest purpose that U.S. grand strategy toward Russia and Europe can serve in the years ahead—and it is a very worthy purpose.

Countering Russian Disinformation, Propaganda, and Cyberwar

Any analysis of national security risks posed by Russia must also delve into the world of disinformation and propaganda. With these tools, in addition to simple harassment, Russia seeks to sow discord in the West, weaken the world's democracies, and improve the electoral prospects of candidates friendly to its ambitions. Such machinations may not be the most dangerous type of potential Russian aggression against the West in the future, but they are the most likely, and they demand vigilance.[60] They could also rise to the level of a true national security threat, in a worst case, by challenging the basic functioning and reliability of key NATO polities.

There is little reason to think Russian efforts have relented of late. For example, Senator Jack Reed reports that on a single day in October 2019, Facebook took down fifty accounts associated with Russia's Kremlin-linked troll organization, the Internet Research Agency.[61] Most Republicans in the United States fully acknowledge the menace as well, even if President Trump was inconsistent in his own words on the subject.[62]

Daniel Fried and Alina Polyakova have recommended a number of measures that could help importantly in the struggle against such methods. They include:

- Government-imposed transparency standards on sources of information about world affairs and current events;
- Cooperation by social-media platforms in labeling sources by their known sources of support and reliability as well as demoting or eliminating accounts of known perpetrators of false data;
- Collaboration with nongovernmental entities that monitor and understand new methods of information warfare such as deep fakes; and
- Creation of transnational, official clearinghouses that track and rebut malevolent and unreliable sources of information on the internet and elsewhere.[63]

In addition, all this should be complemented and trumpeted to the American public by a major public information campaign. Before a given crisis in a given election in the United States, when partisan distrust among Americans themselves is high, voters need to understand just how much mischief Russia and other foreign actors seek to generate.

Ideally, this public education effort should *not* be run out of the White House, because doing so makes it more political and therefore less credible to a large swath of the country. University consortiums, bipartisan congressional task forces, or even elements of the U.S. intelligence community might be better lead agents.

And there is the crucial matter of election security. Fortunately, the means of preventing electoral tampering are well known. They center on ensuring paper records for voter registries as well as actual votes themselves, plus a rapid means of validating results (partly a question of ample personnel available to do physical vote counting). And an effective national organization, the Elections Assistance Commission, exists to help promote best-practice standards around the country. Unfortunately, as of 2020, not all states had taken measures to carry out such basic validation measures—and it is states that have the ultimate responsibility and control over what happens with voting within their respective jurisdictions. About 90 percent of American voters now have paper backup to their ballots, for example.[64] That is good, and better than before, but not yet adequate.

Conclusion

My final observation about Russia, and Europe, policy is a warning. Many in American strategic circles consider China to be the growing threat and Russia the fading one. That is a strange way to view a nuclear superpower that spans eleven time zones and has a population of 140 million (even if shrinking) as well as world-class traditions in science and engineering—to say nothing of a geostrategic ax to grind. In recent years, Russia has shown how to dominate the news and outmaneuver the world's only comprehensive superpower as well as a broader NATO alliance that outspends it on defense by about twenty to one, throughout a swath of eastern Europe extending down to the Levant region of the Middle East.

If we again become complacent about the state of U.S.-Russia relations or take too much comfort in our various national and alliance measures of superiority over the Russian Federation, we could easily

find that Moscow rather than Beijing becomes our major challenger—
or, to be more specific, our major peril—in the coming years and even
decades.

Fortunately, some measures have by now been taken to redress the
situation. NATO and the EU have, for the most part, proved their mettle
through targeted military buildups and the sustained imposition of economic sanctions—as well as a cohesion that has survived the period of
the Trump presidency. We need to sustain this resoluteness, which may
have some chance of bringing Putin and other hardline Russian nationalists to their senses, especially as the Russian economy flounders in the
age of sanctions, coronavirus, and low oil prices. At the same time, we
should seek to use our own policies to defuse tensions—perhaps through
advocacy of a new security architecture for eastern Europe and an end
to further NATO expansion.

FOUR

The Pacific and China

When I last visited China, in 2018, I was part of a small group of American scholars, meeting with fellow Chinese think-tankers to explore possible collaboration for handling the North Korea nuclear crisis. It felt very collegial and professional. Our nations' goals in Korea are not identical, to be sure, but they are generally compatible, and certainly neither Beijing nor Washington wants war. It was one of many times when I have felt that the Chinese, even as they seek a greater role for themselves in the broader Pacific region, do not harbor truly aggressive designs against us. For me, the writer Evan Osnos captures the mentality best, in his award-winning book, *Age of Ambition: Chasing Fortune, Truth, and Faith in the New China*.[1] Note the subtitle. Most Chinese I know are indeed ambitious but not really in classic realpolitik or Machiavellian terms. They want to be prosperous. They also want their nation to be secure and powerful. Yet they are also generally sane enough not to want war—and to know that the United States remains committed to allies and core interests in the region. For all of China's growing assertiveness in recent years, its military spending remains well below 2 percent of GDP, even once adjusted to count things that Western countries include in standard defense budget measures. China's restraint in its nuclear force modernization is another case in point; at this juncture, the world's top manufacturing power could clearly aim for nuclear superpower status if it so chose, yet it appears content with a nuclear arsenal less than a tenth the size of America's or Russia's.[2] These data points make me hopeful.

But there is of course another interpretation. Especially because China is nondemocratic and nontransparent in many ways, it is hard to dismiss. Many of the Chinese with whom Westerners interact are those who speak English, who may have studied or worked in the United States for a while, and who are schooled as "barbarian handlers," to use the old Chinese adage. They know how to talk with, and soothe, Americans. They may be much more conciliatory than hardliners who rarely interact with foreigners—and whose appetite for power could well be growing with the country's GDP. Moreover, top Chinese leaders sometimes have a swagger that can verge on dangerous overconfidence. Consider how then-national security adviser H. R. Mc-Master described a meeting with Li Keqiang, China's titular head of government, during President Trump's state visit to China in 2017: "If anyone in the American group had any doubts about China's view of its relationship with the United States, Li's monologue would have removed them. He began with the observation that China, having already developed its industrial and technological base, no longer needed the United States. He dismissed U.S. concerns over unfair trade and economic practices, indicating that the U.S. role in the future global economy would merely be to provide China with raw materials, agricultural products, and energy to fuel its production of the world's cutting-edge industrial and consumer products."[3] McMaster's observations are neither partisan nor unique. They echo, in fact, the observations of President Obama's last secretary of defense, Ashton Carter, about how Chinese thinking has evolved—and how its leaders' swagger has increased—as the country has become much more powerful.[4]

In addition, the economic policies that a centrally planned economy may undertake to build up strategic industries when still a fledgling power can become dangerous once it becomes a global superpower.[5] And while I understand China's strong desire to reunify with Taiwan, its actions and its official policy in the South China Sea suggest hegemonic temptations of a much more sweeping character. Claiming effective ownership of international waterways, as China does with its infamous nine-dash line, is something that virtually no country has attempted in the post–World War II era. Such ambitions aim a dagger right at the heart of the rules-based global order. We have our work cut out for us in managing the relationship with the PRC in the years and decades to come.

The other great geostrategic challenge for America besides Russia is clearly China. Russia may be the angrier and more nuclear-armed of the two. But China is much more powerful on balance and much more ascendant.[6] The United States needs a plan to avoid what Harvard professor Graham Allison calls "Thucydides trap"—the historical fact that when a rising superpower meets an established superpower, conflict is likely. Allison calculates the odds at about 75 percent, basing his estimates primarily on cases drawn from European history.[7] But it is not inevitable that we relive history. Washington and Beijing have more shared interests than most great powers of the past had with each other, including the importance of together addressing the second set of 4+1 dangers that I discuss in chapter 7. They also have more knowledge about how deadly war can be than did great powers before the world wars. The additional element of nuclear deterrence in today's world may reduce the chances of open conflict—though there are downsides to relying on such a modern-day sword of Damocles for keeping the peace. We need a smart strategy toward China that recognizes the inevitability of its rise but develops tools to channel and constrain that rise while redirecting it in relatively nonthreatening directions, in order to keep that sword from falling.

Admittedly, such a policy might not succeed if China had already decided on maximalist ambitions and was impervious to a combination of positive and negative incentives that might be presented to it. But while Chinese leaders certainly have an ambitious vision for themselves and their nation going forward, it is doubtful that they have charted out a specific plan for getting there. It is also doubtful that they have decided to pay any price, bear any burden—including comprehensive economic decoupling and even a risk of war with the United States—to achieve those goals. They exude a certain arrogance but not recklessness. Much more likely, Western policy can influence how Chinese leaders translate their abstract ambitions into a specific policy agenda. More often than not, human leaders are in large part opportunists, and even most ideologues have a heavy streak of pragmatism. Otherwise, most would not have navigated the path to power within their own countries or held onto that power once they had seized it.

China did not rate highly in George Kennan's strategic map of the early Cold War years. Indeed, in previous eras, grand strategy toward Asia policy generally focused on ensuring openness and access to the region, then on defeating Japan in World War II, then on allying with and helping rebuild Japan, and later on checking communism in Korea and Vietnam—rather than on countering a huge peer rival.[8] But things have changed dramatically.[9] Kennan's logic today would require putting China at the center of American foreign policy.

China's rise over the past four decades—or, more precisely in historical terms, its return to earlier greatness—has been stunning. It went from an impoverished agrarian society to the world's top manufacturing power, number-two military power, number-two research and development power, and top trading nation for every country in Asia.

Few peoples have as favorable a view of themselves, their culture, and their innate importance as do the Chinese.[10] Few feel they have been as mistreated and suppressed by others.[11] Few have as much of a chip on their collective shoulder.

To date, China has also been *relatively* restrained, by the standards of the history of rising superpowers, in its use of military force. Notably, it has not fought a war since 1979 despite doubling its GDP and military spending every seven to ten years since the 1980s. Forebodingly, however, tectonic shifts in geopolitics of this magnitude have often produced war in the past.[12] Conflict could happen in numerous ways. For example, China's leaders and people might seek a chance to get back at Japan over historical grievances.[13] The two sides still have relatively minor, but potentially incendiary, territorial disputes. Combine China's ambitions and newfound power with Japan's pride and sense of increasing encirclement, and there is no telling where this situation could go in the years ahead. The U.S.-Japan alliance makes war a far less realistic option for Beijing than it might otherwise be. But it does not make it impossible altogether. More likely still, the United States and China could fight over Taiwan or over access to the South China Sea—or as the inadvertent consequence of war on the Korean peninsula that initially pitted their respective allies, the Republic of Korea and the Democratic People's Republic of Korea, against each other.

China's rise is among the most remarkable economic accomplishments in the history of the world—and a great success for American foreign policy, since the open economic order that the United States created and protected after World War II made it possible. The United States sustained roughly a four-decade period of bipartisan consensus in favor of engaging China and inviting it into that rules-based order. The strategy dated back, of course, to the Kissinger and Nixon opening to Mao Zedong's China in the early 1970s—a move that had its strategic logic in Cold War realpolitik but continued well after the Berlin Wall fell. The hope was that China would liberalize and become a supporter of the rules-based global order—and that it would liberalize and reform *faster* than its growing economic and military power would make it a potential threat. Alas, that calculus has not been vindicated of late, and so the long-standing American consensus about engaging China has eroded on both sides of the political aisle. The good will and mutual admiration that were cultivated between the American and Chinese peoples in recent decades have been seriously eroded as well. For example, in recent polls, publics in both countries have more negative than positive views of the other nation, and that was before Covid-19. After Covid, Pew polls show nearly 75 percent of Americans as having a negative view of the PRC, with little difference between Democrats and Republicans.[14]

In recent years, general concerns about Chinese power in the abstract have been intensified by a number of specific actions by Beijing. China's behavior in places like the South China Sea has become much more menacing, as it effectively claimed ownership of that sea through its nine-dash line and increasingly harassed U.S. Navy ships, Filipino fishermen, and others trying to use the international waters.[15] It did not relent even after the Permanent Court of Arbitration in The Hague ruled categorically against its claims and its recent behavior in that body of water.[16] President Xi Jinping's preparations for staying in power much longer than recent predecessors, his other efforts to exercise greater state control over the country's citizens, and his strongman behavior toward groups like the Uighur minority in the country's northwest as well as residents of Hong Kong have cast serious doubt on China's potentially reformist ways.[17]

The American response to these developments goes back roughly a decade now. It began with President Obama's attempt at a pivot or re-balance to the Asia-Pacific region starting around 2011. The rebalance focused largely on economics and diplomacy, though it included mili-tary dimensions, too, highlighted by a decision to increase the fraction of the U.S. Navy devoted to the broader Pacific region from the modern 50 percent norm to 60 percent.[18] That was followed by much greater focus on China at the Department of Defense during President Obama's last two years in the White House. The effort picked up further steam during President Trump's 2017–21 term in office. Over the past half dozen years, the U.S. armed forces have prioritized great power competition, and the restoration of American conventional military deterrence, above all other missions. As noted earlier, largely because of China's rise, some reinter-preted the 4+1 threat framework as a 2+3 paradigm, with Russia and China at the top of the list.[19]

The coronavirus crisis provides a timely and telling microcosm of the broader challenge. As usual, President Trump was less than decorous—but still not wrong—to describe the novel coronavirus as a "Chinese virus." That said, China then addressed the problem effectively, using strong-armed measures including severe internal and external travel re-strictions, as well as forced quarantines, in a way that may make its own model of governance look more effective than the slower responses in

Iran, many countries in Europe, the United States, and elsewhere.[20] China also provided modest amounts of help with medical care and equipment to countries such as Italy, once its own crisis had begun to relent. Just how this will play out in the broader court of public opinion globally, it is too soon to say. But the most likely outcome is that the argument will continue for years. We had better get used to such complexity and nuance in our dealings with China—being willing to disagree firmly and resolutely when necessary but avoiding demonization or any expectation that most other countries will simply line up with us against Beijing on the big issues of the day.[21]

Former deputy secretary of state Jim Steinberg and I wrote a book called *Strategic Reassurance and Resolve* attempting to address the question of how the United States should handle China's rise. We maintained that resoluteness *and* constant attempts at reassurance would be needed to keep the relationship on track. Having dealt with U.S.-China relations throughout his government career and having studied China's history extensively, Steinberg saw the challenge coming before many others did: America's sense of global purpose and responsibility, combined with China's reemergence as a great power and confident view of itself as the planet's Middle Kingdom, could put the two countries at direct strategic loggerheads.[22]

Several years later, Steinberg and I revisited our assessment. There was a certain amount of progress. Some recommendations that we, and others, had made to the U.S. side were implemented. The Pentagon's concept of Air-Sea Battle was recast, to avoid analogizing China of today with the Soviet Union of Cold War times (since the United States and NATO had developed Air-Land Battle doctrine for the latter). The United States also showed restraint in deployment of national missile defense systems. Some suggestions we made to the Chinese side, such as continuing to show restraint on nuclear modernization, participating more fully in peacekeeping and other collaborative multilateral military operations, and using hotlines as well as codes of conduct to govern close approaches of military assets, were also partly heeded. Both sides are also showing general restraint in testing of nuclear and antisatellite systems.[23]

However, if the glass might be partly full, at this point it is also at least half empty. Assertive Chinese behavior in the South China Sea has intensified over the past seven years. No real lessening of tensions has occurred between China and Taiwan. There have also been occasional risky encounters between U.S. and PRC naval ships, provoked by China as it has sought to increase its claims to the South China Sea. Dialogue between Beijing and Washington over Korea contingencies has been inadequate (even in semiofficial channels). And there have been no new major confidence-building measures like the "open skies" concept Steinberg and I proposed for aerial surveillance, as well as no breakthroughs on the cyber front.[24] China has expanded its territorial and military ambitions and activities in the South China Sea. It has tightened the network of Chinese entities that seek to gain intelligence and intellectual property for the country, and its military forces, by hook or by crook. Huawei's 5G network technologies also risk providing China with access to intelligence and hacking opportunities in many countries around the world—especially in light of China's "military-civilian fusion" law that requires private companies to share information with the People's Liberation Army (PLA), the Chinese combined military force.[25]

One thing is sure: America's relationship with China will be complex, dynamic, and hugely consequential for world affairs for the rest of the lifetime of anyone reading this book. Thus, grand strategy toward China will do better not to bite off too much. I do not purport here to create a full road map for future U.S. policy toward the PRC. My focus is on two issues that must be of paramount and immediate concern. First, we must reduce the chances of major war in scenarios that seem the most likely and worrisome. Second, we must ensure that long-term trends in economics, science, and technology do not work so adversely against the United States and its allies that China's geostrategic position gradually becomes advantageous and more threatening. The reassurance agenda Steinberg and I proposed is also useful and important to pursue—but perhaps less likely to produce transformative results at this point in the relationship. Accordingly, in the following I first examine the balance of power between the United States and China, on military and economic matters, and then use this net assessment to discuss how to handle various types of possible crises. Additional implications for U.S. defense policy are also explored in chapter 8.

Ensuring Favorable Trends
in Chinese and American Power

Before delving into policy specifics on military planning and crisis management, it is important to take broader stock of the strengths as well as the weaknesses of both the United States, together with its many important and powerful allies, and the People's Republic of China. It is crucial that America and allies ensure a favorable future balance of national power vis-à-vis China.

The United States has never had to face a rival that was effectively its equal in economic weight and clout. Nazi Germany, though highly industrialized in the 1930s and 1940s, was a much smaller country with a GDP well under half that of the United States. The Soviet Union was formidable—especially at first glance—but it turns out that its economy was much weaker and less dynamic than often believed in the early Cold War decades, and its GDP was only about half as great as America's.[26] China's GDP is already 70 percent that of the United States. (In fact, it exceeds U.S. economic output if one uses purchasing power parity measures to do the calculations—though GDP calculations using official exchange rates are probably the more accurate gauge of international power since they reflect resources that are convertible on the world stage.)

While China's per capita wealth and overall level of economic development lag substantially behind the West, its ability to direct resources into key strategic sectors will create many areas of excellence. Recall Li's comment to McMaster, Trump, and others noted above. On the more positive side, America's allies and close security partners together have roughly the same cumulative level of military spending as the United States and roughly twice the U.S. GDP. Nonetheless, the U.S. alliance system is somewhat diffuse and loose. One cannot simply lump the whole Western world together when doing power comparisons vis-à-vis China; any net assessment must be more nuanced.[27]

The United States enjoys roughly a three-to-one advantage in military spending over China. And the gap has been growing in America's favor of late. More specifically, the United States took its annual national defense budget from about $600 billion in 2015 to nearly $750 billion in 2020. Over the past decade, China has increased its own as well, of course, but by slightly less—perhaps from the range of \$125 billion to \$150 billion in 2010 to \$100 billion more than the 2010 figures by 2020.[28] But U.S. military power in some sense needs to be deployed across three main regions of the world, including East Asia, whereas China can concentrate mostly on East Asia.

The most notorious current Chinese modernization programs include the DF-21 and other antiship ballistic missiles, Kilo attack submarines and Sovremenny destroyers purchased from Russia, aircraft including the J-11B and J-20 and J-31, and the PLA's first operational aircraft carriers.[29] More generally, China's army has been streamlined and professionalized in recent decades, making it an even more formidable potential foe on the Korean peninsula than it was from 1950 through 1953. In recent times it has emphasized greater use of information, combined arms and joint operations, and mobility, while also improving training and logistics. The PLA still has a way to go in many of these areas, of course.[30]

The two countries have roughly comparable navies in terms of number of ships. Those of the U.S. Navy are generally much larger and more capable (and include ten large aircraft carriers and effectively another eleven smaller ones, in contrast to a couple for China), leading to an aggregate advantage in fleet tonnage for the United States of well over two to one—though again, American assets are distributed across three major parts of the globe, whereas China's are more concentrated. The United States has considerable advantages in stealth aircraft and stealthy submarines, but China is catching up in meaningful ways. Its ballistic and cruise missiles of short to medium range are numerous and accurate; existing missile defenses could not handle a serious Chinese salvo. The United States has many more, and much stronger, allies as well, of course, and a nuclear arsenal more than tenfold the size of China's.[31]

The U.S. armed forces of today have far more combat experience than China, which has not fought a war since 1979. But the American combat experience is mostly from irregular warfare in the sands of the broader Middle East, which may not be particularly relevant to a great power showdown in the Western Pacific.

Adding together the pieces, on military matters, the United States is ahead by most objective metrics. That said, China has two major advantages. One, most presumed scenarios pitting the two countries against each other would occur near its shores. Two, trends in technology mean that precision-strike ordnance is now much more widely available, even to countries with fewer aggregate resources.

In chapter 8, I discuss the future U.S. military with recommendations on how to sustain current advantages and mitigate vulnerabilities. But it is important to bear in mind, as discussed later in this chapter, that restoring the degree of American military superiority that prevailed during earlier eras against China is simply unrealistic. As such, the course of some combat scenarios near China's shores will be harder to predict, and harder for the United States to win, than in the past. These central facts must inform U.S. war planning much more than I believe they do today.

In economics, China now leads the world in overall manufacturing and in a number of key industrial sectors such as steelmaking and vehicle production. It is gradually catching up in some other areas, such as aerospace. It has also prioritized leading-edge technologies such as artificial intelligence in its future economic and military plans.[32] The United States remains a formidable manufacturing power in high-tech areas such as aerospace and chemicals, not to mention its excellence in R&D and product design, even in areas where China leads in production, such as consumer electronics.[33] The United States is blessed with many economic advantages that are favorable not only for its prosperity but also for its resilience to hypothetical future forms of economic warfare. It is endowed with ample water, farmland, and rich mineral deposits, together with hydrocarbons. It has neighbors in the Western Hemisphere with both similar and complementary resources.

When Germany, other EU countries, Japan and South Korea, Canada and Mexico, and other friendly nations are factored in, the U.S.-led Western alliance system substantially outproduces China in overall industrial output. In shipbuilding, for example, China is often in front of South Korea in total tonnage of production, but the gap is narrow, and Japan also produces a large fraction of the world's total.[34] In vehicle production, China easily produces the most units per year, but the output of all Western nations combined outdistances China's, even without taking into account differences in the relative value of the individual vehicles.

The United States continues to outspend any other major country or group of countries in aggregate research and development, public plus private. Although China is catching up to the United States, the Western world retains a substantial lead overall. In rough numbers, the United States spends a bit more than $500 billion a year on R&D, China ranks second at $450 billion (using purchasing power parity measures), the EU spends about $400 billion in all, Japan logs in at $170 billion, South Korea spends $80 billion, and Russia spends $40 billion annually.[35] The United States also has far and away the best universities in the world, with one recent ranking placing fifteen of the world's top twenty institutions of higher education within U.S. borders.[36]

The United States remains at the top of the charts, among major economies, in the World Economic Forum's competitiveness rankings, scoring second overall, behind only Singapore in 2019. The rating, whatever its precision, reflects America's large consumer market, culture of innovation, adequate infrastructure, good legal protections for investment and trade, strong financial system, outstanding universities, use of English as the main language of business, and other enduring attributes. The other large countries that give it a run for its money with that index are allies Germany, the United Kingdom, and Japan (all also in the top ten), not China or Russia (which rank twenty-eighth and forty-third, respectively).[37]

That said, the United States does have dependencies that could constitute weaknesses or vulnerabilities during protracted economic warfare. One set of vulnerabilities relates to natural resources, notably certain minerals, as well as energy. A second area of vulnerability is in key manufactured goods, either finished products themselves or crucial inputs to other technologies, including advanced military systems. A third area, though perhaps less concerning on balance, is in finance. And in regard to all of these, the United States must think about not only its own dependencies but those of key allies.

In regard to minerals, the United States has a number of dependencies that must be satisfied through imports. It would be possible to economize, recycle, and substitute in many cases, were supplies to become tight. Thus a certain modest dependence on supplies from China, Russia, or certain other actors is not necessarily a major concern. But for those minerals where the U.S. import dependence approaches 100 percent and China or Russia is the lead supplier, attention and remedial action may be warranted. This is the case today with arsenic, gallium, graphite, mica, quartz, bismuth, tantalum, scandium, yttrium, and other rare earths, which are largely produced now in China, though there are substantial potential sources in Australia, India, the United States, and elsewhere, too.[38] There is some reason for real if lesser concern in regard to germanium, antimony, and barite. Cobalt may be a concern because of its use in advanced batteries, though that may change with time and technology.[39] China is the major supplier of many of these strategic minerals to the United States.[40] The Department of Defense has begun to subsidize U.S. producers, with processing sites in California and Texas that would lessen the dependence on China; this idea is overdue.[41]

Regarding energy, the picture is better, but largely because of the dependencies of many American allies, it is still quite mixed. The United States produces more than 85 percent of the energy it consumes.[42] And it has greatly increased its production of oil and related petroleum liquids, as categorized by the Energy Information Administration, to more than 15 million barrels a day—the largest daily output in the world.[43] In addition, the U.S. Strategic Petroleum Reserve of 660 million barrels would buy weeks, months, or longer, depending on how it was employed.[44] However, U.S. consumption still averages about 20 million barrels a day, so the country is still a net importer. Indeed, because it exports some of its production, it winds up importing about 10 million barrels a day.[45] Some 40 percent of imports come from Canada; other major suppliers include Saudi Arabia, Iraq, and Mexico.[46]

China is an enormous importer of crude oil by dollar value, buying more than $100 billion a year in recent times. China is much more vulnerable to interruption of foreign energy supplies than is the United States, with nearly 80 percent of its oil and nearly 50 percent of its natural gas being imported.[47] It will likely remain highly import dependent for the next couple of decades at least.[48] It is attempting to mitigate the strategic consequences of the dependency by developing energy sources that the road networks in its Belt and Road Initiative can reach, but it starts from a difficult position.

Alas, so do a number of American allies. The EU countries as a whole had nearly a 90 percent crude oil import dependence in 2015. Almost 30 percent of overall EU oil imports came from Russia. Europe has similar or somewhat greater dependencies on Russia for natural gas and coal.[49] Japan, China, and Korea also import a great deal of natural gas.[50] South Korea and Japan import more than 80 percent and more than 90 percent of their total energy, respectively. Most oil and natural gas consumed in Japan comes from the Middle East, with additional substantial quantities coming from Russia; most coal comes from Australia, Indonesia, and Russia.[51]

Then there are global supply chains, where interdependencies are everywhere.[52] Main categories of U.S. merchandise imports from China with potential technological sophistication and sensitivity include communications equipment, computer equipment, and semiconductors plus other electronic components.[53] These are the areas that need to be watched carefully for possible dependencies that could give China a potential stranglehold on the U.S. economy, infrastructure, industrial base, or military machine.

The situation with semiconductors is illustrative in this regard. Today's situation is reasonably favorable: American companies own half of the production base of the global semiconductor industry, even if only about one-sixth of the world total is found on U.S. soil. Much of the rest is in friendly places such as South Korea, Japan, and Taiwan (indeed, those three entities together account for about two-thirds of all state-of-the-art production). China is attempting to produce more, and design more, semiconductors—and will surely continue to progress in this regard, sometimes by hook and crook, sometimes by sheer force of effort.[54] But at present it is largely dependent on the outside world for such components (which it then assembles into finished products and, for the most part, sells abroad—in fact, China now accounts for more than half of all purchases of semiconductors globally).[55] These realms of the world economy are dynamic, however, and bear constant and close scrutiny. The recent push in Congress to consider subsidization of greater semiconductor manufacturing capacity on American soil is a policy initiative worthy of serious consideration and, quite likely, support.[56]

A final important area of international interdependence and potential dependency is finance. China holds huge amounts of American treasury securities—about $1.1 trillion in 2019, or about one-sixth of the amount held by all foreign entities combined. Could Beijing coerce Washington by refusing to keep buying more or by dumping existing holdings to drive down their price on world markets? As China expert and Columbia professor Tom Christensen notes, doing so would also cause huge harm to Beijing, by weakening the economy of the huge American market and otherwise disrupting global trade patterns that work enormously to China's advantage. In the context of a true trade war, such steps may not be out of the question. That said, the U.S. Federal Reserve Board has many measures it could take in response to any dumping of U.S. securities, such as adjusting interest rates and potentially buying bonds, so China may find this weapon to have limited potency.[57]

This survey of economic realities and trends suggests several key policy priorities and specific steps for the United States.

First, it is crucial to sustain America's, and the West's, excellence in science and engineering. This has implications ranging from education policy to budgeting for research and development to immigration policy and to other realms that are discussed further in chapter 7.[58]

Second, it is important to correct the Econ 101 view of the world that is agnostic about where manufacturing occurs, provided that it is economical and therefore supposedly Pareto optimal. Many defense analysts have done the nation a disservice in recent decades by underestimating the difficulty and likely costs of war. Similarly, many economists have failed to account for the importance of national power and long-term economic health when making arguments about trade and manufacturing. In this regard, however imperfect some Trump administration tactics have been in trying to level the economic playing field with China, they have not been fundamentally wrongheaded. As a matter of national security, the United States needs to maintain a certain amount of industrial infrastructure and manufacturing capacity and limit its dependencies on potentially hostile parts of the world.

As Ely Ratner has suggested, it is important that the United States maintain diverse alternative sources of key components for strategic products like those just discussed. Its dependencies today on both Russia and China are still too great, at least in selected areas.[59] The U.S. government should track the production of such products and their components, perhaps through the development and updating of what Ratner calls a National Economic Security Strategy. It should have a combination of regulatory and financial tools to mandate or encourage diversification in sourcing for commodities, key components in global supply chains, and end products, when national security considerations so dictate.[60] This is especially important in high-technology domains of particular relevance to the armed forces and national security writ large of the United States. Greater use of the Committee on Foreign Investments in the United States to limit Chinese acquisitions of American technology firms broadly defined is probably a good element of any such strategy.[61] The same logic might apply to potential Chinese acquisition of energy companies and other high-frontier elements of the economy.[62] It is important to create benchmarks for just how much dependence on China the United States can afford to develop—25 percent? 50 percent?—in any key technology. The Covid-19 experience underscores that this way of thinking should extend not only to defense technologies but also to civilian infrastructure and to health care supplies.

In addition, the United States created a stock of strategic mineral reserves during the Cold War called the National Defense Stockpile. It is now maintained by the Defense Logistics Agency. Its aggregate value in 1980 was about $15 billion. American dependence on imports of various minerals has only grown since then, but the stockpile with its thirty-seven main types of components was reduced to only about $1.4 billion in total value by 2009 and was further scaled back to $1.1 billion in 2016.[63] To put these figures in context, the United States imported about $4.5 billion in strategic raw materials in 2016, a nearly identical value in scrap, and some $122 billion in processed metals and chemicals (with a combined raw material content of perhaps $10 billion to $20 billion, too).[64] Thus the strategic stockpile would clearly represent less than 10 percent of a typical year's requirement. To be sure, in a true national emergency, prioritization and substitution would occur. The U.S. Geological Survey, in its annual *Mineral Commodities Summaries,* lists substitutes for virtually every strategic mineral that it considers.[65] Still, to allow more time to find substitutes or alternative sources, and to endure a crisis that could last many months or more, stockpiles roughly ten times larger than at present would seem a reasonable starting point.

Third, the United States needs to encourage key allies to mitigate their own economic dependencies and develop means of sustaining resilience in the event of a crisis.[66] Most noteworthy here is the energy dependence of key East Asian allies, but that is only one aspect of a broader challenge that should be addressed now. By the time a crisis hits, it is already too late.

Security Crises and Combat Scenarios

With all this as backdrop, how could war erupt between the United States and China? This is a crucial question for U.S. grand strategy, which must place preventing large-scale conflict against another nuclear-armed nation at the top of its list of priorities.

For all of China's flaws, it is hard to see the PRC trying to overrun the main populated islands of Japan, for example, or even nearby Korea. Taiwan is a special case—and a dangerous one. China views the island as a renegade, core part of its territory and will not let it slip away. That issue requires considerable attention.

Yet what worries me most are small-scale skirmishes over small stakes that then escalate, in a way neither Beijing nor Washington nor other key capitals manage to control. What would the United States and its regional allies and partners do, for example, should China elect to use force to seize one of the uninhabited specks of rock that China claims as the Diaoyu Islands and Japan claims as the Senkaku Islands? China has intensified its presence near those islands in recent years. In 2013, it declared an Air Defense Identification Zone that includes Senkaku airspace and that demands of nearby planes that they ask for permission to transit.[67] The United States, paradoxically, has no official view on whose islands they should rightfully be—yet has promised to help Japan defend them. This is a confusing mix of policy positions that invites deterrence failure. Related problems could arise, for example, over competing Chinese and Filipino claims to small islands or land formations in the South China Sea.

When a reporter posed the same question concerning the Senkaku/Diaoyu Islands to the senior American marine in the region several years ago, Lieutenant General John Wissler noted that the United States (and

Japan, of course) could surely take them back.[68] Indeed, article 5 of the U.S.-Japan Treaty could make such a response seem quite natural, if not virtually essential in the eyes of some. Article 5 begins as follows: "Each Party recognizes that an armed attack against either Party in the territories under the administration of Japan would be dangerous to its own peace and safety and declares that it would act to meet the common danger in accordance with its constitutional provisions and processes."[69] President Obama was the first U.S. president to say explicitly that article 5 applied to the Senkaku/Diaoyu Islands. Secretary of Defense Jim Mattis reiterated the commitment in February 2017.[70] General Wissler implied that bombing might be the preferred military tactic for responding to any hypothetical Chinese seizure or occupation of one of the islands.

Wissler's comments were militarily well informed. They reflected a serious consideration of the tactical options that would be available to the United States and Japan in such a hypothetical situation. It is also probably good, for deterrence purposes, that Beijing understand that such options could be on the table. Indeed, Japan might respond forcefully on its own, though one would hope that the two allies would consult each other and agree on a joint plan of action.

Nonetheless, Wissler's words also produced a bit of a diplomatic brouhaha, and for understandable reasons. Once blood had been spilled, with perhaps several dozen or more Chinese troops killed, it is not obvious how such a conflict would be ended. (The initial Chinese seizure of the island in question would likely not cause casualties since no one lives on these islands and no Japanese or U.S. military personnel are routinely deployed on them.) The situation could be even murkier and more fraught if, for example, China emulated Russia and its maskirovka tactics and feigned the rescue of a group of tourists or fishermen who just happened to be near the islands when a storm hit that left them stranded. Such a *Gilligan's Island* scenario could provide China a pretext to go ashore—and it would perhaps then keep finding reasons to remain there indefinitely.

Rather than counterinvade or bomb, Americans and Japanese might consider a blockade of the Chinese troops on the island. This approach would in some ways follow the precedent of the Cuban Missile Crisis. However, although a company or two of PLA soldiers on an uninhabited

Senkaku island would be less menacing than nuclear weapons in Cuba, the potential for serious escalation among nuclear-armed powers would exist in the Senkaku/Diaoyu case as well. While the imposition of a block-ade may sound relatively benign compared to a bombing raid, there would be nothing benign about it. China might interpret the blockade as an act of war, since it claims ownership of the islands in question. A blockade is generally considered an act of war under international law. Because ownership is disputed in this case, interpretation of whether a blockade constituted an act of war would likely be disputed, too.

How might such a standoff end? Would China try doggedly to sneak supplies ashore, perhaps by planes or submarines or in small boats disguised as commercial vessels? Would Japan and the United States be prepared, if necessary, to use lethal force to impede such resupply? Would China shoot at the American and Japanese planes and ships en-forcing the blockade? One thing seems clear: the potential for escalation to violent conflict would exist in this scenario. It is hard to say who would have the upper hand militarily, given the geography.[71] Thus, either side might be tempted to pursue maximalist ambitions rather than seek a compromise resolution.

The escalation could also broaden geographically. For operations in this region, China would depend on coastal bases in the central and southern parts of its littoral. The United States and Japan would depend on bases on Okinawa and other parts of the Ryukyu Island chain, on Guam, and perhaps on Kyushu Island as well as other locations on main-land Japan. These facts raise the possibility of broader attacks by each country against military bases in densely populated parts of the adver-sary's homeland, as well as against ships and aircraft operating in the overall area.

It seems implausible that tiny uninhabited islands could lead to general war involving the United States, Japan, and China. But it also is hard to predict with confidence just how this scenario, once started, would end. And either side that found itself on the losing end of a con-ventional engagement might consider—or at least threaten—nuclear escalation. The United States might believe that its tenfold nuclear supe-riority over China gave it nuclear escalation dominance; China might decide that geographic proximity gave it a larger interest in the matter.

Either way, one side or the other could find a credible basis, based on history and nuclear theory, for thinking that it could prevail in a game of nuclear chicken—or even limited nuclear war. Humans being the gamblers and often the intuitive decision makers that they are, it is difficult to assume that such escalatory options would be ruled out just because they seem reckless and beyond the pale of what any reasonable assessment of the stakes at issue would justify. Moreover, an entire Cold War history of American nuclear strategy, weapons development, and crisis management suggests that even the leaders of the greatest democracy on Earth can look to gain leverage from a real or perceived nuclear advantage. Many esteemed strategists have taken the possibility of limited nuclear war very seriously. I think it entirely possible that not only the United States but China, too, might consider limited nuclear weapons use rather than accept defeat in a purely conventional war, whether leaders in Beijing had developed doctrine for limited nuclear weapons employment in advance or not.[72]

China deserves credit for its general restraint on nuclear weapons over the years, especially in regard to the size of its arsenal. But it has been modernizing its forces. It may also have been conducting very small nuclear weapons tests (effectively in violation of the de facto testing moratorium that has remained in effect since the mid-1990s even though the Comprehensive Nuclear Test Ban Treaty has never come into force).[73] China's nuclear capabilities should not be assumed away in these kind of limited-war scenarios, whatever Beijing's rhetoric and official doctrine might claim.[74]

The situation could be even more fraught in the South China Sea. There, the United States also has a treaty ally, the Philippines. Even if that alliance is now on somewhat shaky ground, Secretary of State Mike Pompeo did promise in 2019 that the U.S.-Philippines Mutual Defense Treaty of 1951 would require the United States to come to the Philippines' defense if its ships or aircraft were attacked by China. Whether that pledge goes so far as to protect the Philippines' active implementation of its claims to South China Sea islands is more ambiguous, especially given the rhetoric and policies of President Rodrigo Duterte in Manila. Forebodingly, war games postulating disputes over such land formations often suggest the distinct possibility of escalation, even to nuclear war.[75]

What is not ambiguous is that the United States and major allies also have crucial economic interests in the form of the South China Sea shipping lanes, through which some one-third of global maritime commerce flows.[76] Maintaining access to those blue waters also follows inexorably from Washington's long-standing insistence that freedom of navigation is a central pillar of the rules-based international order. It transcends any particular region or potential adversary, and it does not depend on the interests of any American ally.

But China has declared almost all of that sea, including not just islands but open waters, to be a core national interest. It has also delineated its infamous nine-dash line, supposedly rooted deeply in history, to lay claim to the area. And the PRC has been asserting its claims more vigorously, not only by constructing artificial islands and militarizing them (despite earlier promises not to do so) but also by interfering with the ships of other nations and at times the U.S. Navy. Should a conflict begin, even over relatively small tactical stakes like the collision of two ships, it is again difficult to know how it might end.[77]

A Taiwan scenario would be even more foreboding. Should Taiwan push for independence, or should China get tired of waiting for reunification, trouble could again ensue. Beijing might convince itself that a blockade-centered operation against Taiwan, designed to force it to reverse whatever purportedly offending action or rhetoric might have caused China's reaction in the first place, would present acceptable risks. In principle, China could scale back or suspend enforcement of the blockade at any point if it needed to, and it could do so while saving face, especially if the blockade was conducted principally by submarines. Moreover, Beijing might believe that even a partially effective naval blockade could be a potent instrument of coercion against Taiwan.[78] China would not need to stop all commercial ships transiting into and out of Taiwan. It would simply need to deter enough ships from risking the journey that Taiwan's economy would suffer badly. The goal would likely be to squeeze the island economically to the point of capitulation. This solution might seem quite elegant from Beijing's point of view: it could involve little or no loss of life, little or no damage to Taiwan itself, and the ability to back off the attack if the United States seemed prepared to intervene or if the world community slapped major trade sanctions on China in response.[79]

In any such blockade, China might well combine various elements of military power, including cyberattacks, into a multidimensional operation.[80] It could attack Taiwan's command and control capabilities; if the United States intervened, it could seek to neutralize America's space-based assets too. The centerpiece of the approach could be the PRC submarine fleet introducing a significant risk factor into all maritime voyages into and out of Taiwan by occasionally sinking a cargo ship, either with submarines or with mines it had laid in Taiwan's harbors.[81] The PRC submarine force has improved by leaps and bounds in recent decades. Over the past twenty years, China's fleet of modern attack subs has grown from roughly two to forty.[82] China's precision-strike capabilities have improved to the point that China could conceivably use a preemptive missile and air attack against Taiwanese airfields and ports and associated infrastructure to hobble Taiwan's ability to strike back (though it might choose not to attack Taiwan's territory in the first instance).[83]

To allow humanitarian supplies to reach Taiwan, Beijing might offer countries the option of first docking in a PRC port for inspection before sailing to their destinations. In this and other ways, it could limit the dangers to innocent civilians. Since this strategy might require the Chinese submarine fleet to sink only a few ships to achieve the desired aims, even in a worst case Beijing might believe that it was acting humanely—threatening the lives of no more than a couple hundred commercial seamen. Given the perceived stakes involved, Beijing could well consider this a reasonable risk.

If they chose to try to break the blockade, the basic concept of operations for the United States and Taiwan would probably be to assemble enough forces in the western Pacific to set up a protected shipping lane east of Taiwan. To carry out that mission, the United States together with Taiwan and perhaps Japan would need to establish air superiority throughout a large part of the region. The United States and Taiwan, and perhaps others, would also need to protect ships against Chinese submarine attack while coping with the threat of mines near Taiwan's ports. And they might have to do all this without assured access to some of their satellite architecture. That is because China's abilities to shoot down or disable low-Earth orbit satellites, through direct-ascent interceptors or directed-energy weapons or other means, have improved in recent years (even as some aspects of U.S. access to space have become more distributed and resilient).[84]

Twenty years ago, I examined this scenario and concluded that the United States, with or without allied help, could confidently prevail in such an engagement, albeit perhaps losing several ships along the way. Today I am much less sure. China's cyberweapons, antisatellite weapons, and general swagger mean it would have numerous potent strategic capabilities—and perhaps a greater propensity to consider nuclear escalation if losing the conventional fight.[85] Even in domains where the United States might still be expected to dominate, such as air-to-air warfare, the advantage is less than before—and the growing vulnerability of major U.S. bases to accurate missile strikes complicates the calculus substantially.[86] In undersea warfare, China's enormous progress in fielding quiet submarines also changes the situation substantially. Make no mistake, the United States remains ahead in this domain of warfare. Given the gauntlets it would have to run, the typical Chinese submarine would do well to survive for two or three round-trip missions from base.[87] But it might succeed in sinking several valuable, and vulnerable, surface ships before meeting its own demise.[88]

What all the above means for military force planning and war planning is complex. The United States should not signal to Beijing that it is somehow intimidated from coming to the defense of Taiwan because of the likely difficulty of the operation. It would be a difficult and very risky conflict for China, as well, and there is no point in depriving the United States of instruments that may contribute to deterrence. That said, for the United States, it would be desirable to have other options, too—especially early in any crisis or conflict and especially if there were ambiguity about which side was most at fault in producing the conflict.[89]

Unlike the Senkaku, or South China Sea, scenarios, any fight over Taiwan would immediately jeopardize the well-being, if not necessarily the physical survival, of twenty-four million people. Even a blockade would run major risks of destitution and economic collapse. Thus, the goal for the United States would have to be to end the blockade. Unlike the other cases, where punishment of a limited transgression as a disincentive of any further encroachment could be seen as adequate for deterrence purposes, in this case it would indeed be necessary to create leverage to force China to back down.

In addition to reserving the right to conduct a counterblockade operation, therefore, the United States should think creatively about other forcible but perhaps indirect military responses. Ideally, they should be relatively nonescalatory, in the sense of threatening relatively few people. They could also be geographically asymmetric, so as to play to U.S. strengths and avoid fighting on home turf for the PRC.

Specifically, ships transporting oil or gas from the Persian Gulf to China could be either seized or incapacitated using precision ordnance— or even advanced nonlethal weapons. Even if it could not always be known which vessels were headed for China, since supertankers sometimes set sail before buyers for their oil have been determined, such methods could still be effective.[90] The assets of companies that continued to trade with China, or ships that had been determined to be previously involved in evasion of sanctions, could be subsequently targeted in a blockade that strengthened over time.

Nearly twenty million barrels of oil transit the Strait of Hormuz daily, between the Persian Gulf and the Gulf of Oman. This flow could involve anywhere from just a dozen super-large tankers to several dozen at a given moment in time, depending on the specific vessels in question (with each ship typically having a crew of up to a couple dozen people).[91] Establishing American air supremacy around the broader Persian Gulf region could probably be handled by two aircraft carriers within a couple hundred miles of the coast, since standard doctrine suggests that two carriers, alternating primary responsibility for the mission, can maintain coverage against a limited threat. But because of the stakes involved, the nature of the crisis, and the potential capabilities of the principal adversary, it might be considered more prudent to devote four to six carriers to the mission, with land-based airpower in the region and in Europe providing support. Such a show of force would discourage any wishful thinking by China that a lucky shot by one of its attack submarines, for example, could cripple Western military capability in the region and lead to a termination of the mission. If several dozen tanker ships per day had to be physically boarded, that could imply a need for one to two dozen additional ships (including coast guard variants) in addition to the carrier force. Alternatively, reprisals could be emphasized for ships that had previously been known to be involved in evading sanctions, with no boarding necessary. Admittedly, China has more military presence in the broader Middle East than before, including a base in Djibouti, but its capabilities in this area are still a far cry from those of the United States—and a far cry from what Beijing can do in the Western Pacific.[92]

Chinese retaliation of various kinds would have to be anticipated in such a situation. These considerations therefore put a premium on enhancing the resiliency of key U.S. allies, especially against the limited harassment attacks and partial supply cutoffs that would seem the most likely Chinese recourses.

As noted, although the essence of my proposed strategy is to avoid direct combat near Chinese coasts, in some scenarios the United States and allies might have to consider breaking a blockade to ensure Taiwan's survival. Being able to sustain some of the necessary patrolling, anti-submarine warfare operations, and naval supply and maintenance operations from bases in the broader Western Pacific would make sense. To create the means for such an option, if a crisis of the kind postulated here actually began, the United States should quietly brainstorm about how it might pursue ideas such as those below, should future circumstances so dictate:

- Creating bastions on western islands in the Philippine archipelago, should Manila assent, to include airfields with hardened shelters and underground fuel and munitions stocks, protected by air and missile defense systems and enough ground forces to discourage raids by PLA special forces.
- Homeporting of more American surface warships and submarines in places such as Japan, the Philippines, Guam, and even Vietnam as a way to facilitate sustained forward operations at acceptable strain on the fleet. Increased military cooperation, including rotational deployments, exercises, and joint naval patrols, with various countries in the region could also make sense.[93] The United States should be wary, how-

ever, of developing new alliances in places like Vietnam that are geographically hard to defend, strategically less than central to its security, and politically especially sensitive in regard to relationships with Russia or China.

• The expedited development of unmanned ships to play a growing range of roles, making it possible to carry out reconnaissance and even strike operations with less risk to American military personnel and ideally also at lower cost per ship in some cases.[94]

• The creation, over time, of some U.S. merchant marine capability that could, if necessary, resume under military auspices some of the commercial ship traffic that China had managed to scare away from Taiwan with its partially tight blockade.

• Appeal to European allies to assist more fully in military operations in the broader Persian Gulf, with naval and coast guard capabilities as well as land-based airpower and missile and air defenses, so that U.S. forces are not overstressed by their expanded operations in the broader Persian Gulf region (and thus unable to expand operations in the Western Pacific).

The pace at which such options might actually be implemented would, of course, be a function of how the crisis unfolded. It is possible that it could last years. However, there would also be powerful incentives for all sides to undertake more serious and creative diplomacy as this kind of scenario, with its extensive economic pain and nontrivial military risks, played out.

Conclusion: America, China, . . . and India

In concluding this discussion of grand strategy toward China, a word on India is in order. India, now among the world's top ten economies, one of the world's nine nuclear-weapons nations, and soon to be its most populous country, will be a crucial player in future geopolitics.

India will certainly factor heavily into how we will collectively handle many of the new threats—the other 4+1—discussed in chapter 7. In addition, in terms of classic geopolitics, its main relevance for the United States in the years ahead will likely result largely from how we collaboratively handle a rising China. That will be particularly true if India can stay true to its own democratic and inclusive traditions and prevent a strong turn toward an ideology such as Hindu nationalism of the type that Prime Minister Narendra Modi sometimes seems to indulge. The United States and India already have a long history of dealing with China together. There is little reason to think that will change in the years ahead.[95]

The United States has been wisely and patiently improving its strategic relationship with India for two decades, dating back to the end of the Clinton administration (when the United States pressured Pakistan to stand down during the 1999 Kargil crisis).[96] But Washington also needs to understand the limits of the relationship. India values close ties with Iran and Russia, for example. India's domestic challenges, despite much better growth rates in recent decades, are enormous. The coherence and conviction with which it energetically pursues a global or even regional strategy wax and wane, partly as a result.[97] And India values its independent streak in foreign policy. Despite rapprochement with the United States in recent times, extending to its new status as a "major defense partner" (a term contrived especially for India, to attest at least symbolically to its much greater importance in modern times), it is hardly interested in being viewed as a U.S. ally. Nor should the United States want more binding security commitments with major Eurasian powers.

To be sure, India will continue to buy arms from America, much more than before. The economic relationship will also continue to expand. Washington's recent distancing from Pakistan may improve things somewhat further as well, given the ongoing tension between Islamabad and New Delhi. President George W. Bush's decision to find a way to accommodate India's nuclear-weapons program and thereby allow civilian nuclear cooperation also helped.[98]

But India will not take sides between China and the United States definitively. The country whose side it will take, to paraphrase a former top Indian official, is India's. For example, the above positives will not stop India from buying arms from Russia or oil from Iran. India will not likely participate in multinational maritime patrols to push back against greater Chinese military presence in the South China Sea or even the Indian Ocean unless under U.N. chapeau. It will seek to calibrate its responses to any new moves by Beijing, turning the pressure up or down like a rheostat without making bold moves that cross major thresholds—at least, not until China itself crosses big and bold new thresholds. Even after the tragic and lethal encounters between Indian and Chinese forces in disputed border regions in 2020, New Delhi has sought to avoid escalation or any other major strategic reaction—though it has surely also taken notice and adjusted its expectations about the future of the Indo-Chinese relationship.[99]

The same basic logic applies to other countries with which the United States may collaborate in the Asia-Pacific region in the future. Nonviolent military steps such as expanding training, and even basing, can be considered with countries such as Vietnam and Indonesia if China's behavior deteriorates to the point where that is of mutual interest among Washington, Hanoi, and/or Jakarta. So can various uses of economic pressure and sanctioning, if for example China becomes more violent about opposing other countries' claims to their islands in the South China Sea. The United States may not choose, and would not be obliged, to enter into any direct conflict between China and such countries, but it would have the luxury of pursuing other more indirect and longer-term responses. That is actually an advantageous position to be in, and it should remind Washington of the number of factors that work to its favor over the long term and the long game ahead.

FIVE

Korea

It was a gorgeous September morning in Seoul, in "the land of the morning calm," and I was up early like many Americans when adjusting to Korean time. Jogging up the hill, through gardens and past small streams and ponds, to the famous North Seoul tower in Namsan Park, I was struck by the beauty of the place, as lush rolling hills stretched out in all directions, big buildings in the spaces in between. Seoul was literally glistening in the morning sun. One of the largest, most impressive cities on Earth (if also cursed with some of the worst traffic), the giant metropolitan area is home to half of the Republic of Korea's fifty million people. When my father served in the U.S. Army in Korea in 1960, the country was mostly made up of subsistence farmers and run by a dictator; the typical South Korean was no better off financially than the average North Korean. That is why George Kennan and other American strategists of the early Cold War did not prioritize Korea—that is, not until North Korea, with Soviet and Chinese blessing, invaded the South.

Today, the vast majority of North Koreans still wallow in poverty and suffer widespread oppression at the hands of their leader, Kim Jong Un (who succeeded his father, Kim

Jong Il, and his grandfather, Kim Il Sung). South Korea, by contrast, is a high-tech power and the eleventh largest economy on the planet. Its living standards approach those in Japan, Europe, and the United States. Recently, its response to Covid-19 has been impressive and instructive. None of this could have happened without the U.S. alliance, as well as the open global economic order that American power has fostered and protected.

But I was there in the fall of 2017 (and twice since), when all this progress, however impressive, also felt so fragile. If war broke out in Korea, given the density of populations and the extreme lethality of deployed weaponry, literally millions could die—making a future Korean war much worse than Iraq or Afghanistan in total casualty count. In the weeks before and after my visit, Kim Jong Un and President Donald Trump were threatening each other with military action. Insults like "little rocket man" were flying back and forth across the Pacific; Trump talked of "fire and fury" and bragged that his nuclear button was bigger than Kim's. American military officers told me, then and since, of the real military preparations that were under way just in case—extra stocks of fuel and ammunition positioned in South Korea, American combat forces continuously on standby alert. I know for a fact that at least some top-level American military commanders thought the chances of war to be well into the double-digit percentages. We dodged a bullet then. Soon, the North Koreans were engaged in a charm offensive during the Seoul Olympics. A few months later, Trump and Kim met in Singapore, the first time a sitting U.S. president had ever come face-to-face with a North Korean dictator and only the first of three meetings they have now held. But as that diplomacy falters, could the possibility of war return again?

North Korea's government is probably, quite literally, the worst on Earth. No leader is more brutal toward his people—even his family members—

than the young and flamboyant Kim Jong Un. In recent years we have also witnessed the depravity of the North Korean regime in the death of American student Otto Warmbier. No place on Earth more resembles a police state of the type Joseph Stalin would recognize.[1] Few nations mismanage their economies quite so egregiously. The country today continues to spend as much as 25 percent of its GDP on its military—far and away the highest ratio on the planet.[2] It is the only country on Earth that has tested nuclear weapons this century—and it has done so six times, under three American presidents, in 2006, 2009, 2013, 2016 (twice), and 2017. The last test was likely of a thermonuclear or so-called hydrogen bomb with a yield of at least 100 kilotons (at least six times that of the Hiroshima bomb).[3] Those six nuclear tests, plus three long-range missile tests in 2017, caused even Moscow and Beijing to respond.[4] The United Nations Security Council has imposed very tough sanctions on North Korea in recent years, shutting down a large chunk of the country's trade.

The new Kim seems to want a more modern and prosperous state, and he aspires to prosperity as well as security through his doctrine of *byungjin,* literally "parallel development." He is trying to turn the capital, Pyongyang, into what my colleague and former top Kim watcher at the CIA, Jung Pak, calls "Pyonghattan." But he also shares the brutal, autocratic, and highly insular ways of his father and grandfather, and he is probably not a reformist in any meaningful sense of the word.[5] In addition, he has developed a keen awareness that leaders who faced the United States in war without first possessing nuclear weapons, like Saddam Hussein or Muammar el-Qaddafi, usually wound up out of power—or worse.[6] When he talks of denuclearizing the Korean Peninsula, he is likely placing primary emphasis on an end to the U.S.–Republic of Korea military alliance, backed up as it is by American nuclear weapons.[7] Indeed, he may still have faint aspirations of coercing South Korea into reunification on Pyongyang's terms, if the U.S.–ROK alliance can be ended and the South Korean people or political elite intimidated into acquiescence. To paraphrase Jung Pak, in her seminal work *Becoming Kim Jong Un* (based in part on her earlier long article "The Education of Kim Jong Un"), part of our job in the United States, South Korea, and elsewhere is to educate Kim. That is, through resoluteness and consistency of purpose and message, we need to disabuse him of any unrealistic ambitions—in part by offering him a realistic path forward that, by necessity, will have to be one of coexistence.[8]

Long-standing U.S. sanctions essentially prohibit trade with, investment in, and aid to North Korea. They involve the United States and American citizens and businesses, as well as international organizations in which the United States participates. These U.S. sanctions are codified in numerous laws from the 1940s, 1950s, 1960s, and 1970s (such as the Foreign Assistance Act of 1961, the Arms Export Control Act of 1976, the Export Administration Act of 1979), and in more recent legislation, such as the Iran, North Korea, and Syria Nonproliferation Act of 2000.[9]

United Nations sanctions have intensified in the years since North Korea broke out of the Nuclear Non-Proliferation Treaty in 2003. United Nations Security Council Resolution 1718 of 2006 banned arms trade of any kind with North Korea and placed requirements on member states to inspect cargo that might violate this prohibition. In 2009, UNSCR 1874 started to restrict illicit finances and the bank accounts of key regime actors. Various efforts were subsequently made to toughen earlier measures and tighten their enforcement, both for weapons of mass destruction and for ballistic missiles, such as UNSCR 2087 of January 2013, and for weaponry in general, such as UNSCR 2270 of March 2016. Most recently, U.N. sanctions have targeted commercial sources of revenue for the North Korean regime and the assets of individuals and companies from North Korea or doing business with North Korea—again, UNSCR 2270, plus Resolutions 2371 and 2397 of 2017, with their strict limitations and toughened enforcement measures on imports and exports of fuel, seafood, machinery, textiles, and other traded goods.

Combine those effects with a badly mismanaged command system, and the weak North Korean economy continues to flounder badly. The Seoul-based Bank of Korea has estimated its economy contracted at an annual rate of 3 to 4 percent in both 2017 and 2018.[10]

Yet the North Korean economy is somehow strong enough to keep producing many dozens of missiles a year (mostly of shorter range, though they could still strike South Korea, where more than two hundred thousand Americans live, or Japan).[11] North Korea probably also produces a half dozen or so more nuclear bombs annually, according to Siegfried Hecker and other experts at Stanford University, as well as the 38 North

Project.[12] The armed forces remain enormous, with hundreds of artillery able to range Seoul from current positions.[13] All of this happens partly because China, while generally nervous about its North Korean ally's behavior, also does not wish to see the country collapse: that outcome would create major instability on its border, as well as a possible opportunity for the United States to expand its influence in Northeast Asia. Beijing and Washington have many similar interests in regard to North Korea. But they prioritize those interests differently. And in fact, their interests in regard to the Democratic People's Republic of Korea do diverge in some important ways.

In this complex and dangerous environment, military deterrence is crucial, and the United States plays a central role in creating it. Resoluteness should still be the watchword for doing so, going forward. In 1950, trying to avoid American strategic overextension, Secretary of State Dean Acheson said that the United States would *not* defend South Korea. (Kennan was complicit in this misjudgment, it must be noted, having also ruled South Korea outside the strategic core of U.S. interests in his various writings.) A few months later, taking Acheson's words as a green light to attack, North Korea's founder Kim Il Sung sent legions of infantry southward, where they crossed the Han River, conquered Seoul, and took much of the peninsula. General Douglas MacArthur's Inchon landing seized back the momentum for South Korean and allied forces later that year. But we then pressed our luck, with U.S.–South Korean forces moving northward up to the Yalu River and the Chinese border. At that point, Mao authorized a counterattack led by his own People's Liberation Army. Extremely bloody fighting, and military stalemate, ensued. Eventually, an armistice was reached, dividing the peninsula about where things had begun in June 1950. That is where we remain today, except that the Cold War is over—and North Korean nuclear weapons are now part of the strategic equation.[14]

President Trump was the most radical American president toward Korea since at least Jimmy Carter, who thought about ending the alliance or at least pulling U.S. forces off the peninsula back in the 1970s when South Korea was an oppressive dictatorship. Trump has foolishly mused about himself bringing American forces home and has quarreled and quibbled with South Korea over the so-called host nation support that Seoul pays the United States to defray many of the costs of that U.S. presence on the peninsula. South Korea is already generous; Trump's demands have been outlandish. And Trump's three meetings with Kim—in Singapore in June 2018, Vietnam in February 2019, and the DMZ of Korea in June 2019—later petered out into a moribund diplomatic process with no sense of positive momentum.

As tempting as it is to blame this all on Trump, that would not be quite fair or accurate. North Korea's nuclear arsenal grew fast throughout the Bush and Obama presidencies, too. And at least North Korea has not been testing nuclear weapons or long-range missiles since 2017.

The United States should base future North Korea policy on two pillars that combine resoluteness with restraint and patience: first, a firm and steady commitment to the military alliance with South Korea; and second, a flexible and pragmatic diplomatic approach toward North Korea, with an initial emphasis on preventing crises from turning violent and on capping rather than quickly eliminating the North Korean nuclear arsenal. Over time, such an approach might gradually give Pyongyang incentives to behave more humanely toward its people and the world—but that goal will have to wait, since preventing war on the Korean Peninsula must be the top priority.[15] This approach may or may not quickly produce a deal. But it avoids wishful thinking about the inherent goodness of Kim Jong Un and adopts a durable approach toward the problem.[16]

Before delving into the smart options, though, it is important to rule out a few—especially because we were so close to taking them seriously a relatively short time ago. With the breakdown in nuclear negotiations (and the new uncertainties over Kim's health that began in 2020), some may want to bring them back into the conversation soon. That would be a potentially catastrophic mistake by the Biden administration.

Military Options?

Despite North Korea's overall weakness, there are really no good military options of a preventive, preemptive, or optional nature. Deterrence, not victory and regime change through war, must be our goal in Korea— deterrence, plus a capping of the North Korean nuclear problem and then the gradual use of economic pressures and incentives to induce better, or at least peaceful, behavior from Pyongyang.[17] To see why, consider first what any U.S.–ROK military actions might look like, especially the limited or bloody nose tactics that may resemble what the Trump administration was considering in the second half of 2017.

One military option would be to prevent North Korea from completing any more long-range missile tests to perfect ICBM (intercontinental ballistic missile) technology. This idea was proposed in 2006 by two Democratic secretaries of defense, William Perry and Ashton Carter.[18] The ICBMs could be preemptively destroyed by precision munitions launched from aircraft. Or they could be shot down in flight by a U.S. missile defense system. Based on previous testing, any such shot might have a 25 to 75 percent chance of success, roughly speaking, given the test record of the midcourse interceptor system based today in Alaska and California.[19]

However, in response, North Korea might accelerate its development of solid-fueled ICBMs, which may already be close to testable status, as well as types of liquid-fueled ICBMs that can be prepared for launch less visibly.[20] The United States might not be able to preempt such ICBMs effectively. Furthermore, this idea does not address North Korea's growing inventory of shorter-range missiles that already put South Korea and Japan at risk, including the three hundred thousand or so Americans living in the two countries today.

A blockade by the United States and allied navies could seem a logical way to ensure that international sanctions were respected. Of course, a military blockade is, by standard international law, an act of war. Enforcing it could require the use of lethal ordnance against any North Korean or other ships that refused to allow boarding and inspection. In response to such a blockade, North Korea could be expected, at a minimum, to shoot at any nearby ships that were targeting its vessels, risking American casualties. There could even be risks of a clash between the United States and China, given the proximity with which their respective navies could be operating in any such effort. Even more important, this option would not curtail trade across North Korean land borders or airspace. Thus, it would neither reduce the existing threat posed by North Korea nor likely slow further future growth of nuclear and missile arsenals. It would tighten the economic squeeze but fail to reduce the military threat. It might or might not have an important effect on North Korea's international proliferation of sensitive weapons technologies, either.[21]

Just as Israel preemptively attacked Iraqi and Syrian nuclear reactors in 1981 and 2007, the United States and/or South Korea could take aim at parts of North Korea's nuclear infrastructure, most likely with stealthy attack aircraft. Specifically, nuclear infrastructure that is under construction but not yet operational could be destroyed without dispersal of highly radioactive material, as could known uranium centrifuge complexes.

Unfortunately, such preventive strikes could not eliminate any uranium enrichment facility that North Korea may have built at an unknown site. Nor could they humanely destroy the operational research reactor that has produced all of North Korea's plutonium to date. An attack on such a site would create a miniature Chernobyl or Fukushima-like outcome, lethally spreading highly radioactive reactor waste over an area of hundreds of square miles downwind. Most of all, such an attack would be unlikely to reach any of the several dozen warheads North Korea already likely possesses, since U.S. officials probably do not know where they are located.

Finally, like the start of Operation Iraqi Freedom in 2003, when the George W. Bush administration attempted to kill Saddam Hussein in an early shock and awe strike, the United States and South Korea could target Kim Jong Un.[22] Federal law prohibits assassinating foreign political leaders. But if Kim were declared the military commander of a nation still technically at war with the United Nations and in violation of its cease-fire obligations (due to frequent repeated aggressions against South Korea over the years), this issue might be finessed, at least legally. However, the United States might miss Kim in any such attempt, as the 2003 Iraqi case demonstrates. Whether the attack is successful or not, North Korea might respond with similar attempts against Western leaders. It might even consider using a nuclear weapon, probably in a relatively remote location at first, to signal how seriously it objected to the attempt. After all, strategists often conclude that nuclear weapons are most likely to be used when regime survival is on the line. And where would even a successful operation get the United States? Unless U.S. officials were able to message virtually all other senior North Korean leaders in advance and persuade them to accept amnesty and exile if they chose not to resist, killing Kim might just lead to the replacement of one extremist leader with another. Given the poor state of detailed American knowledge about North Korea's political elite, this is a particularly unlikely prospect. Worse yet, North Korean military command and control might also splinter, with some elements opting for a violent response against the United States and the ROK rather than for surrender. We do not know enough about DPRK nuclear command and control to predict with any confidence how this process would likely play out.[23]

In short, whatever their individual appeal, each of these options would appear to promise only mediocre effects against the North Korean threats that matter most to the United States. Moreover, each would risk a war that could kill millions if it went full-scale.

In the event of hostilities in Korea, China would likely intervene. Fearing refugee flows, if not the leakage of nuclear or chemical materials from the DPRK, Beijing might wish to seal its border with North Korea. And if protecting the border were the goal, doing so from a forward position could strike many Chinese military minds as sound policy.[24] Creating a buffer zone several dozen miles into North Korea might appeal.[25]

Chinese decision making would also be influenced by assessment of the longer-term consequences of North Korea's collapse. Beyond concerns about border security, Chinese leaders could be thinking about postconflict force dispositions on the peninsula. Expecting that the United States might try to retain forces in Korea even after reunification and stabilization efforts were complete, they might seek to establish leverage against that possibility. This scenario is particularly credible in light of two Chinese views. The first view is that an American military presence on the Asian mainland is inimical to the long-term Chinese interests of creating a greater sphere of influence and security for itself while avoiding encirclement by a pro-U.S. coalition.[26] The second is that Korea historically falls within any such Chinese sphere as a tributary state.[27]

Creating a fait accompli of tens of thousands (or more) of Chinese troops on Korean territory might seem a good bargaining chip in this context. Beijing's argument, explicit or implicit, might be that it would of course be happy to remove its troops from Korean soil once the peninsula was again stable—provided that the United States agreed to remove its forces as well. Such a motivation might lead China to seek to deploy its forces farther south than might be required for a border-related operation, and perhaps to employ larger numbers of troops than it otherwise would have. It is also possible that China would hope to retain some kind of North Korean state after hostilities, as a buffer between itself and the United States and Republic of Korea, even if it recognized that such a North Korean state could require a new government.

China's military modernization efforts in recent years have focused more on maritime domains. But a number of its programs could empower—and perhaps embolden—PRC leaders to consider a direct role in a conflict in Korea.

A PLA intervention in Korea could be a prescription for disaster. That is especially true as the U.S. and Chinese militaries have had little contact or discussion about Korea over the years. Many in both South Korea and the United States could be expected to call for a firm, even forceful response by the Combined Forces Command to such a Chinese encroachment.[28] Inadvertent escalation owing to miscommunication, or the assertive actions of local commanders, could also result. Even if top-level political leaders did not advocate or authorize escalation, any ambiguity they conveyed in their orders might allow it to happen.

For a Chinese military that has not gone to war in a generation, it is possible that the dangers of combat might be downplayed or underappreciated. As the scholar Andrew Erickson has pointed out, the modern Chinese military has not gone through its own version of a Cuban Missile Crisis—meaning that it has not been sobered by a deeply unsettling and frightening experience.[29] Overconfidence could result. So could an inadequate appreciation of the dangers of war or a hope that new technologies would permit shorter and more decisive wars than in the past—a tendency of many militaries and leaders over the generations.[30]

The above considerations also suggest that both sides not only have much to lose by failure to coordinate their response to crisis but, indeed, might have a lot to gain through coordination. This fact is perhaps better understood today in Seoul and Washington than in Beijing, which regrettably refuses to discuss such scenarios. China should reassess, perhaps starting with unofficial or semiofficial dialogues (Track 2 or Track

1.5). Coordination could lower the risks of inadvertent war. It could also reduce U.S. and ROK troop requirements for stabilizing the northern part of North Korea. China too has much to gain from prior coordination with the Republic of Korea and the United States, although this would necessarily need to be highly confidential, given the likely anxiety such communications would cause in Pyongyang.

But none of this can be constructive absent a strong American capability, including an enduring peacetime military presence on the peninsula combined with the capacity to deploy corps-scale reinforcements rapidly. The United States needs to be in a strong position vis-à-vis China to maintain the leverage and influence required to make collaboration with the PLA a truly sound idea. Beijing should not be allowed to gain the perception that it would be the most important and influential outside player in a future Korean war. Should China come to such a conclusion, its incentives for asserting its own prerogative to act as it saw fit might increase. In addition, any war and any postwar stabilization effort in Korea would be difficult enough that substantial American reinforcements for South Korea's fine armed forces would be required throughout.[31] South Korea would provide most of this stabilizing force, likely in the range of a half million or more troops, over time. But it would have its own country to worry about, too, given the likely casualties and damage a war could cause to Seoul and environs. A substantial U.S. role would be essential in war—meaning that it is prudent now, for credible deterrence.

The U.S.–Republic of Korea alliance helps keep the peace in the economically and strategically dynamic region of Northeast Asia in a time-tested way. Although it has probed with limited means in modern times, North Korea clearly has not dared to attack, or attempt to blackmail, combined U.S. and South Korean forces in recent decades. We simply do not know what it would do in America's absence. However, the fact that North Korea *has* threatened or attacked the South in relatively recent times, as with the sinking of the ROKS *Cheonon* in 2010 that killed forty-six sailors and the landmine attack in 2015 that maimed two South Korean soldiers near the DMZ, suggests that adventurism and attempts at coercion would likely increase.[32] It is not worth the experiment of finding out. There is no reason to change what is working so well—and at relatively modest peacetime cost to the United States, measured perhaps in the range of $10 billion to $20 billion a year.[33]

OPCON Transfer

Because of the strength and proven success of the U.S.–ROK alliance, I am very critical of a long-standing idea, dating back to the early 2000s, for transfer or transition of operational control (OPCON) within the U.S.–ROK alliance. For over a dozen years, the United States and South Korea have been planning to transform their military command structure known as Combined Forces Command—a remarkably integrated and effective system constructed during decades of alliance cooperation. It is the most tightly woven system of integrated command and control the United States possesses anywhere in the world. Throughout the armed forces of the two nations, South Koreans would command Americans, and vice versa, at all levels of tactical operations. In the unthinkable event of war against North Korea, ultimately more than one million South Korean soldiers (counting reservists) and several hundred thousand Americans would fight together in defense of South Korea. Separate American commands in Japan and the broader Pacific region, along with a United Nations command, would provide support and reinforcements as well as protection for threatened regional interests such as the nation of Japan and the U.S. island territory of Guam. The current plan would replace the American military officer who runs the overall alliance in times of war with a South Korean four-star officer instead.[34]

For many South Koreans, putting an officer from their own country atop the Combined Forces Command would be an important symbol of the restoration of their full sovereignty, even though the American general already takes his orders equally from civilian presidents in both countries.

The concept dates back to the George W. Bush administration in the United States and the Roh Moo-Hyun administration in South Korea—neither of which was a particularly consistent or stalwart supporter of the alliance. Today, President Moon Jae-In of South Korea would like that change to occur on his watch—meaning by 2022, at the end of his single five-year term—even though previously agreed preconditions for transfer include a stable Northeast Asian region, which clearly shows no signs of arriving anytime soon.

Rather than simply delay implementation of this plan, which was originally supposed to happen around 2012, it is time for Washington and Seoul to scrap it. No amount of lipstick on a pig can change the fact that it is a bad idea, for several reasons ranging from good old military common sense to strategic conditions in and around Korea today to broader global concerns and to U.S. domestic politics.

Even though the Republic of Korea has a very fine and battle-tested military, it is and will always remain the junior partner in the alliance. (That is true even though it devotes a higher percent of its GDP to military spending than almost any other U.S. ally.) Common sense dictates as much when one country has a $40 billion annual defense budget and the other spends more than $700 billion, owns five thousand nuclear weapons, and possesses the world's only military with truly global reach. American military leaders may not be any smarter or braver than their South Korean counterparts. But they tend to have this broader, global perspective, informed by previous tours in the broader Middle East, Europe, or elsewhere.

And even though any war between North and South Korea would have the peninsula itself as its first prize and main battleground, such a conflict would inevitably have huge regional and worldwide consequences. For starters, North Korea now has dozens of nuclear weapons, some of which may even be deliverable beyond the peninsula. Moreover, North Korea's main ally is China, and South Korea's is the United States. Even though Beijing and Washington would not want a direct clash between their respective militaries in such a war, it cannot be ruled out. Nothing could shape the future of planet Earth in the twenty-first century more consequentially than U.S.-China war. A Korean conflict would not be just a local or peninsular affair.

Currently, the American commander of Combined Forces Command is also in charge of U.S. Forces/Korea and the multinational United Nations Command focused on upholding peace on the peninsula. That is desirable and consistent with key military precepts of simplicity and clarity of command and control, as emphasized by the landmark 1986 Goldwater-Nichols legislation in the United States. Division of responsibilities into separate commands with different leaders runs at cross-purposes with this core principle of good military operations.

If South Korea is to assume the top command position in the alliance from American allies, where will the process stop? Why would Britain, France, and Germany not all demand their turns at running NATO command in Europe, for example? Each of those countries spends more on its armed forces than does South Korea. Ever since the so-called Pershing rule dating back to World War I, the United States has sought to maintain overall authority for any major military operation in which it participates. One need not be a chauvinistic American to see that this basic concept makes sense in a world where U.S. military power is vastly predominant over that of any ally.

Some policy proposals are just bad ideas. OPCON transfer belongs in that category. It should be gracefully either put on the back burner or, better yet, scrapped altogether.

Defanging North Korea

Assuming that the bipartisan, binational consensus in support of the U.S.–Korea alliance can be sustained and bad ideas from both sides of the Pacific about how to disrupt it avoided, we can turn to the crux of the matter in Korea: diplomacy over North Korea's nuclear program and perhaps, ultimately, even the ongoing state of hostilities on the peninsula. Over time, negotiations could develop a broader mandate to extend to such matters as conventional and chemical arms control and even human rights—if momentum on the first issues can be established.

The recent toughening of international sanctions on North Korea makes sense. But we need a more promising negotiating strategy, too.[35] The right strategy will, in fact, leverage the sanctions in pursuit of a nuclear deal.

There have been whiffs of progress. Over the past three years, North Kora has stopped, at least for now, testing of nuclear and long-range missile forces. For their part, the United States and South Korea have frozen or scaled back large-scale annual military exercises on the peninsula—in particular, the large exercises named Ulchi Focus and Foal Eagle that involved tens of thousands of troops. Those freezes on testing and large-scale exercise should be continued. The suspensions are a good deal for Washington and Seoul, they reduce the likelihood of escalating crises, and they promote an atmosphere more conducive to successful negotiations.[36]

Alas, despite the partial détente of recent years, North Korea continues to build more nuclear weapons. And it probably remains very frustrated by the enduring state of sanctions. The current semitranquillity on the peninsula should not lull us into complacency.

Washington and Seoul should pursue a big deal on nuclear weapons with North Korea. But while the deal should be ambitious, it should not aim for the moon. Circumstances are not ripe for complete North Korean denuclearization. Kim feels that the nuclear program is a proud legacy of his father and grandfather and a key symbol of state power. Kim also knows what happened to Milosevic of Serbia, the Taliban leadership of Afghanistan, Saddam Hussein of Iraq, and Qaddafi of Libya when they fought the United States without nuclear weapons. All were quickly overthrown; some wound up dead.[37]

To be sure, given the dangers of nuclear weapons in the hands of dictators, it would be far better that North Korea not have the bomb. In a nod to George W. Bush, who overthrew Saddam Hussein out of fear that the Iraqi dictator would someday get the bomb, one could even argue that it would have been worth the risks associated with preventive war before North Korea had an arsenal. But now it is too late—and ironically, it was probably Bush who had the last meaningful chance at preventive war against North Korea. Even the team of Bush, Dick Cheney, and Donald Rumsfeld was unwilling to risk the destruction of Seoul with conventional weapons that such a move might have risked, however, and so they watched North Korea withdraw from the (admittedly badly fraying) 1994 Agreed Framework, kick out IAEA (International Atomic Energy Agency) weapons inspectors, and prepare to reprocess enough plutonium for perhaps half a dozen bombs without taking military action to prevent any of the above. Today, with the locations of North Korea's dozens of nuclear bombs almost certainly varied and unknown, the option is simply not there in military terms.

So we need to be more pragmatic for now. The basic idea should be to end, verifiably, North Korea's ability to produce more nuclear weapons in exchange for a suspension and then lifting of the U.N. sanctions that have been imposed over the past four years or so—since North Korea's most blatant and dangerous nuclear and missile tests of 2016 and 2017.[38] In other words, we should seek to cap the North Korean nuclear arsenal at its current size and quality while providing some degree of economic relief. This approach would allow North Korea to resume normal trade and investment with China, South Korea, and other neighbors—a big carrot, since the vast majority of its foreign trade has been with the first two of those countries for many years (and today especially China). Yet it would withhold most American, Japanese, and European cooperation and technical as well as developmental assistance until complete denu-clearization might someday occur. There is good reason to think that this kind of pragmatic proposal would also meet with favor in President Moon's Blue House in Seoul.[39]

Provided that verification is good and that some sanctions are re-tained even after such an agreement was struck, this would be a smart deal. This agreement would not achieve the complete denuclearization of North Korea that Trump initially insisted on. But it would identify, and pursue, the intersection of what is realistic with what is desirable. It would prevent the North Korean nuclear threat from growing further, or modernizing, and would give Kim a stake in sustaining a state of at least partially reduced tensions on the peninsula.

Under this framework, the U.S. sanctions that have been imposed on North Korea over the decades would remain in effect. Most Ameri-can aid, trade, investment, and interaction should still be banned under such an accord. So should assistance from organizations like the World Bank, where the United States has a major influence. North Korea would not be formally recognized as a nuclear-weapons state. Any peace treaty and any U.S. diplomatic presence would be viewed as matter-of-fact mechanisms to enhance future communication, not as great accom-plishments to celebrate. North Korea would still be viewed as a pariah nation, armed to the teeth and brutal in its treatment of its people. Only when North Korea gave up all its bombs, scaled back its threatening con-ventional and chemical weapons, and started to open up its gulag-style prisons would truly normal relations become possible with the United States. Only then would the U.S. sanctions be lifted. That day may not arrive for decades, admittedly. It is not clear how much Kim even wants it at present. But he would have enough opportunity to improve his economy through a lifting of U.N. sanctions that he may take the deal nonetheless, even as the United States stood firm on the principle that it could not have a normal relationship with a nuclear-armed and brutal North Korean regime.

The nuclear pact would have to extend not just to North Korea's known plutonium production facilities but also to uranium enrichment capabilities. We would need some reasonable degree of confidence that most or all of North Korea's hidden capabilities had in fact been declared to inspectors and frozen, ultimately allowing dismantlement. Cross-checking what we know about North Korea's high-tech imports against assets at declared centrifuge facilities could be a key part of this effort. So would the so-called Additional Protocol that the IAEA now uses in places like Iran, where it has the prerogative to investigate suspicious activities even at nondeclared sites. These methods might not be adequate to preclude any and all remaining secret nuclear sites in North Korea. But they could dramatically reduce the production capacity of the DPRK by dismantling known facilities and making it very hard for Pyongyang to build and hide any remainder. Unlike bombs themselves, nuclear production facilities are large. Reactors also give off telltale thermal signatures.

Even without large-scale military exercises, the United States and South Korea can and should continue smaller unit-by-unit training without any reduction of its overall intensity. Exercises that were once large in scale can be broken down into their component parts for most purposes, with tabletop command exercises connecting the various parts and pieces from time to time. The American military trains its combat forces stateside with exercises and activities that involve up to a few thousand personnel—but generally not more. Thus, there is reason to think the same approach can be successful with Combined Forces Korea. Whatever small degradations to combat performance may result pale in comparison with the limitations that permanent testing moratoria would have on North Korea's still relatively immature nuclear and missile programs.

Seoul and Washington should, cooperatively, drive a tough bargain with Pyongyang. But we should not fear to negotiate. Nor should we fear that an interim deal might not get us to complete North Korean nuclear disarmament for years or decades. That latter goal can and must remain official policy; North Korea cannot be recognized as a formal nuclear weapons state, given the damage that such a concession would do to global nonproliferation policy. But an interim, partial deal would leave us better off than the very dangerous path we were on in 2017—a path we could soon retrace absent progress in this extremely dangerous part of the world. And it may align reasonably well with Kim's priorities. We can only find out by clearly, consistently proposing the idea and testing the proposition.

The Future of the Alliance

Any book claiming grand strategic heights should also address the question of the long-term future of the U.S.–ROK alliance. Specifically, if and when the North Korean threat can be defused, should we even want that alliance to continue? As much as Dean Acheson's 1950 comments about Korea not being important to America came back to haunt the United States, it is still a fair question in the abstract whether a distant superpower should want to ally formally with a small and exposed peninsula attached to the giant Eurasian landmass—via China and Russia, no less. Is it worth it? Is it prudent? The question could even arise in nuclear negotiations soon, so it is important to think it through now.

On balance, I think the case is strong from an American perspective—provided that South Koreans agree. That said, if South Koreans (or all Koreans, in a reunified country) do not agree, the United States can accept that outcome, too, given that geographically speaking, Korea is a small, faraway, and difficult place to defend.

First, with the planet's eleventh largest economy, South Korea is quite important in today's world. As I argued above in challenging the idea of offshore balancing, alliances with such powers are generally worth preserving for the simple reason that the United States should not want to go back to the anarchy that prevailed in Europe as well as East Asia a century ago, when major powers often had weak and shifting relationships with each other but no real enduring bonds. The result, of course, was two world wars followed by conflict in Korea.

Not only is South Korea the world's eleventh largest economy in general, but it punches far above its weight in other ways. It is among the world's top three producers of ships, of semiconductors, and of numerous types of advanced electronics. It is also the second most powerful country in the Indo-Pacific region overall, after Japan, with which the United States has a security alliance. Given the dynamism in the Asia-Pacific region that has given rise to President Obama's rebalance or pivot and been sustained in a number of ways by the Trump administration, Korea's role in America's global system of alliances takes on an even more important light.[40]

American and Korean publics seem to understand and agree with these observations. Both peoples see the other in a favorable light and support the alliance.[41]

Second, in more concrete regional terms, the U.S.–ROK alliance is crucial to American posture in the broader Asia-Pacific or Indo-Pacific regions. While American allies are plentiful around the world, they are most numerous in Europe and, in different ways, in both Latin America and the Middle East. They are far scarcer in Asia.

In terms of fully functional and binding alliances, in fact, the United States has only three in Asia—its bilateral relationships with Japan, the Republic of Korea, and Australia. The U.S. security arrangements with the Philippines, Thailand, New Zealand, and Singapore (and, in a different way, Taiwan) are either less formal politically and diplomatically or less muscular militarily or both. Of the big three allies, only South Korea is part of the Asian landmass. That is, as noted above, a liability in some ways, given the difficulty of defending its territory. But it is also an advantage in that it keeps the United States on the Asian landmass, providing presence and influence and various types of leverage.[42]

Third, in more specific military terms, the U.S.–ROK alliance has proven its mettle not only on the Korean Peninsula but from Vietnam to the Middle East and beyond. The United States has some sixty allies and security partners. But of those, arguably only Great Britain, Australia, and perhaps Canada and France have shown the same commitment to collaborative global military operations with the United States, combined with the same mass and fighting capability, as South Korea has demonstrated.

Indeed, although it is streamlining the size of its armed forces at present, South Korea today has the largest military of any American ally.[43] It probably has one of the three or four toughest and most combat-ready armed forces. It ranks fifth in military spending among formal U.S. allies (sixth if one counts Saudi Arabia). Leaving aside U.S. security partners in the broader Middle East, none of which are formal allies, South Korea also is at the top of the list for burden sharing among American allies. It devotes some 2.5 percent of GDP to its military—the most of any U.S. ally in East Asia, Europe, or the Americas with the exception of Colombia (and Trinidad and Tobago)—well in excess of NATO's goal of 2 percent or actual average of 1.5 percent. For future security missions ranging from counterterrorism to protection of sea lanes to cyberdefense, the alliance offers great benefits for the United States.

During the Vietnam War, South Korea maintained two combat divisions in alliance with American combat operations for an extended period of time. In recent years, South Korea has deployed a mechanized infantry battalion to the U.N. mission in Lebanon, an engineering company in South Sudan, and a special forces training contingent in the United Arab Emirates, among other efforts abroad. It also sustains a small contribution to the U.S.-led international mission in Afghanistan, where it had once deployed several hundred troops at the height of the Afghanistan surge. It has a reasonably large navy with some two dozen major surface combatants, as well as mine warfare ships and some amphibious capability. Many of these forces could be used as part of larger multilateral operations elsewhere if need be.[44]

Fourth, there is the matter of South Korea's immediate security— and most of all, its relationship with China. Over the past three decades, the ROK and PRC have become very important economic and diplomatic partners. Indeed, on matters of how to handle North Korea, they often align at least as much with each other as either does with Washington. Thus, there are elements of harmony in the current relationship that many elements within the South Korean polity, especially but not only on the left, would seek to preserve and enhance.

These happy considerations are reinforced by sober calculations in South Korea about size, power, and threat. Even a reunified Korea would have only 5 percent the population of China. From that perspective, the

PRC is not an enemy Koreans can afford to have. In this light, the United States has sometimes been too quick to try to draw Seoul into its broader disputes with China, notably over Taiwan, such as when the George W. Bush administration requested strategic flexibility so that it might have advance permission to use American forces based in Korea for combat operations in the broader region. More generally, the United States needs to appreciate South Korea's strategic circumstances toward China, which are clearly not the same as its own toward China or even particularly similar to Japan's.[45]

Yet if South Koreans want to get along with China and are careful about not angering the PRC, many also have a certain fear about the giant to their north and west. Put simply, China is probably not a country most Koreans prefer to have to trust and deal with on their own. Notably, over the past decade, South Korean favorability toward China has averaged slightly less than 50 percent in polls, twice dropping below 40 percent after disputatious periods.[46] In ancient times, some Chinese dynasties included land from the Korean Peninsula within their perimeters, raising a latent worry among some Koreans that China could be a threat again. Korea was viewed in Beijing as a tributary state for centuries. It has also often experienced conflict, given its location at the nexus between zones of Japanese, Russian, and Chinese hegemony for centuries.[47] Recently, the dispute over a U.S. THAAD missile deployment to South Korea, which led to Chinese economic retaliation against South Korean companies and citizens, was a stark reminder to Koreans that China is not a reliable friend.

And while China may be the greatest regional concern for Koreans, it is not the only one. Japan continues to claim islands also claimed by Seoul. Korean views toward Japan remain wary after the brutal occupation from 1910 until 1945, as well as Tokyo's difficulties in consistently and sincerely atoning for that tragic period. Some kind of alliance with the United States would thus likely help reassure Koreans about their future security in their own neighborhood for multiple reasons. But again, as acknowledged above, this last major argument in favor of a long-term U.S.–ROK alliance is one the Korean people must think through themselves.

If the North Korea threat can someday be defused to the point where it no longer constitutes a major concern for planners in Seoul and Washington, what if any American military presence on the peninsula might make sense? I begin with the perspective articulated in chapter 2: the arguments in support of a permanent military presence are very strong in regard to deterrence.

Today, as noted, the United States has almost 30,000 uniformed service members assigned to posts in Korea. Some 19,000 are soldiers, and almost 9,000 are U.S. Air Force personnel. There are also modest numbers of navy, marine corps, and special forces presence, largely for advance planning, training, logistics coordination, and preparation for absorbing an incoming U.S. force that could exceed 300,000 GIs in the event of war.[48] Today's total is down from some 60,000 in the early Cold War decades and some 40,000 in the 1980s and 1990s.[49] The biggest change since the Cold War ended, in terms of numbers of U.S. troops, resulted from Secretary of Defense Donald Rumsfeld's decision to pull one of the two U.S. Army brigades normally deployed to South Korea off the peninsula and instead involve it in the rotation base for forces being sent to Iraq and Afghanistan. The biggest changes since the end of the Cold War in terms of force posture and disposition were, first, to remove U.S. tactical nuclear weapons from South Korea during the George H. W. Bush presidency and, second, to relocate most U.S. ground forces southward from positions in Seoul and north of Seoul near the DMZ to a giant base called Camp Humphries. The army presence centers around a mechanized infantry brigade but also has large contingents focused on air and missile defense, long-range counterartillery detection and artillery fire, battlefield mobility, and logistics preparation for any massive reinforcement. The air force presence is primarily at the Kunsan and Osan bases—like Humphries, below Seoul, but also in the country's northwest. It centers on tactical combat forces that would be crucial both in early attacks against North Korean artillery and missile launchers and in subsequent efforts to mount a joint counteroffensive against the DPRK.

Looking to a future peninsula, two different concepts are straightforward to imagine. One would be a slimmed-down version of today's. The other would be fundamentally revamped to be more multilateral, regional, and expeditionary in character. It would also probably be much smaller. Either way, Seoul and Washington would likely determine that it would be better for their longer-term relationship with Beijing not to station any Americans north of today's DMZ.[50]

We do not need to answer all these questions now. But it is not too soon to begin the debate. Indeed, Donald Trump and some members of the South Korean government have arguably started it already, when contemplating in 2018 if they would be willing to offer up the very existence of alliance to North Korea as part of a nuclear deal. It would be good to have some thoughts on this subject before future negotiations get to a similar place and a decision of lasting consequence for regional and, indeed, global order has to be made quickly.

Still, as noted, the question of a long-term U.S. military presence in Korea is very interesting in strategic terms and eminently debatable in policy terms. And the United States can do very well with either outcome, someday, in terms of grand strategy. What is important, now and into the future, are the twin goals of preventing war and constraining nuclear weapons proliferation. It is on these two matters where Korean issues must most strongly have their imprint on U.S. grand strategy today. And with both, the philosophy of resolute restraint offers clear and useful counsel to retain a strong U.S.-ROK alliance, and to seek a pragmatic, partial deal on North Korean denuclearization.

SIX

The Middle East and
Central Command Theater

Ken Pollack, Tony Cordesman, and I had an amazing experience in July 2007—we were among the first strategists and scholars ever to see the Iraq surge in action. Traveling around the country, mostly by helicopter, for about ten days, we visited sites that had become infamous in the American lexicon over the past four years: Fallujah and Ramadi, the Baghdad triangle of death, and the densely populated slums of Baghdad that were often laced with lurking fighters and improvised explosive devices. We took some small risk, but of course it was nothing compared with the dangers encountered every day by the brave young men and women of the American armed forces and the citizens of Iraq.

Thankfully, the news on that trip was good. As Ken and I later wrote in the *New York Times,* "Today, morale is high. The soldiers and marines told us they feel that they now have a superb commander in Gen. David Petraeus; they are confident in his strategy, they see real results, and they feel now they have the numbers needed to make a real difference. Everywhere, Army and Marine units were focused on securing the Iraqi population, working with Iraqi security units, creating new political and economic arrangements at the local level and providing basic services—electricity, fuel, clean water and sanitation—to the people. Yet in each place, operations had been appropriately tailored to the specific needs of the community." Alas, such successes are rare in the Middle East. Even in Iraq the progress proved largely reversible.

Another image also stays with me, this one from Afghanistan, where I traveled on more than a dozen occasions on research or election observation trips over the years. A number of times, thanks often to the good graces of Ambassador Ronald Neumann, I had the privilege of meeting with the country's presidents, Hamid Karzai and Ashraf Ghani. In one conversation with Karzai, a charismatic and gifted if often difficult man, he challenged the Americans present in the room, noting that we had the best military in the world yet didn't seem able to defeat a bunch of poorly clad and badly trained insurgent fighters. Perhaps, Karzai mused, that was because we Americans didn't really want to leave such covetous strategic terrain as the Hindu Kush, from where we could keep a wary eye on China, Russia, and Iran? (He has said similar things on the record many times, so I am not betraying any confidence to report on this conversation— I am only confirming that his private conversations seemed to track fairly closely with his public pronouncements.) I tried to push back gently, offering that the United States had better ways and better places from which to watch those countries than Afghanistan. Yet in some broader sense, I have come to think Karzai was partly right about one thing: we Americans are fairly bad at winning wars in places like Afghanistan. But then again, maybe winning is the wrong and unrealistic standard for these of conflicts, most of the time.

The Middle East was not central in George Kennan's global strategic map of the late 1940s. In ensuing decades, the Middle East became much more important as the epicenter of global hydrocarbon production. It

also became the place where Israel struggled for its security. And it became the region from which the United States suffered numerous terrorist attacks against its peoples, forces, interests, or even national territory—
in Beirut in 1983, at Khobar Towers in Saudi Arabia in 1996, against a
U.S. Navy ship in port in Aden, Yemen, in 2000, on the home front on
September 11, 2001, and then throughout the prolonged so-called war on
terror ever since.

But today, things are changing again. The region, while surely important, may be slipping in strategic import. Perhaps it is not quite in a
second tier—but it may well now be in Tier 1.5. American strategy needs
to adjust accordingly, as writers including Ambassador Martin Indyk
and Brookings scholars Tamara Wittes and Mara Karlin have been persuasively arguing of late.[1] In a way, however, they have only been putting
a clear theoretical and conceptual chapeau around what was already
happening by the second Obama term, and since.[2] The United States is
correctly placing the Middle East in a middle ground of strategic priorities. Washington has realized that this is a region where it is important
to have numerous partners and points of strategic and military access—
but where it is also important not to get bogged down or overcommitted.

Ever since Iraq, Afghanistan, and the Arab Spring of 2011, it has
been clear that large-scale military efforts in the region are generally not
worth the cost. Ever since the shale oil and gas revolution, it is also increasingly clear that the stakes in the region are at least somewhat less
than before, too. Arab-Israeli issues are also less central to America's
relations with the broader Islamic world than before.[3] In addition, and
much less happily, the Israeli-Palestinian standoff seems nearly impervious to American efforts at peacemaking at present. That said, the United
States still has a moral and practical debt to the Palestinians, in my mind,
that it must try to find creative ways to address in the future (even if Israel's regrettable plans for West Bank annexation make that much more
complicated an endeavor than before).[4] But it is not clear that this matter is a top-tier *national security* imperative for the United States so
much as a matter of fairness and humanitarianism.

The United States does not have the luxury of leaving the Middle
East or the broader Central Command theater extending as far east as
Pakistan. The region still produces a quarter of the world's oil, and it

contains at least twice that fraction of proven reserves, as well as huge amounts of natural gas.[5] Even if the United States itself does not need this energy nearly as much as before, the world economy still does. The region also is not inherently stable or self-regulating. It has produced the world's worst violent extremist movements in recent decades, as well as a number of nuclear-weapons programs—at least six by my count— most of which, but not all, have thankfully been thwarted, forcibly elim- inated, or otherwise kept in check to date.[6] Thus, the United States can- not quit the broader Middle East. However, Washington should find ways to sustain its most crucial interests there at a modest level of effort.

"Tell me how this ends" is what then major general David Petraeus said to the journalist Rick Atkinson soon after the U.S. invasion of Iraq in 2003. As far as we can see today, the answer to General Petraeus's prescient rhetorical question appears to be that it does not. That is true not only for Iraq policy but for U.S. engagement in the broader Central Command and Middle East theater. This is a region with serious sectar- ian and religious tensions—but also with plenty of old-fashioned strate- gic rivalries and ambitious leaders that make for a tempestuous mix.[7]

We have tried various ways to escape this morass over the years. President George H. W. Bush watched as Saddam Hussein reestablished order (albeit brutally) in Iraq after Operation Desert Storm, rather than have U.S. troops do the job. A dozen years later, Bush's son decided that the strategy had not worked and removed the butcher of Baghdad. Alas, a quick invasion soon turned into a protracted occupation. President Bill Clinton used cruise missiles to go after al Qaeda in the wake of the 1998 bombings of U.S. embassies in Tanzania and Kenya, but that ap- proach missed its main targets and only allowed the problem to metas- tasize. President George W. Bush tried to minimize the U.S. footprint in Afghanistan after the overthrow of the Taliban, but by 2007, it had become clear that the Taliban were returning, which led to a U.S. surge. Presidents Obama and Trump continually promised to leave Afghani- stan until they learned and relearned that there was no good option for doing so.

Even though this recent history may be somewhat dispiriting, there is a silver lining. America's strategic position around the globe is strong enough that maintaining a long-term, modest military presence throughout the broader Middle East, even into the Sahel in Africa and Afghanistan in South Asia, is entirely feasible. That presence should include intelligence capabilities as well as aircraft, unmanned aerial vehicles, and special forces to strike at the most worrisome and imminent threats when needed. It should also provide trainers and liaison officers to help "build partner capacity" among indigenous forces in the region.[8]

We should certainly promote political and economic reforms that make Mideast societies healthier and, therefore, the problem of violent extremism less serious over time. But those reforms have proved elusive for decades and will take a long time. There is no magic path to aiding the political change process abroad. Some of what it requires can be budgeted through aid programs for economic and political development. But those programs only work with the right partners in the region. Waiting for—and recognizing and then supporting—such reformist leaders requires patience. Even with such leaders, progress will be slow in a region with many deep-rooted grievances, weak economies, and dysfunctional politics.[9] Sometimes there will be setbacks, as for example with Saudi Arabia in recent years. Under its young leader, Muhammad bin Salman, however promising he may have seemed for the cause of reform, the U.S.-Saudi relationship has suffered. Riyadh's mistaken war in Yemen, brutal killing of Jamal Khashoggi, and generally autocratic ways have set things back considerably.[10]

Fortunately, Washington has flexibility in this region. In military terms, for example, the United States has enough basing options in the future that it should not allow itself to feel so dependent on any one location or country as to need to kowtow to any given government in the interest of preserving access. It certainly does not need to stay in Saudi Arabia, for example, as proven by the fact that it did not base forces there for about fifteen years, starting shortly after the overthrow of Saddam and continuing into the early Trump years.

Can we keep up an open-ended strategy indefinitely? Although it is often argued that Americans are impatient, I would dispute this. The United States waged the Cold War, with numerous periods of hot combat, for forty years. What many strategists predicted would be a generation-long struggle against Islamic extremism and sectarianism in the Middle East is now well into its second generation. It has been two decades since President George W. Bush, after the attacks of 9/11, told Congress and the nation that "Americans should not expect one battle but a lengthy campaign unlike any other we have ever seen." The "forever war," as the journalist Dexter Filkins coined it in his 2008 book of that title, is still living up to its name—more than a dozen years after that book with such a dispiriting title was published. All this is highly frustrating, especially given the apparent lack of progress in the overall military and political campaign. Yet we are still at it, and most Americans seem okay with that—not because it is a desirable situation but because there are no better options. Even when conflicts like the war in Afghanistan poll badly—and how could they not?—the intensity with which Americans demand change of their leaders is modest. There are no million-person marches on the Capitol Mall to demand an exit from the Middle East.

To wage these wars, there are currently still thousands of U.S. troops stationed in Afghanistan, as well as similar numbers in Qatar and Kuwait; thousands as well in Iraq, Bahrain, and Djibouti; and anywhere from several hundred to two thousand in Saudi Arabia, Syria, Jordan, and Turkey. Add to this some ten thousand sailors and marines afloat in the region, as well as coast guard personnel and civilians.[11] That amounts to about 5 percent of the American armed forces deployed in and around the broader Middle East. That is significant, to be sure, but it is also not an enormous requirement or an unsustainable burden. This approach means relying primarily not on main U.S. ground combat troops but instead on special forces, drones, aircraft, trainers, intelligence operatives, and standoff forces. This accords the Middle East its proper strategic due—as an important region but not one that George Kennan or most modern strategists would put in the top tier of American interests.

One reason that Americans are putting up with these seemingly endless wars is that there have been relatively few U.S. casualties since 2015, averaging a total of twenty to thirty deaths a year, including accidents. For most of us, the war is far away and impersonal, even as we owe a huge debt to the all-volunteer American military, as well as intelligence, foreign service, and development experts. Enough patriotic and dedicated Americans of this new greatest generation want to serve that even with so many deployments, recruiting and retention are holding up well. In fact, without pushing the point too far, a certain number of deployments are not inconsistent with developing combat readiness— or making military service appealing—provided that they are purposeful and effective and not involve inordinate risk.

None of this means that the United States should put Middle East policy on autopilot or accept being bogged down in the region without any glimmer of hope. Country by country, innovation and progress are possible.[12] Indeed, the pursuit of them is necessary in any serious strategy. It is just that we need patience, too, for most efforts will take many years to show promise, as we await effective leaders (like the king of Jordan or the late sultan of Oman) and try to work with them.[13] That means we need to tailor the implementation of grand strategy toward the Middle East in country-specific ways, as discussed in the rest of this chapter. My approach is not comprehensive but focuses on the half dozen countries of greatest direct relevance to U.S. military operations past, present, and/or future—beginning with the country where American forces have been at it the longest and where they are still deployed in substantial numbers as I write these words in late 2020.

Afghanistan

America's role in the Afghanistan war is now two decades old. Afghans themselves will have been at war continuously twice as long, if one dates the beginning of the modern conflict to the Soviet invasion there in 1979.[14]

Americans are understandably tired of this war. It has by any measure been a frustration, especially when measured against the more ambitious nation-building goals of the first Obama term (goals I largely shared at the time). But it has not been an abject failure.[15] The Afghan government continues to hold all major and midsized cities as of this writing, and a modest majority of the population lives in areas it controls (much of the rest lives in contested areas).[16]

Even more to the point for Americans, the United States has not again been attacked by a group that plotted or organized its aggression from within Afghan borders. The United States probably has the ability to do its part to sustain these modest, yet real, accomplishments at far lower cost in blood and treasure than before. The bad news is that there is likely no near-term exit strategy; this reality should be faced head-on. The good news is that, in strategic and military and budgetary terms, the cost of the mission is sustainable.

The United States needs a policy that recognizes Afghanistan for what it is—a significant, but not a top-tier, U.S. strategic interest—and builds a plan accordingly. That overall strategy should still seek peace, but its modest military element should be steady, stable, and not set to a calendar. Roughly five thousand U.S. troops for at least five years could be the crude mantra.

A future force of 5,000 U.S. troops in Afghanistan, aided by 2,000 to 3,000 other NATO military personnel, would contrast with the late-2019 figure of 13,000 GIs there; it would roughly equal the late-2020 figure. It would be 95 percent less than the 100,000 U.S. troops, along with roughly 40,000 more from other foreign countries, commanded in Afghanistan by General David Petraeus and then General John Allen at the peak of the American presence in 2010–11. This level of 5,000 might be reduced further, though the glidepath could be slowed if conditions required, or modestly reversed if Trump has cut too far.

The advantages of this approach go well beyond the reduction in force numbers. By laying out a plan designed to last for several years, Washington would be avoiding the drama and the huge consumption of policy bandwidth associated with annual Afghanistan policy reviews that typified the latter Obama and Trump years.

The number of U.S. forces could decline even further if a peace deal eventually were struck—in which case it might even ultimately wind up near zero. The size of the deployment could also be reduced further if the Afghan military started to develop greater strength and battlefield momentum. But for planning purposes, "5,000 for 5" would be the core premise; it could entail a modest increase from latter Trump levels.

Some will say that terrorism in and near Afghanistan can be checked without an American military presence on the ground, even if our departure leads to all-out civil war and/or a victory by the Taliban within the country. Perhaps any future al Qaeda or ISIS presence on Afghan soil could be handled with long-range strikes or occasional commando raids that emanated from ships in the Indian Ocean. Or perhaps we could be confident that such groups have no substantial future interest in basing themselves in Afghanistan.

But that latter argument ignores history, as well as the geographic suppleness of global extremist movements in general. Few saw the ISIS caliphate coming in Iraq and Syria before 2014, but then, all of a sudden, it was there. And the former argument shows a poor appreciation of how counterterrorism intelligence is developed—usually by cooperation with partners on the ground—as well as an unrealistic appreciation for the geographic remoteness or ruggedness of the Hindu Kush. Stand-off counterterrorism is generally an oxymoron.

Casualties to Afghans are way too high today, at the rate of as many as ten thousand police and soldiers per year killed in action. This news is tragic at a human level and discouraging at a campaign level. But it is a strange reason to concede a war to the enemy who is responsible for most of those casualties. (Taliban losses are probably at least as great.)

The peace deal announced with the Taliban in early 2020 is no panacea. It risks placing too much trust in the Taliban, with U.S. and other NATO forces racing for the exits in ways that will be much harder to reverse than any purported Taliban pledges to oppose global terrorist movements and work sincerely toward peacemaking with the Afghan government.[17]

Rather than implement the existing deal indiscriminately, without reference to future Taliban behavior, Washington should be patient. There are plausible models of power sharing and compromise available to Afghan negotiators, though they will likely take many months or years to agree on.[18]

It is also worth noting that any eventual deal may well require some kind of U.N. observation force, however without military enforcement capacity or authority, to help monitor the various combatants for a time. It is not particularly plausible that Taliban and Afghan security forces will be quickly and seamlessly merged into one cohesive and peaceful whole.

Meanwhile, a modest U.S. and NATO military presence can continue in country. With five thousand American troops (and some additional civilians and contractors) in Afghanistan, the United States could maintain two or three major airfields and hubs of operations for intelligence, airpower, and special forces/commandos—at Bagram near Kabul in the nation's center, near Kandahar in the south, and perhaps around either Khost or Jalalabad in the east. It also could maintain a modest military advisory and training presence in Kabul to help the Afghan army and police carry out the bulk of the fighting against extremists. The annual cost of this presence would be perhaps $7 billion to $8 billion—not trivial, but only 1 percent of the defense budget. It would require several billion dollars more in annual assistance to the Afghan government to maintain its army and police and to pursue modest development goals, though other donors could be expected to provide most funds for the latter purposes. Committing to such a presence for half a decade would also signal to Pakistan and the Taliban that the new president would not be expecting a Hail Mary peace deal as a viable near-term exit strategy. Perhaps such a promise would even improve the seriousness with which one or both might then engage in peace talks.

Pakistan

How should the United States adjust its Pakistan policy? Inherently, given its size, internal schisms, ongoing tensions with India and Afghanistan, and nuclear weapons, Pakistan may be the most important country of all in the broader Central Command region (as well as its easternmost state, given how American military commands are demarcated).

Pakistan has been a frenemy for the United States in regard to Afghanistan policy in particular since 9/11. Over time, that fact combined with its nuclear program has led to a nadir in U.S. aid to Pakistan—now next to nil. Military collaboration is circumscribed, too. Pakistan tolerates and, in some cases, may support the forces that target and kill U.S. military and civilian personnel, other foreigners, and many Afghans. The Taliban has safe havens within parts of Pakistan and access there to funds and equipment. The United States needs to oppose Pakistan's role in these dynamics at every turn.[19]

Some believe that Pakistanis tolerate the Taliban out of conviction that America will again desert them—just as it did in 1989. This may seem strange given that the United States has already stayed in Afghanistan twenty years. In fairness to Pakistanis, however, Americans should bear in mind that we did leave them holding the bag, pulling out of the area completely, after the United States and Pakistan had cooperated in successfully supporting mujahedeen fighters who defeated the Soviet Union in Afghanistan in the 1980s. It was arguably one of the great betrayals by the United States of any modern ally—and ironically, it happened during the first Bush administration, widely (and rightly) seen as highly professional and decent. The second Bush administration quickly lost interest in Afghanistan after the overthrow of the Taliban, turning most attention and resources toward Iraq instead. President Obama built up forces there but brought most of them home almost as fast. Then, in his second term, and also during President Trump's four years in office, the United States has threatened to end the American presence in Afghanistan on an almost yearly basis.

Washington should do whatever it can, however, to allay Pakistani fears that it will again face an Afghanistan in chaos or an Afghanistan dominated by its rival, India. An Afghanistan policy such as what I outlined above would help. But either way, stay or go, our purpose should be to change Pakistan's calculus over time—recognizing that whatever policies we adopt, Islamabad will likely not change its Afghanistan policy quickly (even if civilian leaders in Pakistan decide they favor that outcome).

What options does the United States now have? In 2016, a group of former American commanders, ambassadors, other public servants, and scholars addressed the question and laid out the following ideas:

- The United States could take further steps to pressure Taliban sanctuaries within Pakistan (with or without the support of Islamabad). The May 2016 killing of Mullah Akhtar Mansour, the head of the Afghan Taliban, while he was traveling through southwestern Pakistan indicates the kind of direct action against the Taliban and Haqqani Network that could make an important difference.
- The Obama administration and Congress have reduced coalition support funds to Pakistan in recent years and curtailed the use of foreign military financing. But today's reduced amounts of U.S. assistance could be cut even further.

- More controversially, targeted economic sanctions could be selectively applied against certain specific organizations and individuals in the Pakistani government; Washington could encourage other countries to consider similar steps.
- Even more controversially, Pakistan could be designated as a state sponsor of terrorism, a finding that would not only be embarrassing to the country but also harmful to its economic prospects, given the likely influence on potential investors.[20]

In more positive terms, Washington might also sketch out a vision of an improved relationship with Pakistan if Islamabad would show more forthright and consistent support for the goals of NATO in Afghanistan. This outcome would be highly desirable for broader American interests, given Pakistan's central role in the stability of the entire region—and its ability to upend that stability. The most obvious elements would be perhaps a return of the early 2000s levels of assistance, renewed arms sales, and possibly even a free-trade pact. Washington should underscore that this relationship could be realized only *after* Pakistan had verifiably acted to end its policies of sanctuary and support for the insurgents and sustained that policy for a time.

Indeed, not all hope has been lost. Despite his anti-American rhetoric as candidate, Pakistan's leader, Prime Minister Imran Khan, in office since 2018, has been relatively pragmatic as leader. In addition, Pakistan's democracy has done better since the Pervez Musharraf period, avoiding coups even as the military has retained considerable leverage on national security policy.[21] All that said, progress against extremism is fragile so far, and Pakistan's willingness to help stabilize Afghanistan and avoid conflict against India remain uncertain at best going forward.[22]

Syria

In the great grand strategy scheme of things, Syria, like most of the broader Middle East, is in a second tier of importance. Indeed, it may even be third tier, given its relative unimportance to global oil markets and its (current) lack of a program to develop nuclear weapons. That said, Syria already disproved those who considered its war of the past

decade a strictly humanitarian matter. The pressures it put on close Western allies and friends, to include Turkey and Jordan and ultimately even
western Europe, as well as the dangers it created for Israel, are of strategic significance. They could again worsen, too.

In 2019 and 2020, humanitarian catastrophe has again been occurring in Syria, where the long-awaited assault against Idlib in the country's northwest, by the Assad regime backed by Russian airpower and
Iranian-sponsored militia fighters, finally occurred. Turkey has struggled to contain the tragedy with its forces, while the United States kept
some six hundred of its own troops in the Kurdish-dominated northeast
of the country. That is a residual presence President Trump was persuaded to sustain despite his preference to end the mission—a preference
that had done much to lead to the resignation of Secretary of Defense
Jim Mattis in late 2018.

The outcome of the decade-old Syrian civil war is not really in
doubt at one level. Assad and allies will win. But lots is still at stake in
this war, starting with the fate of Idlib's three million inhabitants in the
country's northwest. There also remains the possibility of enormous refugee flows into Turkey and, from there, the rest of Europe. Clashes could
erupt between Russia and Turkey inside Syria (since both have forces
there and an earlier cease-fire has broken down); Syrian and Turkish
forces have also recently exchanged lethal gunfire. Perhaps most concerning is the future of the country after the shooting eventually stops.
If the West turns away and Assad dictates terms of victory, he will surely
punish his vanquished opponents. In the process, Assad will breathe
new life into the popular grievances that launched the conflict and boost
prospects for a resurgence of violent extremism in the future.[23]

Neither President Obama nor President Trump has had any interest in getting involved in this conflict, beyond defeating ISIS. Assad will
not be pushed from power militarily at this juncture.[24] Nor will he be
pushed aside politically. The U.N.-sponsored peace process aimed at political transition in Syria is effectively dead—in fact, it has probably been
completely unpromising at least since Russia's military intervention on
behalf of Assad in 2015. From that point onward, there was little prospect
of Assad willfully stepping down in favor of a new government, which
given the country's demographics would probably be Sunni-dominated.

For Assad, an Alawite, agreeing to such a democratic transition would in effect have been snatching defeat from the jaws of military victory.[25]

However, the United States and allies can still pursue these goals:

- Limit the humanitarian catastrophe and refugee flows by supporting Turkish efforts to slow the Assad regime's offensive in Idlib and increasing humanitarian assistance;
- Maintain some influence and leverage over areas like the Kurdish-dominated northeast, including the capacity to help provide reconstruction aid there; and
- Provide incentives for political transition in the country, if not to an elected president then at least to a managed process whereby Bashar al-Assad relinquishes hold of the country that he has so butchered and bludgeoned.

There is in fact much we can still do on each front. To begin, Turkey's intervention in northwest Syria deserves U.S. support. It is designed to save lives and prevent refugee flows by providing protection and relief for affected populations in place. Ideally, Turkey would show Syrian refugees the same hospitality today it demonstrated in earlier phases of the conflict. Yet if Turkey can no longer countenance adding to the nearly four million Syrian refugees already on its territory, establishing a real safe zone inside Syria is crucial for civilian protection. Turkey's inherent right of self-defense under the U.N. Charter, to say nothing of the Genocide Convention, provides ample legal basis for its operations in areas of Syria near its own territory.

American officials have endorsed Turkey's presence in parts of Idlib but done little beyond a few statements from Secretary of State Mike Pompeo. We should be sharing intelligence on Syria with Turkey and publicly leading a diplomatic effort to build an international coalition that supports and legitimates Turkey's efforts to halt the Assad regime's advance. Moreover, Washington should warn Russia that any attacks on Turkish positions will lead to new sanctions under the recently signed Caesar Syria Civilian Protection Act. Of course, any American or Turkish forces coming under direct attack will also retain the right to defend themselves (as U.S. forces did several years ago, with devastating effect, when mercenaries from Russia's paramilitary Wagner Group showed hostile intent against an American position in Syria's east).[26]

By holding territory in northern Syria, governments that oppose the Assad regime gain a valuable bargaining chip, denying Damascus full sovereignty over the north unless it agrees to implement a verifiable and meaningful political transition.

American diplomacy toward this end would be strengthened by further exploiting two key priorities of both Moscow and Damascus: gaining Western aid for postconflict reconstruction and obtaining sanctions relief. To be sure, no U.S. funds should be forthcoming while Assad remains in place. Nor should Washington do anything to loosen its current, effective sanctions policy while the current regime is in power. Broader assistance to Damascus and the country as a whole should only flow once a meaningful political transition is under way and a new government is installed—even if that new government is one that Assad and his Russian patrons have a hand in picking. Indeed, rumors have sometimes circulated that Moscow is advising Assad to prepare for a political transition. Helping Turkey to prevent Assad from retaking Idlib will bolster Moscow's efforts to ease Assad from power. While such a transition will be far from ideal, the right new president and cabinet could strengthen possibilities for stitching the country together and putting Syria on a postconflict trajectory that could pave the way for U.S. and European Union assistance and the easing of sanctions.

This initiative does not require big and bold new investments or risks from Washington. It simply requires the concerted focus and consistency that, alas, the United States has never mustered since this war started in 2011. As a way of ensuring that Syria does not become a grand strategic problem for the United States and its allies and as a partial amends for the negligence with which the United States has addressed this war since it began, the Biden administration should attempt to salvage something out of the mess and mitigate further loss of life.

Libya

Some experts say that Libya is the Las Vegas of the Middle East: what happens there, stays there. I suppose what they mean is that Libya, given its small population, remote location, and eccentric leader for so many years, has little bearing on broader Arab politics. Taken literally, however, the opposite seems closer to being true. Libya supplied a very high percentage of extremist fighters for the wars of the last twenty years in the Levant.[27] Libya has been the source, but even more the way-station, for huge numbers of Africans fleeing trouble at home in an attempt to reach Europe. Through the tragedy in Benghazi in 2012, Libya wound up playing a significant role in the 2016 U.S. presidential election, given the way that issue was used against Secretary Hillary Clinton. Libya is now a site of proxy war among numerous outside players, including Russia, several European states, and numerous neighbors as well. Libya is in fact important. Again, like larger Arab and Maghreb and South Asian countries, even if Libya is a second-tier interest, it is not irrelevant to U.S. security or grand strategy.

President Obama made it clear that he wanted as little as possible to do with Libya. He needed to be persuaded to support intervention there in 2011 in defense of innocent civilians who might be targeted by Qaddafi's forces—and even then, he did so largely to support a NATO operation that he insisted the United States not lead. Tragically, anarchy resulted there, just as it had in Iraq in the aftermath of the U.S.-led invasion eight years earlier, if this time on a smaller scale.[28]

Today, Libya remains in distress. In 2019, a Brookings-led task force with important contributions from the Carnegie Endowment, Atlantic Council, and Center for Strategic and International Studies argued for a city-based model for the country's future. Our proposal was to create a more transparent system whereby Libya's considerable oil revenue could be distributed fairly among those groups locally providing services in the country's various cities—including even militia-affiliated groups, provided that their behavior met modest standards of fairness and nonviolence. In my view and that of some of the report's other coauthors, a U.N. observation mission could help by monitoring oil facilities, key infrastructure, and lines of demarcation between the territorial zones of certain militia groups. It might also monitor the fledgling Libyan coast guard—an institution that foreign donors might also think about strengthening. Other observers, including on-the-ground development specialists, would confirm if and when resources were being used correctly and in a way that justified continuing the flow of resources from central coffers to the city or neighborhood in question. Over time, regional coordination centers for the activities of the various militias could be developed—not to create a national army from the ground up, as had been attempted in the early 2010s, but to help one perhaps eventually emerge as a loose conglomeration of local security forces.[29]

But unfortunately, as often happens in the Middle East, a promising new strategy ran into the concrete wall of reality. To put it differently, a new reality emerged: General Khalifa Haftar's "Libyan National Army," as he called it, went on the offensive. Backed by Russia, Egypt, the UAE, and other foreign powers, it took much of the country's south and center in 2019, before stalling in an attempt to seize Tripoli from the weak U.N.-recognized government of Prime Minister Fayez al-Sarraj.[30] Diplomatic efforts turned to mitigating the risk of a worsening fight for the capital city, with the potential for enormous civilian casualties.[31] Pursuit of an architecture for gradually solving the conflict was placed on the back burner yet again.

Fortunately, Haftar has been pushed back to the eastern half of the country. But he remains influential and powerful. Given Haftar's strength today, a mixed model might be needed. Perhaps a city-based approach to governance, security, and sharing of oil wealth still has relevance.[32] But it might have to be promoted first for the country's west and center while Haftar retains a certain degree of control in the east—as a recognition of the realities on the ground and the practical distributions of power in the country.

Iraq and Iran

Targeted assassinations were a preferred tool of U.S. foreign policy for a crucial period in late 2019 and early 2020. American special forces tracked and killed ISIS leader Abu Bakr al-Baghdadi late in 2019. That raid was followed in early January 2020 by the killing of Quds force leader Qassem Soleimani by U.S. drone strike near Baghdad airport—eliminating a terrible terrorist ringleader, yet throwing into doubt the ability of the United States to keep its five thousand military personnel inside Iraq. This recent history, plus the Covid-19 outbreak in Iran, plus the worldwide effects of the coronavirus-induced recession on any major global oil exporter like Iran or Iraq, sets the context for policy in this crucial part of the world.

Iraqi politics have become fascinating and complex; they are no longer dominated just by Saddam Hussein or just by sectarianism. In some ways, they are more promising—though they are also as turbulent as ever. In 2019, demonstrations by Iraqi citizens—aimed mostly at corrupt and ineffectual politicians from their own country but also at Iran and its unfortunate influence within Iraq—led to hundreds of deaths, as Iranian-linked snipers shot generally peaceful civilians exercising their constitutional rights of speech and protest. Iraq's prime minister at the time, Adel Abdul Mahdi, accepted responsibility and promised to step aside once a successor could be chosen through proper parliamentary procedures (not new elections).

To divert attention, and pressure America, Iranian-sponsored groups then began shelling U.S. facilities within Iraq more than they had in many years. The United States, understandably frustrated at this situation, blamed the Iraqi government for allowing the violence and took matters into its own hands, bombing five sites in western Iraq where the Iran-sponsored militias kept lethal supplies in December 2019. The Iraqi government, understandably frustrated itself by this infringement on its sovereignty (since the U.S. forces carried out the raids without forewarning), objected strenuously. Abdul Mahdi, by this point acting as a caretaker head of government, tried to bridge the chasm. But the parliament passed a nonbinding resolution asking U.S. forces to leave—which the Trump administration subsequently promised to ignore. Then, just when the situation was already so fraught, the United States opened the new year with the strike on Soleimani, killing him and an Iraqi militia leader near the main airport in Baghdad.

It is hard to oppose the Trump administration's decision to target and kill Qassem Soleimani, the head of Iran's Quds force within the Islamic Revolutionary Guard Corps organization.[33] In effect, he was the most important military leader in Iran and perhaps the country's second most powerful leader overall. Soleimani's machinations had led to the deaths of hundreds of American troops in Iraq. That happened largely because the Quds force funneled explosively formed penetrator devices and other technologies to the militias and insurgents that were fighting Iraqi and U.S. forces there, especially in the early years after Saddam was overthrown in 2003. Killing Soleimani was therefore arguably more akin to shooting down the plane of Japanese admiral Isoroku Yamamoto in World War II than attacking a civilian leader.

Iran's lack of restraint in killing Americans also removed one major argument against political assassination in general—the fear of legitimating a form of attack that will then be used against our own country or citizens. It was Soleimani, not the United States, that crossed the assassination threshold first and often—attacking Americans (and others) with abandon. He succeeded earlier Iranian leaders who had done equally heinous things against Americans in Beirut in 1983 and at Khobar Towers, Saudi Arabia, in 1996. America's history toward Iran is checkered, to be sure, in our support for the shah of Iran before 1979 and in our support for Saddam (at times) during the Iran-Iraq war. But over the past thirty years especially, it is Iran that has used lethal force against the United States much more than the reverse. And for the past twenty-two years, Soleimani was the chief plotter and mastermind in much of this. Given the believable intelligence reports that he was planning additional attacks against U.S. assets and personnel in Iraq (even if the Trump administration likely exaggerated their probable scale) and given his central role over the years in many similar atrocities, it is difficult to object to this U.S. action.

Yet that is hardly the end of the story. However justifiable the attack may have been, we do not yet know if it will turn out to be advantageous to our interests; future policy decisions will largely determine whether that proves true.

The most pressing matter is preserving, if at all possible, the U.S. military partnership with Iraq now that Iraq has a new leader, Prime Minister Mustafa al-Kadhimi.[34] For all that country's many challenges, it has in fact started to cohere as a polity and has avoided descent back into large-scale civil war; there is considerable hope for its imperfect and struggling democracy.[35] If we are thrown out of Iraq by that country's parliament as a result of this action, it will be a net win for Iran, since there will no longer be a balancing foreign power with comparable clout

inside the country. It will also leave Iraq more vulnerable to further sectarian strife and/or ISIS and al Qaeda attack. America's five thousand
troops have played important roles in training, providing airpower, sup-
plying intelligence, and being an honest political broker that has helped
Iraqis of different sectarian groups work together. It may be too late to
salvage our role, and our presence, in Iraq. But we should try. We should
also try to sustain a military presence and substantial amounts of reconstruction and development aid to Iraq long enough to help that country
really get on its feet in the aftermath of Saddam, the sectarian civil war
and al Qaeda catastrophes of the 2000s, the ISIS debacle of the mid-
2010s, and ongoing challenges from Iran throughout Iraq's entire modern history.[36]

Notably, the United States should pledge not to conduct airstrikes
like those of December 2019, against five facilities in Syria and Iraq of the
Kataib Hezbollah (KH) militia, again. We should undertake any further
unilateral actions within Iraq only in direct, immediate tactical defense
of our people there. We should also offer to help develop a plan, with
the new government of Iraq, to pressure the most reckless KH groups
economically as a first resort in the future. (Perhaps Iraq's government
could cut them off from the payments they now receive as a semiofficial
part of the Iraqi security forces.)

And Washington needs a more realistic Iran strategy for the longer
term. The Trump administration has had a policy of economic constric-
tion of Iran that leaves no real daylight for leaders in Tehran. Trump and
Secretary Pompeo have stated that, if Iranians want sanctions lifted and
their economy restored, they should be expected to abandon virtually all
nuclear-related activities, give up categorically their regional machinations from the Levant and Lebanon to Yemen and beyond, accept major
constraints on their missile programs, and recognize Israel's right to
exist—all this according to a speech by Pompeo in the spring of 2018. At
a moral level, most of these demands are reasonable. At a practical level,
taken collectively, they stand virtually no chance. We need to prioritize.

One possible approach could look like this. The United States could
offer to lift sanctions on Iran if it would extend the 2015 nuclear deal's
restrictions to have indefinite duration (rather than eight to ten years for

most of them, as is currently the case). Iran would also have to acknowledge a state of nonaggression with Israel in some way and commit not to
develop long-range ICBMs. Agreement on a dialogue on regional security
that would acknowledge Iran's influence in countries with substantial
Shia populations—Iraq, Lebanon, Syria, Yemen—would also be important. Iran's presence need not be fully ended there, but its role in stoking
violence could be addressed on a country-by-country basis. However,
these regional dialogues should not be expected to produce results as a
precondition for an extension of the nuclear deal.

The case for extending restrictions on Iran's nuclear activities indefinitely is strong. Placing temporary restrictions on dangerous nuclear activities is not logical. That is especially the case when a country
like Iran has had a virulent and violent foreign policy for forty consecu-
tive years. Why would we think that a few more years of time would
make that nation less threatening? The world's central nuclear nonproliferation accord, the Nuclear Non-Proliferation Treaty of 1968, was of
unlimited duration—because the spread of nuclear weapons is not a
challenge that becomes less pressing or worrisome with time. That pursuit of permanent nonproliferation should provide the basic logic that
the Biden administration applies to future negotiations with the Islamic
Republic.

The United States has considerable leverage with Iran, given Iran's
weak economy as well as its additional suffering at the hands of Covid-
19. The temptation will be to hope that Iran's economy or political order
may completely crumble.[37] But the reality is that autocracies from North
Korea to Syria to Iraq under Saddam to many others often show resilience. To paraphrase my colleague Jung Pak, their dictators often prove
to have a very high tolerance for other people's pain. To grant Iran relief
from most sanctions in return for an indefinite extension of the 2015 nuclear pact's restrictions, prohibitions, and inspections protocols would
in fact be a good deal for Tehran at this juncture. But it would also
amount to a strengthening of the deal and represent a bipartisan success
for American foreign policy despite the intense partisan rancor that has
surrounded the issue in recent times.

An indefinite extension of the Iran nuclear deal would render much
less likely a choice the United States should never wish to be forced to

make: whether to use preventive military force to destroy as much as possible of the known parts of Iran's nuclear-related infrastructure. Such an attack would almost surely only slow, not prevent, Iran from obtaining nuclear weapons should it devote itself fully to that course of action. There may be some circumstances in which that could be our least bad option—complete breakdown in negotiations even under an American president trying to find a compromise, Iranian breakout from all of its obligations under the nuclear deal with an all-out push to produce weapons-grade uranium (and perhaps complete and start its nuclear reactor), the world united against Iran. But we are nowhere near that point today. And any such military operation would have untold effects on the potential for large-scale Iranian retaliation, most likely through terrorism as well as sabotage of large elements of nearby nations' oil production infrastructure. It is far better, and safer, not to go down this path, even at some risk of ongoing low-grade Iranian regional adventurism.

Congress and Authorization on the Use of Military Force

A final and important subject that is most vividly raised by the Middle East—though hardly limited in importance to that region—concerns Congress's role in deciding on the use of American military power. At present, there are insufficient checks on the president. However, many proposed solutions could do more harm than good.

Congress needs to play a major role in future U.S. national security decision making, including in regard to decisions on the use of force. Many of the nation's best national security ideas in recent decades had origins in the legislative branch: the Nunn-Lugar cooperative threat reduction program that sought to secure Russia's (and others') nuclear materials; decisions to induce authoritarian leaders like Ferdinand Marcos in the Philippines to step down from power over the years; the Senate hearings in 2002 on how difficult Iraq might be to govern after any overthrow of Saddam; and the imposition of tough sanctions on Vladimir Putin and his cronies in Russia as well as the extremist regimes in Tehran and Pyongyang.[38]

Under article 1 of the Constitution, only the Congress can declare war, raise armies and maintain navies, and otherwise provide funds for the common defense. Congress has done well with the latter responsibilities since then. Yet it has not declared war since World War II and has not even formally approved, in any alternative ways (except belatedly through the appropriations process), several of the major conflicts the nation has engaged in since then—notably, the Korean War, Kosovo War, or 2011 Libya operation.[39]

This argument transcends anything specific to President Donald Trump. Indeed, perhaps somewhat ironically, it appears that President Trump's 2017–21 term in office may have ended with him being one of the *less* guilty perpetrators of overuse of commander-in-chief authorities in the post–World War II era.

Today, two decades after Congress passed the 2001 Authorization on the Use of Military Force within days of the tragic 9/11 attacks, we are living on legislative fumes. That 2001 AUMF is all we have to legitimate military operations from Afghanistan to Iraq and Syria to Yemen and Somalia and beyond. Because that law targeted the perpetrators of the 9/11 attacks—Sunni and Salafist extremists under the al Qaeda banner and their associates—it does not even attempt to speak to the current situation with Shia-run Iran.

The nation cannot tie the hands of this or any future commander-in-chief in a way that could leave the nation even temporarily defenseless. But that does not mean the president should get a blank check or that a twenty-year-old law should provide the legal basis for combat today. We need to revise the AUMF legislation of 2001.[40]

The War Powers Act of 1973 is not adequate because it only required a president to seek legislative approval for actions lasting longer than sixty days. It has not been recognized as constitutional by any president to date in any event.[41]

A new AUMF should not be indefinite. It might span five years, for example, after which another new AUMF would be needed. However, in the event that Congress failed to replace it, the previous authorities could remain in effect so as not to leave the country defenseless in the event of Washington gridlock. In these ways, my recommendations echo those of Senators Bob Corker and Tim Kaine in the 115th Congress.[42]

A new law should require that the director of national intelligence certify that any new extremist group had ideology, goals, and/or key membership that were related to al Qaeda or broader violent extremism or Salafism before a president was entitled to strike it. That would prevent a president from using the AUMF for entirely different purposes than its original intent while allowing flexibility if new terrorist groups splintered off from old ones or simply changed their names to avoid being targeted.

The AUMF debate should go beyond the terrorism issue. Congress needs a stronger role in any possible war against North Korea, China, or Russia, heaven forbid. The degree to which American presidents have circumvented Congress on decisions of war and peace in the modern era is hard to square with the Constitution or intent of the founders, and worse, it is dangerous.[43] The consequences of any such uses of force could be far more dire than those of the twenty-first century from Iraq to Afghanistan to other parts of the Central Command theater. Certainly, for any decision that could have existential consequences for the nation, the people's branch of government would need to play a central role *in advance* of any decision to initiate hostilities; checks and balances are crucial. This principle should be reaffirmed in any new AUMF that, for current purposes, retains its own primary focus on the broader Middle East and the struggle against violent extremism.

We should also add more checks and balances to any future employment of nuclear weapons, except in the event of immediate peril to the nation when an enemy nuclear attack is imminent or under way. Richard Betts and Matthew Waxman have recommended requiring that the secretary of defense and attorney general both certify a decision to use nuclear weapons.[44] One might consider extending this requirement either to the Chief Justice of the Supreme Court (or some other justice, should the Chief Justice not be available) or to the congressional leadership. Their role would not necessarily be to rethink the decision, only to ensure that it had some basic acceptability in the laws of war. Certainly, in any U.S. grand strategy, reducing the odds of inadvertent, accidental, or unconstitutional nuclear war should have a place. I return to the nuclear issue in chapter 8.

America will have to manage its interests in the Middle East indefinitely. That will include a nontrivial role for its armed forces and intelligence capabilities. The potential for terrorism, nuclear proliferation, interstate war, and threats to world energy sources is too great for us to pretend we can disengage from the region or somehow treat it as a minor interest. The trick is to try to keep our engagement commensurate with the Tier 1.5 magnitude of the region's importance to the United States and the world.

SEVEN

The Other 4+1—Biological, Nuclear, Climatic, Digital, and Internal Dangers

Never has the planet been more prosperous or a more exciting place to live. Never has it been more vulnerable to an imperiled climate, disease, dangerous technologies, or fragile infrastructure. One image of what can go wrong stands out for me personally. When I was a Peace Corps volunteer in the former Zaire (now the Democratic Republic of the Congo) in the early 1980s, my small city of Kikwit had some amenities. They had declined from the heyday of the Mobutu Sese Seko period of the late 1960s and 1970s, before the corruption of the government and broader global economic trends had wreaked their havoc. But there was still some power and water, as well as a passable road network. And the city was small enough, and natural resources were abundant enough, that people also had backup plans. Most could walk to streams or springs for water, and to nearby fields for food, if they needed to. Their home villages were often just an overcrowded truck ride of a few hours away. Those villages relied on subsistence farming—not an advanced or easy life—but at least there were abundant resources.

Today, as Kikwit's population approaches one million,

the DRC is worse off. Fifteen more years of Mobutu plus civil warfare and governmental ineptitude—not to mention HIV-AIDS, Ebola, and now Covid-19—have decimated what was left of the still somewhat happy land of the 1980s that I knew. Because of burgeoning populations and mega-cities, the nation's inhabitants no longer have insurance policies against a possible breakdown of the urban economy like they once did. It is hard just to pick up and return to the village in tough times.

Heaven forbid that what has happened to Kikwit, and Congo, and the wonderful Congolese people could be a har-binger of what awaits the planet writ large. We have higher standards of living than before, but much of it is built atop fragile infrastructure and a complex, fragile global economy vulnerable to technical, pandemic, and other insults. We have now been forewarned. Just in terms of biology and pandemics, to say nothing of many other types of threats, the string of new diseases and pandemics over my adult lifetime—starting with HIV-AIDS and Ebola but then con-tinuing through SARS and MERS and West Nile Virus and Zika and the novel coronavirus among others—must be a wake-up call for the planet as a whole.

For the Pentagon as an organization, and for a long-standing student of the Pentagon like myself, it is natural when analyzing threats to think first in terms of nations, as well as blocs or alliances of nations. The last generation has also taught the American national security community to view terrorist organizations as potentially serious security concerns themselves. Groups like al Qaeda, ISIS, Hezbollah, Lashkar-e-Taiba, and even certain parts of national governments, like Iran's Quds Force or parts of the Pakistani Inter-Services Intelligence, come to mind.

But in the twenty-first century, we need to think about threats in a new, orthogonal way as well. This chapter focuses on a separate 4+1 list of dangers: biological weapons and pandemics, nuclear weapons, climate change, nefarious aspects of digital technologies, and America's own weakening internal cohesion and strength. This last one is different from the others, in that it chiefly concerns the United States itself, so it is the "plus one" on the 4+1 list.

None of the above are scheming enemies in the traditional sense. But they pose serious challenges nonetheless. When they interact with the classic list of threats, they can make every problem more serious. They can exacerbate, intensify, or accelerate the dangers posed by more classic, human adversaries; they raise the stakes enormously. They also therefore challenge the Pollyannaish claim that humankind is inexorably headed to a better future. Any effort at understanding the security environment of the twenty-first century, and determining a corresponding grand strategy for the United States, needs to factor them centrally in its cognitive framework.

Not all of these threats are new, of course. But most are becoming more concerning in light of the ballooning human populations and remarkable advances in technology that characterize modern times. Bigger populations and more advanced technologies are themselves not bad things; they can, in fact, be very desirable. But they can certainly accelerate and intensify many dangers in the world even as they allow for more prosperous and potentially happier lives for more people than ever before in human history.

To put all this in broader perspective, the twentieth and twenty-first centuries are likely to go down in the broad sweep of human history—assuming we as a species survive them—as the two hundred years when people filled up and dominated Earth. In 1900, there were fewer than 2 billion humans on the planet. By 2020, we exceeded 7.5 billion. By 2100, we are likely to reach a plateau of around 11 billion, with almost all the net growth between now and then in Africa.[1] For adults alive today, over the lives of our great-grandparents, grandparents, parents, children, grandchildren, and their children—roughly six or seven generations—this is the greatest demographic explosion in the history of the planet. Nothing like it has been seen before, and nothing like it is imaginable for the far future either.

Those people will increasingly live in close quarters, too. In 1950, of the world's 3 billion people, only one-third lived in cities. By 2050, of the world's projected 9 billion people, two-thirds will be urban inhabitants. In other words, the world's urban population will go up sixfold over that time, from 1 billion to 6 billion people.

Dozens of cities are becoming megacities, with populations of 10 million or more. They often include large, sprawling, and poorly serviced slums. Large numbers of the cities are near coasts, where flooding is increasingly likely due to rising oceans. And inhabitants across the globe are increasingly interconnected, not only electronically but also physically. The connections are wonderful in many ways. Yet they also ease many of the tasks of organizations like transnational criminal cartels and the spread of scourges like disease, drugs, and weapons.

This is not a prediction of apocalypse or a lamentation about human progress. We should not give up on civilization and become survivalists or modern-day Henry David Thoreaus. Today's sets of conditions, and challenges, are preferable to those of any previous era in human history. But we would be badly mistaken not to recognize the enormous dangers in today's world, either.

When assessing future threats, we should not adopt a sky-is-falling mentality. Only some are likely to be serious national security problems. To be a true national security threat to the United States as well as its friends and allies, something on this list has to have a plausible chance of killing, displacing, or harming a significant fraction of a given nation's population. If the term "national security" is to be useful, and precise, that is what it should be interpreted to mean. Other kinds of security are important, too, but they are not necessarily *national* security.

For example, civil wars kill more people than any other kind of violence on Earth today (except criminal murder). But they generally happen most in countries where the ripple effects are limited primarily to nearby neighbors. Transnational criminal organizations need a functioning, viable global transportation and communications infrastructure to thrive, so their incentive to try to destroy the nation-state and global economic system is usually low. Thankfully, many of the advanced information and communications technologies that they use to move people and goods can also be used against them.

Pollution and environmental degradation are big problems, from the concentrations of plastic in the oceans to the contamination of freshwater in China to the overfishing of the oceans to the toxic air of India's cities. Many people will die who need not. Many national treasures on this planet will be compromised. Yet these should be thought of generally as serious human, humanitarian, ecological, and economic problems rather than national security ones, for the most part. They will typically not arise so suddenly or acutely as to put entire territories or populations at physical risk in a way that could threaten the nation.

Or, to go in an entirely different direction, possible asteroid strikes may be worth doing something about in theory. But the likelihood of a serious strike is probably about one in a billion per century (if Earth's history is a guide). Overinsuring against this extremely unlikely threat, especially with today's fairly fledgling technologies, would likely not be smart. Earthquakes can be major tragedies if they hit megacities, but they are likely to be localized, as always—and thus not really threats to the national security, properly defined. Supervolcanoes could end life on Earth if serious enough; but again, the expected time frames are calculated in the range of tens or hundreds of thousands of years or more. Moreover, like asteroids, they are better thought of as threats to the planet than to national security; they are more likely to be aimed at Earth writ large than the United States, more likely to target humans in general than Americans in particular. Research and monitoring makes sense, perhaps on an expanded scale, and at some future date, the capacity for building defense mechanisms may make sense, too.[2] But these matters probably do not belong on a short list of U.S. national security threats and thus should not be what American grand strategy is built to prioritize.

By contrast, the threats on my new 4+1 list could, especially when juxtaposed with those from the classic 4+1 list of real or possible U.S. adversaries, wreak huge damage. It is important to ask what we could realistically do about each—and what each teaches us about the art of war in the modern age.

Pandemics and Biological Weapons

The 2020 coronavirus crisis may be only a harbinger of what could come next in either natural or artificially created pandemics. And the stakes are potentially enormous, as we are all now viscerally more inclined to believe than before—even if Covid-19 itself changed little about what epidemiologists already knew to be possible. Historically, disease has at times been instrumental in the rise and fall of nations.[3] The string of new viral diseases stretching back to the 1980s has been remarkable and is probably not a fluke in light of the proximity and density of human and animal populations that characterize the modern world.[4]

Biological weapons may become more dangerous too. Gene splicing has become much, much easier in modern times, thanks to the development of such methods as CRISPR. Fortunately, it is in fact still very difficult to engineer extremely dangerous pathogens, because it is hard to know the effects of any rearrangement of genes in advance. Moreover, most nation-states will have only limited reason to consider the attempt (especially in a world where nuclear deterrence provides a backstop against most such threats). It takes a great deal of luck to produce a pandemic that will cause so much more damage to other nations than to one's own way as to be somehow, in a sinister and evil way, geostrategically advantageous to the perpetrator. For a nation-state, it would take some combination of great brilliance, remarkable moral depravity, and/or extreme recklessness to venture down such a path.[5]

That said, there is also no basis for complacency. It is possible that mad scientists with enough time and resources will hit on an engineered pathogen that combines the contagious qualities of the flu with the lethality of smallpox or Ebola or something similar. They could hope that they might find a disease that treated their own ethnic group less harshly. Or they might hope to develop a vaccine for their own nation's use before releasing any bug on the world. Sheer trial-and-error methods are easier to pursue in an era of rapid and easy gene-splicing technologies. It is terrifying how many millions could be killed in plausible ways in this fashion. And even old-fashioned anthrax can be extremely deadly if delivered efficiently.[6] To discourage and deter the pursuit of new types of pathogens, John Steinbruner proposed a type of societal verification—that is, collaborative oversight of biological research around the world. If geopolitics improves enough to make it feasible, the idea merits serious consideration.[7]

Whatever the threat of biological weapons, the central lesson of

2020 is that *natural pandemics* are a top-tier threat to humankind. Indeed, they are so daunting that they should encourage us to put traditional geopolitics on the back burner and focus on the common and potentially catastrophic dangers of this twenty-first century, with a planet full of people and pathogens alike. Whether that proves possible, one thing is clear: the United States, like other countries, has not done enough by way of preparation. And this moment when minds are concentrated must not be lost.

For example, the Strategic National Stockpile of medical equipment and supplies, dating back to 1998, was certainly a worthy idea that was expanded by President George W. Bush after the 9/11 attacks.[8] In general, resourcing for preparations against biological pathogen dangers was fairly good in the late 1990s and early 2000s.[9] But it was not consistently taken seriously enough by the administrations and Congresses that ensued.[10] To be sure, stockpiling the right types of basic supplies is a daunting challenge.[11] Yet some elements of a stockpile are quite predictable.

The kind of preparations needed to mitigate a future pandemic are by now so frequently discussed that to the ear of a reader in 2021 they almost sound hackneyed. But to summarize:

First, early detection and early identification–isolation–contact tracing for initial victims are far and away the most desirable ways to mitigate any pandemic—essentially to contain and exterminate it before it can reach the broader population, at least long enough for a vaccine to be developed. This method requires ample test kits, the number being a function of how widely the virus has spread before widespread testing becomes available; Scott Gottlieb and colleagues at the American Enterprise Institute estimated in late March 2020 that up to 750,000 tests a week would soon be needed in response to the novel coronavirus outbreak.[12] It also requires strong public health institutions that can do the legwork associated with contact tracing and quarantining of the infected and potentially infected.[13] Febrile thermometers for screening of individuals going into public buildings or aircraft or trains are needed in abundance, as are smartphone apps to help track movement and contacts.[14]

Second, it is crucial to maintain adequate stocks of the basic protective and lifesaving supplies that were in such limited availability, due to inadequate preparation by the Obama and Trump administrations in particular, in the Covid-19 case. These include N95 masks and ventilators, not only for first responders and health care workers but the population writ large—with adequate supplies not only to care for Americans but to help others abroad (on humanitarian grounds and because there is no other way to eradicate a pandemic in the age of globalization). The number of necessary ventilators is a function of course of the nature of a given illness; for Covid-19, one estimate was that roughly twice as many ventilators would be needed nationwide as the nation initially possessed.[15]

Third, the nation needs the manufacturing capacity to ramp up production of key supplies quickly. For some situations, this may require peacetime subsidies to keep capacity ready. We need the ability to expedite production of tests, vaccines, and various antiviral treatments that could mitigate the effects of the illness on anyone who gets sick. And, in an emergency, the country should commit to production of promising treatments even before safety trials run their course, with government incurring the financial risk associated with production of vaccines and medicines that may have to be discarded rather than used.[16] One-time costs in a crisis could range into the tens of billions of dollars. But compared with the stakes, and compared with the costs of other kinds of emergencies, this is not out of proportion to the magnitude of the threat by any means.[17] The government has tools ranging from the Defense Production Act to simple subsidies to address this challenge.[18]

We also must build up public health infrastructure needed for surveillance of possible future disease outbreaks, isolation and treatment of affected populations, and sharing of information across regional and national lines. Much of this can be on-call for emergencies; it need not all involve full-time employees. It might be juxtaposed with various concepts for national service as well. The effort must also extend to other countries and should be combined with general global efforts to improve health care and health infrastructure around the world.[19]

We need ongoing work to mitigate the risks of future outbreaks occurring. That means strong restrictions on the kind of live-wildlife markets in places including China that have contributed to some of these kinds of outbreaks and better protection of the natural habitats of species that tend to foster and harbor dangerous diseases so that interactions between animals and humans are better regulated and limited.[20] The World Health Organization also needs to be empowered with more authority and resources to deploy capable surveillance and treatment teams quickly and effectively to zones where future outbreaks may occur.[21]

It is also conceivable that certain kinds of outbreaks, perhaps more like Ebola than Covid-19, may require a direct response including military forces—for example, to quarantine an area that is badly afflicted (perhaps even a war zone) or to protect medical workers from crime or war as they seek to contain an outbreak. The world has been lucky in a sense in that most Ebola outbreaks to date have occurred in countries that, while recent victims of civil warfare, had ended or at least largely defused their violent struggles before Ebola hit. That is not guaranteed to be the case in the future, of course.[22]

Indeed, it is important to remember that even if quelling civil war around the world is largely viewed as a humanitarian matter, it can have strategic implications for the United States, too, and it certainly belongs in any discussion of grand strategy. The implications could arise if pandemic disease spread out of a war zone where it could not be controlled, for example. They could also arise if, say, Pakistan were the country experiencing the internal strife, with uncertain implications for the safety of its nuclear arsenal (the nuclear question is discussed in the next section).

Fortunately, the world does have rather inexpensive means of mitigating the dangers and tolls of such wars that are commensurate with their importance to American strategic interests.[23]

There were fourteen U.N. peacekeeping operations globally as of 2019. They involved a grand total of some one hundred thousand personnel, including troops, police, civilians, and specialists. Most U.N. operations are in the broader Middle East and northern and central Africa, with additional missions in Cyprus, Kosovo, South Asia, and Haiti. The annual combined cost of these operations is now about $7 billion—a bargain compared with the strategic stakes, to say nothing of the human ones.[24] These operations have a mixed track record; U.N. peacekeeping operations fail to keep the peace about 40 percent of the time. Some conflicts are just too deeply rooted, or face problems of spoilers who seek to maximize their own gains at the expense of any possible peace process.[25]

In addition, the world's collective capacities (and will, especially among the great powers) to address them are often lacking. This is not an argument against such missions—which do in fact succeed in whole or in part some 60 percent of the time and which are far cheaper than American-led military operations of the type witnessed recently in Iraq and Afghanistan.[26] For example, Lise Howard of Georgetown documents the dozen multidimensional missions since the Cold War has ended that have succeeded in achieving much or most of their respective mandates—in Namibia, Cambodia, Mozambique, El Salvador, Guatemala, East Slavonia and Croatia, Timor-Leste, Sierra Leone, Burundi, Timor-Leste again (underscoring that success does not necessarily mean an end to all problems!), Côte d'Ivoire, and Liberia. By contrast, about a half dozen of these complex missions have been unsuccessful—in Congo (in the 1960s), and then since the 1990s in Somalia, Angola, Rwanda, Bosnia, and Haiti.[27] There is a good case to keep up the effort, and improve it where possible, including with limited amounts of American help in some cases—perhaps in training indigenous forces in certain missions.[28]

Covid-19 has been horrible. Its costs are measured in the trillions of dollars for the U.S. federal budget and economy alone and in the hundreds of thousands of deaths in the United States alone—with global effects an order of magnitude or so greater. Alas, while the next pandemics will likely be less severe, based on experiences with previous outbreaks of the late 1990s and early 2000s, they could also be much worse, with the potential for a tenfold greater death rate or more. At that point, one could reach a tipping point in the basic cohesion of society, its police forces, its medical infrastructure, and its military capabilities. For all the talk of "flattening the curve" of number of cases at any given moment versus time to avoid overtaxing a nation's health care system, the greater national-security benefit of limiting the pace at which an outbreak spreads may be in preserving the ability of its basic institutions like police, health care systems, and armed forces to continue to function. Through the early months of 2020, for example, the impact of the coronavirus on American military readiness has largely been limited to temporary disruptions of basic training, putting to port of a couple of ships (the *Theodore Roosevelt* and *Kidd*), and a reduction in training intensity for certain units that may lead to a gradual and partial atrophy in their skills—but no immediate huge effect.[29] Things could be different, however, in a more intense or debilitating outbreak. It is for this reason that pandemics, and their evil cousins biological weapons, must both rate high on the parallel 4+1 list of top-tier threats facing the United States—and the world—in the years to come.

In addition to grasping the inherent importance, and potential dangers, of advanced biological sciences as well as natural pandemics, it is also essential that we seize the Covid-19 moment. History presents opportunities when crises occur because it focuses the collective mind and makes policy makers more prone to take action. Fear is a great motivator. It can be a dangerous motivator when it leads to overreaction against a thinking adversary. But we are less likely to overdo it in reaction to pandemics. Now is the time to prepare aggressively.

Nuclear Weapons and Nuclear Proliferation

The world can get inured to nuclear dangers because they have been around all of our adult lives and because the pace of proliferation as well as of nuclear crises has slowed in the twenty-first century to date. This is no cause for complacency, however.

Some of the world's greatest statesmen and strategists of recent decades—Sam Nunn, Bill Perry, George Shultz, and others—have viewed nuclear weapons as the greatest threat to civilization in modern times. Indeed, some went so far as to support movements that sought to eliminate them entirely early in the twenty-first century, before Russian behavior made such thinking unpromising. What makes the views of these individuals so striking is that they all are sophisticated technically and strategically and politically. They knew how the hardware works; they knew how complex military organizations function; they understood how politicians and political leaders think, in peacetime and in crisis. And they were scared by what they saw.[30]

Indeed, there were enough close calls, during the careers of these and other individuals, to focus the attention. It was not only the Cuban Missile Crisis, when Soviet tactical commanders on Cuba and within a nearby submarine had preauthorization to use nuclear weapons if under attack. There were various other false alarms, for example, in 1983, when a Soviet technician thought he saw incoming U.S. ICBMs but luckily recognized the radar readings as suspect and withheld overreaction. There had been other false alarms in previous years. A number of accidents involved bombs accidentally dropped from aircraft. An American nuclear-tipped missile blew up in its silo.

Proliferation of weapons to countries such as Pakistan and North Korea, which have real disputes with their neighbors, shaky political leadership, and limited resources for safety, causes further concern. It may not be plausible to aspire to nuclear abolition yet. But further relegation of nuclear forces to a less central place in the military postures of great and smaller powers should be a top priority going forward.[31]

Even if proliferation has slowed in recent decades, we should not be complacent. Proliferation can take on the character of a ripple effect once it gets started.[32] Moreover, the spread of more and more advanced technologies around the world, to include 3-D printing and advanced machine tools, as well as the digitization of information related to nuclear weapons production and its dissemination on the internet, means that, as nonproliferation expert David Albright wrote back in 2010, "It's simpler now to obtain the materials, equipment, and know-how to produce nuclear weapons than it was ten years ago, and could be simpler still ten years from now."[33]

Overall, we will be lucky if the nuclear taboo that dates back to Hiroshima and Nagasaki survives well into the twenty-first century. Consider, for example, one scenario by which nuclear war could result in South Asia out of a series of events that no one predicted or desired: India might well retaliate after another terrorist strike like the horrific Mumbai attack of 2008 by a group like Lashkar-e-Taiba.[34] That could happen even if the group had in effect become a Frankenstein's monster, no longer obeying its initial creator, the Pakistani Inter-Services Intelligence directorate. Such an Indian conventional counterattack, perhaps influenced by its so-called Cold Start military thinking, could very quickly put the Pakistani capital at risk, given the narrowness of Pakistan in the northern part of the country.[35] Islamabad and Rawalpindi are a scant 125 miles from the Indian border—meaning that in theory they could be reached within days by a successful Indian maneuver operation. This worry could be the Pakistani perception even if it were not the

Indian intent. And the great city of Lahore is just over the border. In such a situation, Pakistan might well see military logic in the use of several nuclear weapons against Indian troop concentrations, marshaling facilities, choke points, bridges, military airfields, or other tactical targets.[36] If airbursts were employed, meaning that the weapons were detonated, say, 3,000 feet or so up in the air (depending on precise yield), the effects of the explosions could be catastrophic to people and military equipment immediately below and over an area of roughly 2 to 3 miles' radius, *without* creating much fallout that would later descend on populated areas downwind.[37] That is part of why Dr. Strangelove thought nuclear weapons were so usable; at a purely technical and tactical level, they can in fact be limited in their effects. Such thinking might, however unadvisedly, make Rawalpindi think that nuclear escalation was its least risky option. This could, in the minds of Pakistani planners, hold out the hope of simultaneously slowing the Indian advance, showing resolve, and yet at the same time evidencing enough restraint that India would not choose to retaliate against Pakistani cities with nuclear weapons. Such a gamble would be perhaps reckless. But it is far from unthinkable.

Whether such a finely graduated nuclear attack would impress Indians as having been restrained in any meaningful sense can be debated. That might be especially true if any of the Pakistani attacks went off course and caused more damage than intended. Thus, the danger of inadvertent escalation in this kind of scenario could be quite real. Even conventional attacks against warning and command systems could make India or Pakistan believe it was under nuclear attack by the other when in fact it was not—raising the possibility of a nuclear response.[38]

Nor, in an age of apocalyptic terrorist ideologies and groups espousing those views, can we entirely dismiss Dick Cheney's fear that terrorists could get their hands on the bomb. As author Ron Suskind wrote, Cheney felt that if there were even a 1 percent chance of a bomb reaching American shores back in the early post-9/11 period, the risk had to be treated as a near-certainty. One need not agree fully with Cheney to understand why he was so worried at such a fraught moment in American history.[39]

Fortunately, it remains difficult and expensive to produce fissile materials for nuclear weapons—meaning that, when trying to reduce the odds of nuclear terrorism, we should focus most on the safety of those materials that already exist around the world.[40] Indeed, this assessment leads to a strong case for greater nuclear safety and security in general. It will need to be pursued across many fronts, often with slow progress, sometimes with setbacks. In addition to working to address and at least partially defuse the specific dangers with Russia, China, North Korea, and Iran as discussed before, we need a nuclear security and safety agenda that includes:

- Continued arms control and weapons reductions with Russia (ultimately involving other nuclear powers, too—though perhaps in a rolling fashion that does not ask them to do more than cap the size of their respective arsenals in the first instance, given their much smaller numbers of weapons).[41]
- Reductions in nuclear alert levels where possible.[42]
- Additional safeguards on nuclear-related technologies including at power plants and research reactors—not only in Russia and in the United States but also in countries with fewer resources and smaller geographic buffers from their potential adversaries. There has been considerable overall progress globally in this arena since the Cold War, but work remains to be done, and U.S. resource levels (measured only in the hundreds of millions of dollars) have slipped too much.[43]
- Further relegation of nuclear weapons to a smaller role in national security and defense strategy, so that the basic logic of the Nuclear Non-Proliferation Treaty can be sustained, including the so-called Additional Protocol by which IAEA inspections can now examine suspected sites rather than only declared facilities (this topic is considered again in chapter 8).
- Ongoing work on the cooperative threat reduction agenda that dates back to the Nunn-Lugar program of the early post–Cold War years.
- Recommitment to strengthening of export control regimes and careful monitoring of technologies covered by the Nuclear Suppliers Group (and often having legitimate civilian uses, making them dual-use goods). These include advanced

valves, other vacuum technologies, detonators, neutron gen-
erators, high-speed cameras, flash X-ray equipment, and metals and other key components for centrifuges.[44]
- Extreme care in how we handle any expansion of nuclear
energy around the world. While the case for zero-emissions
dependable energy is appealing, as discussed further below,
the dangers associated with careless pursuit of nuclear power
are very serious.

Even beyond the importance of such a specific policy agenda, the
dangers of nuclear weapons need to affect us each and every day both at
the philosophical level and in the broad way we approach great power
military competition. To paraphrase Einstein, they have truly changed
everything except the way we think. That is dangerous.[45] Nuclear weapons may have helped prevent war between great powers for seventy-five
years. But they greatly raise the stakes and risks in any war that does
happen—and they certainly have not yet made such conflict impossible.
Again, the case for a measure of restraint in foreign policy, and specifically in crisis decision making as well as in efforts to control escalation in
any conflict between nuclear weapons states that does somehow begin, is
reinforced by the existence of these modern-day swords of Damocles.

Climate

This last point leads to the subject of climate change. For this huge challenge, nuclear power is often seen as part of the answer, not the problem.
That may be so, provided that the right kinds of reactors and safeguards
are employed. Viable strategies for disposal of waste must be developed
as well (unless we choose to accept, and admit, that we will simply store
it on site for the indefinite future, for perhaps decades or more to come).
Otherwise, we should go very slowly on nuclear power. It is important
not to mitigate one of the problems on this 4+1 list by exacerbating another; all are too potentially consequential to take that approach.

It is worth spelling out just *why* climate change is so threatening
from a national security and therefore grand strategy perspective. The
list of likely effects is increasingly well known, even if the magnitudes of

what is due to climate change remain uncertain in some cases. At home, Americans can expect stronger storms and hurricanes—with perhaps 40 percent of hurricanes now likely to be Category 3 or above, compared with a 30 percent norm historically[46]—as well as the gradual transformation of New York City and Florida into virtual archipelagos of city-states fortified at great cost against the seas. These effects will be costly; they can also damage military facilities and thereby degrade combat readiness. Abroad, many effects could lead to mass displacement of peoples or competition between potentially adversarial states for increasingly scarce resources. Civil wars can be exacerbated, too; some believe that climate-related drought contributed to the outbreak of the Syrian civil war.[47] Crops may be more difficult to grow, not only in an increasingly parched American farm belt but also the Middle East together with parts of Africa. Farmland could be degraded or destroyed in places including South Asia from encroachment of the seas and salination of soils, displacing huge numbers. Human encroachment into remote rain forests could increase the risks of pandemic disease due to contact between humans and animals.[48]

However, to understand the effects for geopolitics, it is still important to translate these changes in climate into security terms. The ways in which ecological, environmental, and human tragedy can also become national security issues begin with intensified competition for scarce and dwindling resources, together with forced displacements of large numbers of people. Some consequences of climate change, such as the potential destruction of small island nations, are more in the category of humanitarian and political catastrophe (that does not make them any more acceptable than direct threats to U.S. national security, of course). Other consequences could in fact implicate U.S. national security and therefore demand attention from any grand strategy.

Many hundreds of millions of people around the world are believed to be at serious risk of displacement in coming decades. By mid-century the figure could easily exceed one billion, and it might approach two billion by the end of the century, given projections that sea levels may rise eight inches to six feet or more by the end of the century, with the most likely range perhaps one to four feet—on top of the rise of eight inches that has already occurred over the past 140 years.[49] Two-thirds of those living within three feet of today's sea levels will be in South Asia, Southeast Asia, or East Asia.[50] Drought will also force movements of people.

These trends will cause displacement, and loss of farmland, in many of the world's most populous regions. They will do so, moreover, at a time when depletion of global fisheries can exacerbate any ensuing problems of malnutrition—an especially concerning situation given that three billion people depend in large measure on the oceans for food. Today's fisheries, in broad terms, are roughly one-third healthy and two-thirds depleted, with most of those that are depleted being further weakened by overfishing.[51]

Climate change is probably already exacerbating some conflicts, even if it is generally not the top driver or cause in most.[52] Further specific manifestations of these trends are not hard to imagine. The uncertain peace between India and Pakistan could be jeopardized by a lack of water from Himalayan glaciers. South Asian and East Asian megacities could go underwater, or have their main drinking water sources infiltrated by sea water, in fairly rapid succession. China could assert its claims to the South China Sea even more aggressively given its needs for food. Even if better water-use methods are employed, drought could intensify in the broader Middle East, South Asia, and North Africa; Egypt and Ethiopia could come to blows over sharing water in the Nile River. Based on current trends, some 40 percent of India's population could lack dependable access to drinking water by 2030. Such conditions exacerbate the risks of civil conflict and perhaps even interstate war (over assets like water flows in the broader Nile River basin or in parts of the Levant or the Ganges and Indus River systems in South Asia).[53]

Some of the above problems could affect either nuclear-armed nations such as India and Pakistan or key U.S. security partners in crucial locations including Egypt. And there could be indirect paths to climate-induced catastrophe for key U.S. allies as well. For example, already-stressed populations in Africa's Sahel region could be forced to migrate in increasing numbers into Europe. Europe's viability for large human populations could even suffer catastrophically if the Gulf Stream shifts direction, leaving most of America's main allies with much colder climates.[54]

Of all the Pentagon's top threats in its 4+1 or 2+3 framework, only Russia and North Korea seem relatively unlikely to be seriously affected by climate change in coming years. China, Iran, and much of the broader Middle East are highly vulnerable. So is South Asia, where the presence of two densely populated, nuclear-armed, and mutually antagonistic powers raises worrisome concerns for the future. Even though the United States does not have alliances in South Asia, the possibility of major war that could even involve exchanges of nuclear weapons is foreboding for many beyond the immediate parties to any fight—especially when one takes further account of the witches' brew of extremism, political instability, and weapons of mass destruction in Pakistan in particular.

Climate change will likely get much worse because we are not anywhere close to reducing our dependence on oil and other hydrocarbons that emit carbon dioxide when combusted. Today, hydrocarbons account for 80 percent of world energy use. The figure is projected to still be around 75 percent twenty years from now. Even though energy efficiency will continue to improve, greater prosperity around the world will likely drive hydrocarbon usage upward for many years to come.[55]

Changing from oil and coal to natural gas and more nuclear energy can be part of the answer, but it will not be enough. Absent a major technological breakthrough that allows for large-scale carbon capture, there will be no choice but to dramatically expand the use of renewable energies, even if this requires premiums of 10 to 50 percent in the cost of energy for a time, if the world is to avoid a serious intensification of climate change and climate-related security dangers.

Carbon taxes must be part of the answer, as well, I believe. I will return to this issue below, in sketching out a broad fiscal and policy agenda for strengthening the United States at home.

Digital Dangers

Over time, new dangers from the computer, information, and internet revolution could emerge. For example, down the road, regulation of artificial intelligence could be very important to ensuring human safety and survival.

But for the immediate and near-term future, one problem is of

overriding importance, even if it is by now quite familiar: the vulnerability of many crucial computer systems on which we have come to
depend to hacking and other attacks. In national security terms, this is
a problem not only for American and allied armed forces but just as
importantly for the national infrastructures on which they depend and
which they are responsible for helping defend.

In regard to computers, the context is well known. Progress has
been extraordinary for half a century and will likely continue. Moore's
law may or may not hold quite as it has for several decades; the capacity
and speed of computers may no longer double every eighteen to twenty-
four months. But rapid progress seems likely to continue. Around 1970,
several thousand transistors could be embedded in a given chip; by
2000 the figure was roughly ten million, and by 2015 or so it exceeded
one billion.[56] Even if the pace of advance slows, it will not stop. And
countless means will be invented to take advantage of the computing
capacity that is already available, with a huge undeveloped potential in
many areas.

With progress in computers, however, has come far greater cyber
vulnerability—and this fact may be even more important for defense
planning going forward, since U.S. vulnerabilities that an enemy per-
ceives before we do may tempt aggression. By effectively building Achil-
les' heels into everything they operate, modern militaries and societies
have created huge opportunities for their potential enemies. The fact
that everyone is vulnerable is no guarantee of protection. Deterrence of
some actions is not impossible in cyberspace, but it is difficult and likely
to fail in many important situations.[57] Vulnerabilities may vary across
countries based on different types of software employed in their military
systems and the different relative abilities of their respective offensive
hacking units. It is distressing to note that the United States may be
among the most vulnerable nations as a result of significant computer-
ization of operations with inadequate attention to vulnerabilities and
often with software of questionable resilience.[58]

An aggressor nation may be able to use cyber attacks very effectively and perhaps even decisively as part of an attack plan in a future
war. This may be less true for possible war between nuclear-armed states,
since an attacking country would have to be highly risk-tolerant to as-

sume that a combination of cyber and physical attacks would so incapacitate an adversary's nuclear forces as to make retaliation impossible.
But the nuclear dimension also heightens the stakes and exacerbates the
dangers, if some country miscalculates.[59]

The situation is potentially quite dire. A military and a national
infrastructure with key systems plugged into the internet, running on
flawed software, and often employing a simple password system for user
access rather than a two-factor authentication system is inherently vulnerable.[60] This is precisely the situation the United States and most of its
major allies face today. With ongoing U.S. vulnerability, in a future conflict
an enemy is likely to roll the dice and attempt large-scale cyberattacks—
even if, in crossing such a threshold, it opens itself up to inevitable retaliation. Because the United States needs to deploy and operate forces far
from its own shores to protect allies and because it depends on a high-
technology advantage that is made possible by the interconnectedness
of assets from space to air to the ground to the oceans and below, an
enemy may calculate that attacking such infrastructure will be advantageous to its interests regardless. And it may well be right.[61]

That said, uncertainty abounds in the cyber domain. Even as software vulnerabilities are patched up, new ones can emerge. Much of the
information about these weaknesses is both highly technical and highly
classified, making it hard to assess a net vulnerability for the armed
forces as a whole.[62] On balance, though, the overall situation today is
worrisome. A Defense Science Board study in early 2017 asserted that
virtually no major U.S. weapons system had cyber systems that could
be confidently vouched for.[63] There are good reasons to think we can get
much better at cybersecurity with cyber methods that involve better defense and resilience, replacement of flawed software (like Windows XP)
never really written to prioritize security, and counterattack options of
various sorts. But we are not in great shape now. I return to this subject
in the next chapter with a particular focus on military modernization.

At least U.S. military systems have the entire resource base of the
Department of Defense and U.S. intelligence community to help protect
them. Key national infrastructure, to include utilities on which Americans depend to stay alive, transportation systems upon which the U.S.
armed forces depend to move about the country and therefore the world,

and electricity systems that make everything else possible are potentially quite vulnerable. So are voting systems, at a time when the country has not yet completed the task of hardening that infrastructure and ensuring hard-copy backups to electronic voting systems in particular. In 2016, for the first time in U.S. history, a foreign power achieved material effects in covertly trying to sway the outcome of an American election. This type of danger should be seen as a national security threat because it potentially places the basic functioning of the U.S. polity in jeopardy. And the problem is not related to Russian sources or causes, of course. Nor is it getting any easier in an era of deep fakes and artificial intelligence.

It may not be prudent to allow a situation in which the Department of Homeland Security must protect all nonmilitary government assets in the United States and the private sector must protect itself. Greater Defense Department involvement in protecting core national infrastructure like electricity grids—and, as a backup, moving toward a more distributed, redundant, and resilient electricity system in the United States—is an idea worth considering in the future.[64] That is true for U.S. allies as well; strong public-private partnerships may also often make sense.[65] Robust protection of electoral infrastructure and machinery is crucial, too. So is a concerted national and multinational effort to counter disinformation.

A related problem arising from ongoing progress in computers and electronics is the vulnerability of domestic infrastructure and of military weaponry to electromagnetic pulses from a high-altitude nuclear explosion. These vulnerabilities may be growing because smaller and smaller electronic devices are progressively more vulnerable to a given electrical insult and because, as the Cold War recedes in time, the perceived likelihood of a nuclear weapon being used to generate high-altitude electromagnetic pulse (HEMP) may decline. Americans may lull themselves into a false sense of invulnerability, believing that a HEMP attack would be seen as tantamount to a direct nuclear attack against populations and hence too risky. It is debatable whether all adversaries would make such a calculation. American vulnerabilities in this area, already quite substantial, could increase.[66]

Digital vulnerabilities, and uncertainties, reinforce the case that any conflict against a peer rival would be, in the modern era, a highly fraught and unpredictable affair. They should make us more hesitant to enter into such conflicts, even when provoked, than we might naturally be inclined to be. Again, there is a case for resoluteness—which in this case means greater resilience being built into a wide array of key U.S. national infrastructure, military and otherwise. But there is also a further case for restraint on drawing first blood, or rapidly escalating, in any conflict. We really do not know what will happen when the shots, and the electrons, start to be fired.

The Domestic Underpinnings
of National Power and Purpose

The United States has had serious internal challenges before. The Civil War was the worst period; the 1960s may have been the second worst. But today, above and beyond what the Trump phenomenon may signify about cleavages in American society, we are facing a threat that has developed more insidiously—and that will be very challenging to address. Yet if we do not do so, the country's willingness to bear burdens and sacrifices abroad in support of a greater good—even if smart for the United States as well—cannot be taken for granted.[67] That makes domestic cohesion and cooperation a top-tier national security concern for the United States—and, I would argue, for the world, since again there is no other power capable of undergirding today's rules-based global order.

Americans supported a strong defense and engaged foreign policy after World War II because they remembered what happened when they were not engaged before that war. They also feared communism. Support for engagement continued even after the Berlin Wall fell because it was not that expensive at the time. But thirty years later, many Americans are wondering if the global security, trade, and manufacturing system that has developed over the years is really good for them. As the election of Donald Trump, with his antitrade and antialliance message, proved in 2016, many are willing to rethink fundamentally the nation's role in the world. If we do not listen to that message, the entire domestic basis for a strong America and an engaged U.S. foreign policy leadership role in the world could evaporate.

Much of the problem arises from economics. Trends in automation and technology do not augur well for the working and middle classes in the future, either, absent major changes in how we think about and reward work.[68] Forebodingly, America also underinvests in its children, in terms of education, child care, early interventions, and many other areas of government activity.[69] In many ways, the American dream is in trouble. As economist Raj Chetty has shown, only half of all children born in 1980 could aspire to live better than did their parents—a dramatic turnaround from the situation forty years earlier, when 90 percent could aspire to such an outcome.[70] Not all economists agree with this perspective, but it is true that wage growth has been uneven and often weak over the last generation, especially in the lower-income quintiles.[71] Life expectancies have even declined among certain demographics, reflecting a deep malaise about life in many quarters, manifested in opioid abuse and suicide in too many cases.[72] The anger among many in rural and working-class America is often very strong, and not unreasonable, against a system perceived to be rigged against them. This phenomenon helps explain not only the election of Donald Trump but the political success of other modern disruptive movements or individuals, including the Tea Party Republicans and Senators Bernie Sanders and Elizabeth Warren.[73] Similar phenomena are of course happening beyond the United States.[74]

From a global perspective, frustrations with globalization in much of the Western industrialized world need to be balanced against the general improvement in world living standards over recent decades as a result of trade, globalization in general, automation, and efficiency.[75] Because of the improving standards, today for the first time, at least half the planet's population can be said to enjoy at least a middle-class life, as Homi Kharas at Brookings has calculated.

Yet without a strong and engaged United States helping ensure global order, future prospects are not good for developing countries, either. Hence we all need what former senator Bill Bradley called a new American story—a big-picture narrative of how this can change for the moment of history in which we find ourselves.[76] We also need a concrete policy agenda for reviving the American dream. I do not purport here to have the capacity to provide either that new American story, at the level of poetry and vision, or the accompanying detailed policy agenda, at the level of prose and detailed analysis. What follows is limited to how, as a Congressional Budget Office veteran and longtime student of the federal budget (with mentors including Alice Rivlin, Robert Reischauer, and Maya MacGuineas), I hope I can at least sketch out the approximate fiscal dimensions of what a serious plan might entail.

The added federal debt, and prolonged economic downturn, from the novel coronavirus impose serious constraints, to be sure. But Covid-19 may also create an opportunity by helping break us free from many of the shackles of old and tired debates. And the acute national distress and division following the killing of a defenseless George Floyd by a police officer in Minneapolis in May 2020 may remove any doubt that we are in need of bold action.

On the deficit, and debt, the task is daunting. As of 2021, publicly held debt now equals the nation's GDP, for the first time since soon after World War II. The structural deficit is now roughly $1 trillion a year, some 5 percent of GDP, even if and when we resume full employment. Under these conditions, aiming for near-term fiscal balance is not realistic, economically or politically. What is needed, rather, is a viable longer-term strategy to reduce debt relative to GDP that tilts key fiscal curves in the right direction and makes time our ally over a period of many years.

Brookings scholar Bill Gale, in a book somewhat whimsically entitled *Fiscal Therapy*, provides an excellent way of thinking about these problems that is even more apropos in the post-Covid-19 era. He avoids the usual shaming and the articulation of draconian, unrealistic proposals needed to bring the country quickly back into budgetary balance. Instead, his goals are more modest. His proposals aim to get publicly held debt down to 60 percent of GDP rather than the 80 percent figure of pre-Covid-2019 or the 100 percent level reached in 2020—and the 180 percent of GDP it might otherwise reach by midcentury. Indeed, that 180 percent figure may now be closer to 200 percent, in the aftermath of Covid-19. Gale seeks to do so in a patient, politically realistic way that also ensures adequate investments in the country's future. He worries less about proposals measured in dollars and cents—since his time horizon is longer-term—and thinks more in terms of percentage of GDP.

For example, Gale advocates adding a total of nearly 2 percent of

GDP to investments in children, education, infrastructure, and non-defense R&D. That would be nearly 10 percent of the pre-Covid federal budget. A compelling Council on Foreign Relations task force report has similar recommendations for R&D, while also increasing scholarships and loan forgiveness for tens of thousands of students in STEM disciplines in higher education—a crucial area where American students continue themselves to struggle compared with other advanced nations.[77]

Gale also promotes reform of entitlements but protection of core benefits, especially for those who most need the help in today's bifurcating economy.[78] This way of thinking is crucial if part of our goal is to revive the working-class and middle-class dreams. That should in fact be our goal. It is the right thing to do by our fellow Americans. And, from a grand strategy perspective, we cannot expect the American people to support an overall federal policy framework that does not watch out for their own well-being. If we wish a national consensus in favor of a globally engaged United States, the preponderance of Americans need to believe that such a foreign policy and associated budget priorities also will help them and their families.

Fortunately, in devising these policies, the United States does have one big advantage compared with what was expected, say, a decade ago. A sustained period of low interest rates has changed what many economists consider a fiscally prudent amount of national debt.[79] While current levels are surely undesirable, we need not consider them the equivalent of national emergencies the way we once might have.

At the same time, complacency must be avoided. We do need to get on with it. Some existing trends and realities are indeed quite worrisome—including in national security and grand strategy terms. As Maya Mac-Guineas of the Committee for a Responsible Federal Budget puts it, it can't really be *desirable* to borrow from your biggest global competitor—and current deficits require that we do in fact borrow a good deal from China, among other foreign powers.[80] Nor, in an era of large deficits and complex financial markets, can we ignore the possibility of another major economic meltdown.[81] Indeed, the damaging effects of Covid-19 themselves will last for quite some time.[82]

Backing up Gale's thinking on domestic investments, a bipartisan group at the American Enterprise Institute and Brookings Institution, including Stuart Butler, Ron Haskins, and Richard Reeves, recommended several major steps to deal with issues of opportunity, fairness, the future of the family, and children in the United States. In doing so, they echoed many of the arguments made by farsighted economists such as Gene Sperling a decade or more before, with a focus on strengthening the family, on making work pay, and on assisting at-risk populations:

- An increase in the minimum wage ("large enough to substantially improve the rewards associated with work among the less-skilled");
- Tougher work requirements in welfare, especially for food stamp recipients;
- More charter schools;
- More resources to help low-income students to and through college;
- A clear public commitment to the importance of marriage for raising children; and
- Greater access to contraception and parenting support.[83]

To this list I would add better vocational and community college training in the United States. This is not quite the same thing as making community college education free. To be sure, many students need more help than they are getting today, and college debt among the country's youth as well as many middle-aged Americans has become a national scandal. But some students do not need the benefit of free tuition. It makes little sense to deprive community colleges and vocational schools that are often short of the necessary revenue that their tuition can provide. Affordability matters, but so does quality.[84]

Sperling's ideas emphasize a higher minimum wage, more generous earned income tax credit with higher income cutoff levels so more can benefit from the EITC, and caps on the cost of child care for working adults of modest means. Together they are part of what he now calls a commitment to "economic dignity" for all. It is hard to challenge the essence of the concept.[85]

And one more element that should be added to this list is criminal justice reform. The huge numbers of incarcerated Americans is not only a drain on federal and state budgets but a tragic squandering of lives and of human resources. Any such reforms need to be undertaken carefully and in a data-driven way that protects the safety of all Americans. But there are very good new and already demonstratively successful reforms that need to be generalized across the country.[86] Moreover, incarcerations for nonviolent drug possession, and for criminals too old to be of much risk to others in most cases, may cost the country as much as $20 billion a year—money that could arguably be better spent elsewhere in large measure.[87]

Consistent with the theme that people are America's most precious resource of all, as well as the most important raw ingredient to economic success, we need to rethink immigration policy. Future policy should have as one goal seeking to attract and keep strong talent. Today, U.S. immigration policy focuses overwhelmingly on reuniting families rather than strengthening the economy and increasing the talent of the workforce. Federal policies have been providing far fewer visas for skilled workers than they did even two decades ago; U.S. percentages are essentially upside-down (in terms of visas for skilled workers versus family members) relative to that of Canada, for example.

Such considerations need to be modified somewhat in regard to individuals from China and Russia. They should perhaps not be encouraged to work in particularly sensitive, cutting-edge sectors of the economy unless they can be confidently expected to remain in the United States down the road. That said, it is worth noting that more than 80 percent of Chinese students receiving doctorates in science and engineering did stay in the United States on temporary visas at least five years, so on balance the attraction of foreign students to U.S. universities in technical fields redounds to the benefit of the country.[88] Comprehensive immigration reform requires tighter control of the border with Mexico, to be sure, as well as rethinking of legal visa and citizenship policies—but it is overdue, regardless.[89]

To this list, if we are interested in domestic cohesion, we must add a restructuring of tax rates to help the working classes further, in recognition of how much income and wealth trends have worked against them in recent decades in the United States.[90] The carbon tax noted above should probably be refunded to the country as a whole, rather than viewed as an additional source of revenue, unless the politics of the matter change enough that it becomes a more popular way to raise federal revenue than other taxes.

However, the central point is clear: as Richard Reeves of Brookings has rightly argued, it is not just the top 1 percent but the top 20 percent or so of Americans who have benefited enormously in recent decades from globalization and other changes in the domestic and world economy.[91] (Also, a word to the wise: the top 1 percent includes families making roughly half a million dollars and up. At the slight risk of contradiction— there are more of you than you think!) That 20 percent group should pay the increased taxes. And reforms of the corporate tax structure should create greater incentives for companies to share profits with employees more than in the past.[92]

Making the numbers add up will take a lot of work, and more money. If structural federal deficits are 5 percent of GDP now, and we need to add almost 2 percent more spending for children, STEM, science, infrastructure, and other long-term determinants of domestic strength and national power, *and* we need to make modest investments in pandemic, nuclear, and cyber safety amounting to a few more tenths of a percent of GDP, that leaves the country with a substantial problem. The deficit would then be over 7 percent of GDP, even once recovery from the novel coronavirus is complete. We need to get that deficit number down to around 2 percent of GDP to follow Gale's guidelines and have the debt shrink over time relative to GDP. That means we need more revenue and/or less federal spending to the tune of an additional 5 percent of GDP, on top of the 17 percent or so of GDP taken in by the federal government before Covid-19 hit.

That is, alas, a lot of money—especially if it is in effect all to be paid by the top 20 percent of income earners in America as well as corporations. Depending on specifics, that means federal tax bills at least one-quarter to one-third larger than today for wealthy Americans—*without* even pursuing most of a Bernie Sanders–like agenda for remaking the domestic economy. Of course, half measures may be more realistic. They would also do some good—but, compared with the magnitude of the need, they would in fact be half measures.

This is a huge ask. But in another sense, it is not an ask at all. Our future way of life, and global stability, may well depend on it. The most important new argument I may be offering in this book is that sustaining our foreign policy with an effective grand strategy in the years and decades ahead may require that much of a fiscal effort—and *not* in the realms of defense, diplomacy, or aid spending so much as on repairing our fissures and strengthening our long-term foundations of social cohesion, economic power, scientific excellence, and power here at home.

EIGHT

The American Armed Forces

What type of American military will be needed to make all the above successful? This is partly a question about budgets, force structures, and overseas deployments. It is also about ensuring that the United States innovates and modernizes its armed forces faster than any other nation can improve theirs in the years to come.

In a post-Covid environment, with economies reeling from the huge hit of the coronavirus and the American publicly held federal debt exceeding GDP, it will be tempting to look to the large defense budget for money to fund other priorities. Secretary of Defense Mark Esper acknowledged as much on several occasions in 2020.[1] While the Pentagon should have to tighten its belt as part of any comprehensive national plan for deficit reduction and economic renewal, this temptation must not be indulged too much. The Department of Defense budget, while large, is far from big enough to become the main bill-payer for a fundamental fiscal realignment in America. It represented about 15 percent of federal spending and 10 percent of all public spending in the United States in the pre-Covid world. In the early 2020 federal budget request, moreover, it was already slated by the Trump administration to plateau in the early years of the 2020s—at a time when many defense analysts have called for sustained real growth of 3 to 5 percent a year to keep up with rising costs and a dangerous world.

Nothing about Covid-19 makes that dangerous world less dangerous. As such, asking the Pentagon to make enough ongoing reforms and tough decisions to handle flat budgets is already a somewhat risky proposition—and indeed, will be itself difficult to achieve responsibly, even if it probably is the correct goal for the foreseeable future. The national defense budget in the United States is reasonably strong now and does not need to grow more; it can even decline relative to GDP. But it should be held steady in real terms, growing roughly with inflation in the years to come.

The Military, Foreign Policy, and American Society

Before venturing into the nitty-gritty of defense budgets and military modernization strategies, it is important to ask the broader question about how the United States employs its armed forces as an instrument of national power in modern times. It is also crucial to take stock of civil-military relations in the United States today, inquiring if the military still knows its place in our constitutional democracy and if policy makers listen carefully to military advice in making key national security decisions.

Some argue that the United States has become too reliant on its military as the go-to instrument of foreign policy. Noting that current military budgets in the United States exceed those of the Cold War and lamenting further that the country seems to be in a state of perpetual combat, they wonder if things are out of kilter.

Certainly, there have been mistakes in the use of force. And this book is premised in part on the view that we can and should look to be more restrained, where possible, in future decisions on everything from alliance expansion to crisis management to war-fighting escalation strategies.

That said, I do not believe that we have lost control of our military or that modern military leaders have become such a strong, cohesive, and tendentious group as to bias the country toward an overmilitarized foreign policy. If there are problems, they come from the broader polity's mistakes, not from the relationship between the American military and society.

In my considerable experience interacting with thousands of military personnel over my career, I am strongly of the view that modern American military officers understand their role in our democracy. They develop strategic sophistication, think hard about the use of force, and otherwise engage in the tough issues of the day. But they also know how to salute and take orders—or, in an extreme situation, to resign if necessary.

In complex wars of the type we have generally experienced as a nation in recent decades, politics and military issues are interwoven. That has been true in places including Vietnam, Iraq, and Afghanistan where nation building was part of the mission.[2] It is also true in wars where complete victory and unconditional enemy surrender are not realistic, such as against a nuclear-armed foe. In such situations, the relationships between acceptable military costs and preferred political outcomes must be constantly scrutinized and reevaluated. Because of these interrelationships, there is no clear bright line between technical military decision making and political decisions about whether and how to fight wars. Officers and civilians will inevitably step on each other's toes in the development, implementation, and evaluation of policy. Harvard professor Samuel Huntington's ideal of the professional, technical soldier who is left to win the nation's wars provided that he or she stays out of strategic decision making therefore does not seem truly realistic to me.[3] But what is realistic, and essential, and intact, is civilian control of the military in the United States—with that civilian control extending beyond the president to the Congress as well.

Fortunately, today there are no modern Douglas MacArthurs or Curtis LeMays pushing the limits of what the armed forces should do in the policy-making realm. Consider a few modern examples. Chairman of the Joint Chiefs of Staff General Colin Powell publicly disagreed with Madeleine Albright over whether to intervene in the Bosnian civil war in the early 1990s. But given the absence of any compelling plan for *how* to intervene successfully, Powell's reservations were understandable, especially coming from a military that had been through the terrible experience of Vietnam only two decades before.[4]

In the next decade, General David Petraeus commanded the surges in Iraq and Afghanistan but did not force them on anyone. In fact it was President George W. Bush, with the assistance of national security adviser Stephen Hadley and others, who truly devised and owned the policy.[5] General Stanley McChrystal asked for more forces for Afghanistan only after he himself was tasked by Secretary of Defense Bob Gates with doing a zero-based assessment of what the mission there might require when McChrystal took command in 2009. And again, it was President Obama, not any military officer or organization, who had decided that Afghanistan should become a higher military priority for the United States.[6] Military commanders (and ambassadors and other senior officials) in Afghanistan gave hopeful narratives about what new strategies there could perhaps accomplish over the years, but they were not deceptive in how they reported the facts. The *Washington Post*'s so-called Afghanistan papers got this central fact wrong, in my view, forgetting that national debates about Afghanistan always acknowledged the huge difficulty of that complex political-military-economic mission.[7]

Military leaders like Chairman of the Joint Chiefs General Joseph Dunford asked for more budgetary resources for the military from time to time—but acknowledged that the nation's fiscal deficit needed to be viewed as a national security concern as well.

When Vice Chairman of the Joint Chiefs of Staff General John Hyten was commander of Strategic Command and was asked in 2017 what he would do if President Trump gave him an illegal order to launch a nuclear attack, he wisely retorted that he would talk to the president and they'd figure out a legal option and then the military would execute that.[8] The previous year, before Trump was president, former chairman of the Joint Chiefs General Marty Dempsey said that "if an order is illegal or immoral, we should and would resign"—exactly the right answer, once such an order is given.[9] Retired General Jim Mattis was careful not to invoke his military credentials when playing the role of civilian secretary of defense in the Trump administration and was careful to be deferential to the president—and to resign when he felt he could no longer do so in good conscience.[10] These are generally the kinds of roles that senior military officers should play in a democratic constitutional order in which they are rightly subordinate to the nation's civilian leaders.

Retired lieutenant general Michael Flynn was wrong to appear at Trump campaign rallies and wrong to support the anti-Hillary shouts of "Lock her up." But he was an extreme outlier in modern times.[11]

Chairman of the Joint Chiefs of Staff Mark Milley and Secretary of Defense Mark Esper both made mistakes in the early days after the May 2020 killing of George Floyd in Minneapolis. General Milley wore combat fatigues to accompany President Trump in a cynical push through peaceful demonstrators from the White House to nearby St. John's Church. Secretary Esper talked publicly about the need to dominate the country's urban "battlespace" during that same period of unrest. But both were called to account by numerous critics—Democrats as well as Republicans, civilians as well as retired military leaders.[12] It appears they learned their lesson. Both opposed invoking the 1807 Insurrection Act to justify the use of active-duty troops to quell protests in the spring of 2020, even when the president appeared to favor such an option, and Milley later publicly apologized for his role in the St. John's episode.[13]

We would be wrong to put our military leaders on pedestals and assume that they can solve the nation's problems on their own. As noted, they do not have the authority to make policy themselves. And of course, they can get it wrong. General Tommy Franks at Central Command effectively went along with the Bush administration's belief that Iraq would somehow self-stabilize after the 2003 invasion overthrew Saddam; other generals in those early years in Iraq followed a failing strategy as well.[14] No one (including me, and many other civilian experts) found the magic formula for the Afghanistan war, despite dogged efforts. There were plenty of other mistakes in which the military had a big share of the blame: General William Westmoreland's search and destroy concepts for Vietnam, the hope shared by the armed forces that limited air strikes could compel Slobodan Milosevic to let up his oppression of the Kosovar Albanians in 1999, and for many years a nuclear weapons planning process that produced, in a competitive dynamic with the Soviet Union, huge overkill capabilities as well as war plans that often bore little resemblance to prevailing civilian doctrine (or common sense).[15]

There are structural problems, too. For all of its many virtues, today's military comes mostly from too small and specialized of a stratum of society. That is not fair to them. It is not optimal for our democ-

racy. And it risks creating a chasm between most civilians and the nation's armed forces.[16] Thankfully, to date, I see no compelling evidence
about any falloff in the quality of military leaders or personnel as a result.
But we are still asking too much of too few for too long.

The Department of Defense can further improve recruiting, retention—and gender balance, since women today still make up only about
16 percent of the total force—in the years ahead. One way to improve the
pool of potential military recruits is to get behind the campaign led by
General Stanley McChrystal to dramatically increase the prevalence of
national service in the country. This would *not* be a draft; no one would
serve in the military except voluntarily. But by supporting a national campaign to significantly increase national service of all types, the military
could benefit for its own specific purposes. In addition, to the extent that
too many young Americans fail to meet fitness standards, how about a
ten-week *pre-boot-camp* concept, as suggested by New York business-
man and philanthropist Marshall Rose, that would grant direct access
to traditional military boot camp if potential recruits passed the fitness
regimens of the precursor course? As for retention, a number of things
should change. Most have to do with the expectations placed on those
who wish to stay in the military and keep seeking promotions; they have
little flexibility in their allowable career paths today, and many with
family or personal or professional constraints wind up leaving as a result. A more flexible personnel system that allowed for sabbaticals or
even departure and reentry, among other options, could do a great deal
to ensure that a wider range of individuals choose to stick with military
service. Such ideas remain largely in the conceptual stages in today's
military.[17] That should accelerate dramatically in the years ahead.

If we have an overall problem in civil-military relations in the United
States today, this is it: the military is too far removed from some parts
of society, and vice-versa. But this is a different problem than worrying
that the military has somehow come to dominate U.S. foreign policy.

The Budgetary Backdrop

The Trump administration, with the bipartisan support of Congress,
achieved large increases in defense spending in recent years. The 2020

national defense budget of nearly $750 billion was much larger than the Cold War average of about $500 billion, adjusted for inflation, or President Obama's last budget of just over $600 billion.

Is that amount too much, too little, or about right? Many who wish to defend the magnitude of Pentagon spending often point out that in recent decades its share of the nation's economic output is modest by historical standards. During the 1950s, national defense spending was typically about 10 percent of gross domestic product. In the 1960s, it averaged 8 to 9 percent of GDP, again including war costs and nuclear weapons costs. In the 1970s it declined to just under 5 percent of GDP, before growing to 6 percent during the Reagan buildup of the 1980s. In the 1990s, defense's burden on the economy went down to about 3 percent of GDP. Then, during the first George W. Bush term, the figure grew to 4.5 percent by 2009, due largely to the wars in Iraq and Afghanistan. National defense spending gradually declined over most of the Obama presidency. It has ticked upward slightly in the early Trump years, to just over 3 percent of the GDP expected before Covid-19—though budget projections as of early 2020 would see it drop below 3 percent in the coming years. (As is standard when talking about the national defense budget, these figures include costs for the wars, costs incurred by military reservists as well as active-duty troops, and the Department of Energy's expenses for nuclear weapons activities; they do not count the spending of the Department of Veterans Affairs of more than $200 billion or funding for the Department of Homeland Security.)

Seen in this overall light, current levels seem moderate and perhaps broadly commensurate with the geostrategic environment.[18] And compared with the broad fiscal needs of the nation outlined in chapter 7, defense resources are also moderate—as noted, again using pre-Covid-19 figures, national defense spending represents only about 15 percent of federal spending and 10 percent of all public-sector spending in the nation. If the Covid-19 crisis leads to a prolonged recession or worse, the above analysis may have to be adjusted—both because a given size military budget will then represent a higher fraction of GDP and because the nation's fiscal plight may be even worse.

Yet even if U.S. defense spending is moderate in some macroeconomic sense, it is large in simple dollars-and-cents terms. The United

States accounts for more than one-third of all global military spending. Its budget is at least three times that of the second global military power, China. As noted before, its current spending levels exceed the Cold War inflation-adjusted average by more than $200 billion (expressed in 2020 dollars, as are all costs in this chapter).[19] With allies factored in, the U.S.-led alliance system accounts for about two-thirds of all world military spending, counting NATO as well as key allies in East Asia and close security partnerships in the broader Middle East.

One might ask—many do rightly ask, in fact—why the United States should shoulder so much of the burden of deterring Russia and China. Shouldn't our allies do more? While some of America's allies have stepped up to the plate in terms of defense spending (for example, South Korea at about 2.5 percent of GDP and Australia, the United Kingdom, Poland, France, and the Baltic states all around 2 percent), many have not kept their military spending levels as high as they had promised. Nor have they consistently spent their resources well. So, without a doubt, the United States must continue to press allies to spend more for their defense.

Nonetheless, complaints about burden sharing should be kept in perspective. For one thing, to complement NATO's goal that countries should spend 2 percent of GDP on their military forces, it is time to create a complementary goal that nations should spend roughly 3 percent of GDP on a combination of their own military forces, security assistance abroad, development assistance, humanitarian relief, and refugee resettlement. Whatever precise goal is established, it will improve the relative performance of most major American allies on this broader metric of promoting global peace and stability. Relative to GDP, most are substantially more generous with their assistance funds than is the United States.[20] Even if American allies should still do more in military terms, moreover, they collectively spend almost as much on their militaries as does the United States, creating a preponderance of military power in what might loosely be called the U.S.-led global alliance network that is unrivaled in human history. That is a considerable strategic advantage for the United States.

Before proposing an overall resource-allocation strategy for the Department of Defense, it is also important to ask about waste, fraud, and abuse. Some might wonder if the Department of Defense, a federal agency not even able to audit its own expenses, is so wasteful that it can preserve or improve combat power with far fewer budgetary resources. While it is true that the department is inefficient, much of the waste is marbled into muscle—difficult to excise without painstaking and patient work, lest major combat capabilities be damaged along the way. For example, the military health care enterprise is probably too large and expensive. But access to high-quality health care is a crucial military benefit that helps attract and retain such a high-quality all-volunteer force. And most proposals for health care reform would, once implemented, save at most a few billion dollars a year—important savings, yet modest relative to the overall size of the nation's military budget and defense needs. Or take base closures. After five generally successful rounds of base closures and realignments since the late 1980s, the Defense Department still has 20 percent more infrastructure than its current force posture requires. More base closures are needed—at least one if not two more rounds. A future round will likely yield eventual savings of $2 billion to $3 billion a year, like the first four rounds.[21] That's real money, but not huge money relative to a $700 billion-plus budget. Also, net savings would not accrue for half a decade; like many defense reforms, base closures are more a question of smart long-term planning than a near-term budgetary fix.

Long-standing Capitol Hill staffer and Pentagon official Peter Levine has written a compelling book about how to understand the process of defense reform. In this, he echoed former Defense Department comptroller Robert Hale, who once wrote a paper entitled "Promoting Efficiency in the Department of Defense: Keep Trying, But Be Realistic."[22] Levine argued that efficiencies and reforms *are* possible but tend to work best when well focused and modest in aspiration—aiming for savings in the tens or hundreds of millions of dollars rather than the many billions.[23] He pointed out several reasons why promises of huge savings from reform are destined to remain illusory: "First, the DoD budget does not have a line item for waste. . . . Second, many of the good ideas have already been tried. . . . Third, any significant change in DoD organizations or processes is likely to encounter significant institutional resistance. . . . Finally, real reform requires an up-front investment of time and resources."[24] So yes, we should keep looking for waste and promoting reform. But it will be a slog, and progress will be measured in the tens and hundreds of millions of dollars of savings, as a rule, and not the tens of billions.

Prioritizing Resources at the Pentagon

Former defense secretary Jim Mattis's National Defense Strategy sensibly calls on the Department of Defense to reinvigorate its capabilities vis-à-vis China and Russia. That includes addressing dangerous vulnerabilities from those countries' cyberspace and outer space weapons, as well as through their "anti-access/area-denial" capabilities from advanced precision-strike weapons and reconnaissance assets.[25] These challenges will be palpable even if Russia and China continue to have difficulty competing comprehensively across the full range of defense technologies, to include advanced aircraft and submarines.[26]

Yet the United States must do these things while sustaining today's wars of the Middle East as well as deterrence of crisis on the Korean Peninsula—as Mattis's National Defense Strategy itself acknowledged. That is a daunting set of tasks for a busy military.

As former under secretary of defense Jim Miller and I wrote two years ago, in a critique that remains true today, one regrettable consequence of this situation is that some military services clamor for more force structure. In particular, the navy seeks to grow to 355 ships from about 310 as of this writing in 2020; the air force seeks to grow from 312 to 386 squadrons. Such increases of roughly 15 to 25 percent in force structure would require unrealistic overall budget growth, in the steady state, of 10 to 20 percent in air force and navy budgets—meaning a total of perhaps $40 billion to $80 billion in the average annual defense budget.[27]

Some targeted growth in certain sectors of the defense enterprise may make sense. However, it makes little sense under a strategy focused on China and Russia to grow the force overall. Some invoke these countries' considerable capabilities to argue for a larger U.S. military, but the arguments are generally not compelling. For example, some allege that China's navy is now bigger than America's—but that is only because the United States builds far larger (and much more capable) ships.

As of the late 2010s, as Jim Steinberg and I calculated with the help of Ian
Livingston, U.S. naval tonnage was more than twice that of China's, for
example.[28]

Innovation in how we manage the armed forces can relieve some
of the strains that result from having a relatively small military carry out
a wide array of tasks around the world. The army verges on being collectively overworked partly because it maintains deployments of several
thousand soldiers in South Korea and Poland through frequent rotations
of multiple units, rather than a better idea: permanent stationing of individual brigades in these locations. The air force could consider similar
changes in how it maintains key units in parts of the Middle East. Several fighter squadrons could, for example, be based in Persian Gulf states
rather than rotated through. The navy still focuses too rigidly on maintaining a permanent presence in the broader Persian Gulf and Western
Pacific regions. More flexible and unpredictable deployments can ease
strain on the force without giving adversaries any solace. Jim Mattis was
right that we should be strategically predictable but operationally unpredictable. The navy can also consider crew swaps (via airplane) while
ships remain in foreign waters, rather than bringing ships home from
deployment every six to eight months, as is now the norm. Having a
small transitional crew remain in place from the end of one deployment
to the beginning of the next can ease this process, given that individual
ships have their own idiosyncrasies and are not all identical even within
a given class.[29]

Other good ideas abound as well—with the caveat that all require
care, and time, to implement, and therefore they promise initial savings
more commonly measured in the hundreds of millions of dollars a year,
or low billions, than the many billions at first.

For example, as he prepared to retire after four years as air force
chief, General David Goldfein was not pushing as hard for a larger air
force, as he had two to three years before (when he laid out a plan to grow
the air force, including active and guard and reserve, from 312 squadrons
to 386). He now said he has "plenty of trucks"—that is, plenty of planes—
but not enough "highway." By the latter, he means reliable and secure
command, control, and communications infrastructure. In fact, in the
312 squadrons of today's air force, he was prepared to retire some indi-

vidual aircraft—10 percent of the total? 15 percent?—that happen to be older or more problematic and use some of the savings to modernize the remainder while also modernizing that "highway." Some portion of the savings might also be returned to the taxpayer.[30]

General Joseph Lengyel, the former head of the National Guard Bureau and a member of the Joint Chiefs of Staff, pointed out in a Brookings event in July 2020 that today's guard (army and air force) is far different from the one he joined thirty years ago. It is much more combat capable, with just as good equipment as the active force. With the U.S. Air National Guard, units are pretty much ready to go all the time, too, he argued. With the U.S. Army National Guard, given the larger size and complexity of main combat units, it takes time to generate full combat readiness at the brigade level. But the units can be very good after a number of months of preparation.[31]

The guard and reserve components of the various services do not save the United States any money when they are activated and deployed. So shifting more force structure to the reserve components makes sense only if the overall military is somewhat less busy than before. However, with the surges in Iraq and Afghanistan long since over, that is indeed the case now, and it figures to be the case in the future, too. Today's military includes about 2.1 million uniformed personnel: 1.3 million and 800,000 reserve component (of that latter number, about 450,000 is in the two guard forces and the rest in the services' reserves). It is worth asking if we can apportion that total of 2.1 million personnel more equally between the active force and the guard/reserve.

Neither of these ideas is going to allow us to cut the defense budget enormously. We would do best to try to keep the current $750 billion national defense budget (using round numbers) at that nominal level in the years ahead—or maybe get it down to $700 billion-ish. But bending the cost curves such that the defense budget can stop rising, and over time become a smaller fraction of GDP, would itself be a huge accomplishment and would contribute to a declining deficit in the years ahead.

Fortunately, the American armed forces continue to repair readiness—and that process is now fairly well along, even if the coronavirus now presents additional challenges. Major aircraft, ship, and vehicle fleets have mission capable rates of 80 to 90 percent—quite good by historical norms. The army also reports about half of its brigade combat teams in the very highest state of readiness—up from just two teams at that level a few years ago. There have been some limited challenges with recruiting of late, but overall the quality and experience of military personnel remains high by historical standards. The Covid-19 economic downturn may help recruiting and retention trends, moreover. Operational tempos and other demands on the force remain high. But they are less severe than a decade ago. American military compensation remains quite good relative to most comparable age, experience, and education cohorts in the private-sector economy.[32]

Increased military spending can serve three possible objectives: better modernization for the future, improved readiness for current missions, and increased force structure. Of these, the last is the least important to the U.S. military for the foreseeable future, given the above considerations—for all the strains and challenges, the all-volunteer force today is holding up well, and innovations can make its burden even more manageable. By draining away resources needed elsewhere, growing the force can actually be counterproductive, moreover. The focus should be on quality and innovation over quantity. It should also be on making forces as survivable and resilient as possible, given the potency of modern technologies that our potential adversaries could use against us. This argument has been a consistent theme of Secretary Mattis, Secretary Esper, Vice Chairman Selva, and others.

Most recently, this view has been forcefully articulated by leaders like the commandant of the marine corps, General David Berger, who has argued for smaller amphibious ships, more long-range high-endurance unmanned aerial vehicles, potent long-range rockets, and other technologies that could be both survivable and lethal in the emergent combat environment. As he wrote in 2020, "Even if there were a strong and credible requirement for large-scale forcible entry operations, such operations could not be carried out in the face of an adversary that has integrated the technologies and disciplines of the mature precision strike regime." When even the commandant of the marine corps, basing his arguments on detailed technology study and war gaming, suggests that the days of large-scale amphibious assault are numbered if not already over, one should take note![33] It is almost as if John Madden had just said that in the NFL, it will no longer be important to run the football.

The U.S. armed forces need to innovate and invest in breakthrough capabilities and to improve immediate readiness for a wide range of missions. They need to keep what General David Petraeus calls "pentathletes," who can do a number of things well. Unexpected contingencies can and do arise.[34] But the armed forces can retain this preparedness at their current overall size. Investing in modernization and readiness rather than growth, paired with more clever and efficient management, can allow today's U.S. military of roughly 1.3 million active-duty troops, some 800,000 reservists, and almost 750,000 full-time civilians to do the job. By giving up most plans for expansion, the military services can ensure that modernization and readiness get the resources they crucially require.

It seems more likely that a potential adversary would risk war with the United States if it felt that it could somehow incapacitate the nation, at least temporarily, through some kind of knockout punch—what Michele Flournoy termed "system destruction warfare." As such, maximizing the size of force structure is less crucial than ensuring that the American armed forces have unparalleled lethality, as well as no major vulnerabilities.[35]

As my recent research has shown, the period of 2020–40 seems likely to see even more change in the technologies and the character of warfare than have recent decades. We need to keep our eye on these for the opportunities, as well as the potential vulnerabilities, that will result. For the period 2000–2020, revolutionary technological change probably occurred only in various aspects of computers and robotics.[36] For the next two decades, those areas will remain fast-moving, and they will be joined by various breakthroughs in artificial intelligence (AI) and the use of big data. The battlefield implications in domains such as swarms of robotic systems usable as both sensors and weapons may truly come of age. In addition, progress in laser weapons, reusable rockets, hypersonic missiles, unmanned submarines, biological pathogens, and nanomaterials may wind up being made very fast. The sum total may or may not add up to a revolution. But the potential cannot be dismissed.[37] Jamming, possible attacks on fiber-optic undersea cables or on satellites, and cyberattacks on the software of the radios and other systems used for communication are all serious worries, to say nothing of HEMP devices.[38] Even when communications systems within a small unit survive enemy attack or find themselves outside the targeted zone of intense jamming, communicating with central authority may suffer. It is because of such concerns that the army's Maneuver Center of Excellence at Fort Benning, Georgia, is examining concepts of future operations in which a brigade might be cut off from divisional or corps headquarters for an extended period and have to function entirely on its own during that time.[39] Regardless, to ensure deterrence, we need to stay on top of all such developments and lead the way with most.

Largely as a result of the computer revolution, robotics will continue to improve dramatically.[40] Already self-driving vehicles are possible, and a number are likely to be used for specific military purposes, such as tactical resupply on the battlefield. The army's Wingman program, the use of armed robotic vehicles guided by soldiers, is one example.[41] Robotics holds much future promise for military applications.

The former vice chairman of the Joint Chiefs of Staff General Paul Selva has argued that the United States could be about a decade away from having the capacity to build an autonomous robot that could decide when to shoot and whom to kill, though he also asserted that the United States had no plans to build such a device.[42] Other robotics with more specific functions are likely to include advanced sensor systems, often functioning in networks or swarms. In the air, they could also involve stealthier unmanned aerial vehicles (UAVs) with a long range that could be used as penetrating sensors.[43] On the seas, future robotics could include unmanned surface vessels for intelligence gathering, mine clearing, and possible local point defense against threats such as fast-attack craft. Indeed, a 2013 RAND report noted that sixty-three unmanned surface vessels had already been developed and tested. Robotic unmanned surface vehicles (USVs), such as the Defense Advanced Research Projects Agency's Sea Hunter, could, for example, perform search functions associated with antisubmarine warfare and mine warfare.[44] It is already possible to talk somewhat realistically about how the U.S. Navy's future fleet might include substantial numbers of UUVs (unmanned under-

water vehicles) and USVs; a team of researchers that includes Bryan
Clark and Bryan McGrath has recommended a future fleet with forty
of each type of vehicle, for example.[45] The navy is increasingly thinking
how to deploy its littoral combat ships with families of unmanned ships
and other robotics.[46] Some UUVs could have long persistence and low
signature even when near an enemy's shores.[47] A $100,000 ocean glider
recently crossed the Atlantic; promising concepts could cut that cost by
a factor of ten.[48]

Inevitably, robotic devices will in some cases be given greater
decision-making authority as to when to use force. This highly fraught
subject requires careful ethical and legal oversight, and the associated
risks are serious. Yet the speed with which military operations occur will
create incentives to eliminate humans from the decision-making loop.[49]
Whatever the United States may prefer, restrictions on automated uses
of violent force would also appear relatively difficult to negotiate (even
if desirable), owing to likely opposition from Russia and other nations.[50]
With Russia and China making progress in AI, it is far from clear that
the United States will be the lead innovator in AI in the years ahead,
with some experts warning that one or both of these countries may soon
set the pace in AI—and thus also in war-fighting robotics.[51]

In assessing all these trends, the rise of China and the return of
Russia raise the strategic stakes enormously. The marriage of rapid technological progress with hegemonic change could prove especially potent.
The return of great power competition during an era of rapid progress
in science and technology could reward innovators and expose vulnerabilities, much more than has been the case in the twenty-first century
to date. These considerations place a premium on emphasizing modernization and innovation over growth in force structure at the Department
of Defense. They should also make us all the more wary of warfare, since
periods of rapid change in technology, war-fighting concepts, and doctrine create even more uncertainty than is usually the case about combat
outcomes. With that uncertainty comes a greater risk of escalation if a
country is surprised to find itself losing—and considers such a result
unacceptable.

Arms control can mitigate some risks—and at least avoid unneces-
sary wastes of resources even when it may not lower the dangers of war.

There are several ideas worth promoting along these lines in the years ahead, along with the proposals for nuclear deals with North Korea and Iran that I discuss elsewhere in this book. Ratifying the United Nations Convention on the Law of the Sea would make sense as a means of increasing pressure on China to improve its behavior in places like the South China Sea. Current efforts of the United States to do so by invoking rulings of the Permanent Court of Arbitration are awkward at best, with the United States not being a formal party to the treaty framework on which the court's rulings are based.[52] If there are elements of the convention that make certain senators wary of ratification, such as the provisions pertaining to economic development of resources in the blue-water oceans, they could be renegotiated—or removed for now. But there are too many other benefits of the convention to leave it in indefinite limbo.

The nuclear testing (de facto) moratorium that all except North Korea have respected this century is still sound, given how confident the United States will continue to be about the basic reliability of its nuclear arsenal and the options it will possess for introducing simple designs that do not require testing as a final insurance against any perceived reduction in the arsenal's dependability. Verification that no tests of any meaningful yield are occurring anywhere on Earth is also well established and quite sound.[53] Ideally, the United States and China—along with Egypt, North Korea, Pakistan, India, Iran, and Israel—would soon ratify the Comprehensive Nuclear Test Ban Treaty so as to pave the way for the treaty to enter into force internationally, thereby formalizing the moratorium.[54]

Other arms control ideas can be important, too. The existing Biological Weapons Convention and Nuclear Non-Proliferation Treaty should surely be sustained.[55] The Outer Space Treaty might be revised to include a ban on explosions or collisions in space above a given altitude (measured in the low hundreds of miles), since such events would endanger satellites. Renewal of New START past 2021 makes eminent sense, and at some point its ceilings on strategic warheads should be lowered another 30 to 50 percent. Codes of conduct that prohibit cyberattacks (including exploratory probing) on the nuclear command-and-control infrastructure of nuclear weapons states make sense, too. A restoration of the INF Treaty, at least for nuclear-tipped missiles, is a sound idea, especially if the PRC can be persuaded to join Russia and the United States in the endeavor.

But most of these measures, however worthwhile, will have limited effects. More ambitious arms control concepts would generally either be too difficult to verify or too uncertain in their potential costs versus benefits to make sense. More sweeping arms control measures could founder on verification difficulties, as in most realms of biological research, cyber and AI technologies, and space weapons—or, in some cases, simply not be desirable on their own merits.[56] Arms control is an important element of national security policy and a crucial complement to military preparedness. But on balance its prospects for helping with the big challenges of the coming years are probably modest at present.

Then there is the issue of not just the goal but the means to achieving it. Beyond ensuring adequate budgets, how, procedurally and bureaucratically, can the United States do a better job of modernizing the U.S. military for the years ahead? One important dimension of this question concerns the fine acquisition system of the Department of Defense, which has been recently reorganized due to efforts by former Armed Services Committee chairmen senator John McCain, congressman Mac Thornberry, and others. In particular, the office of the under secretary of defense for acquisition, logistics, and sustainment has been divided into one part focused on research and engineering and another on acquisition and sustainment.

But if that system is strong, it is only three-fourths so. Major problems remain. Some involve a tendency still to overinsure by buying weaponry that is more expensive than need be at times. This problem arises at the high strategic levels of the decision making of the military service chiefs and their civilian leadership; it is less a weakness of the acquisition system itself. Other problems arise from the excessive bureaucracy and red tape associated with the acquisition process, which drive away certain types of potential providers whose technologies could be of great benefit to the U.S. armed forces. Key recommendations to mitigate these problems include:

- Use Federal Acquisition Regulations (FAR) Title 12 more often, rather than falling back on FAR Title 15. In theory, the

Pentagon is supposed to buy commercial goods, as under the so-called FAR 12 code, whenever possible, and avoid the complex and cumbersome FAR 15 rules that involve negotiated contracts. In these FAR 12 cases, the Pentagon can, in theory, behave like a normal customer and avoid the complex steps and onerous paperwork involved in major weapons procurement. Yet the tendency is still to define requirements in such a way that whatever radio, phone, jeep, or computer is at issue has enough military-unique characteristics that the FAR 15 code is used almost by default.

• Streamline oversight when the Pentagon can rely on competition to discipline firms about price. Today, for example, the Defense Contracts Management Agency has an on-site presence in many factories; its personnel tabulate what it thinks weapons should cost, based on all sorts of details about the production process. This may make sense for complex weapons being built by one supplier. But for cases in which there is a commercial equivalent or two producers, the competitive process can provide the discipline—just as it does in the commercial market—and oversight can be scaled back.

• Follow the Joint Improvised-Explosive-Device Defeat Organization model for other technologies. When so many Americans were being hurt or killed by improvised explosive devices in Iraq and Afghanistan, Congress allowed the Defense Department to create special, expedited acquisition procedures and ultimately the JIEDDO to research and produce relevant technologies quickly. Deputy Secretary of Defense Paul Wolfowitz and others championed the effort, to great effect. This concept could be used, especially for lower-risk technologies that nonetheless are important to build quickly. Another way of getting at the same concept is through existing procedures known as Other Transaction Authority. These approaches could save money in areas such as information technology, on the one hand, where the pace of change is fast—or, on the other hand, in areas such as ground vehicles, where technologies are largely mature.

• Break down information technology purchases into smaller batches. There are times when creating a huge common computer infrastructure with the same machines or software across hundreds of thousands of users may make sense. In other cases this big approach puts too many eggs in one basket. By using open-architecture and modularity concepts, making sure that different systems can talk to each other but allowing more discrete and smaller buys by various agencies, the Defense Department may do better. Over time, this, too, could save money—particularly by avoiding future white-elephant projects that wind up costing the taxpayer enormously yet do not work that well.

• For commercial technologies or close derivatives of commercial systems, allow firms to keep their intellectual property rights rather than sharing all relevant data with the government. This could help convince many companies wary of doing business with the Pentagon to reassess. However, it should not be employed in cases where a specialized defense system is developed by a given company at considerable taxpayer expense, especially in cases where the Defense Department may wish to contract for upgrades or modifications subsequently—because in such cases, competition could be thwarted by such retention of intellectual property rights.

The overall message remains the following: we need a more modern, and ready force, not a larger one. Or, in the words of former John McCain aide Christian Brose, we need "rapid but incremental pursuits of transformational goals."[57] As he and former Pentagon official Kathleen Hicks have suggested, this approach might be pursued by designating several percent of the defense budget to be awarded centrally to the most innovative war-fighting concepts and technologies; that is one possible means to hasten the process.[58] With such an approach, the United States can do very well with a defense budget of the current size; huge increases are not warranted or wise, in light of other pressing national demands. But by the same token, the nation would do well not to slash the budget of the Department of Defense—whatever the politics of the issue may seem to argue come 2021. Coronavirus and other new dangers do not displace or even mitigate most previous defense needs; in some cases, in fact, they may intensify them.

Conclusion

I n 1910, the intellectual Norman Angell published a book called *The
Great Illusion*, in which he claimed that the world could no longer
afford war and should no longer view it as viable policy. Four years
later, political leaders tragically reached a different verdict. In the
summer of 1989, just months before the Berlin Wall fell, the political
scientist Francis Fukuyama predicted an "end to history" as ideologies
besides capitalism and democracy seemed to have been definitively re-
pudiated worldwide. Although his notorious essay was caveated more
than many remember, he nonetheless did write that "large-scale conflict
must involve large states still caught in the grip of history, and they are
what appear to be passing from the scene."[1] By the mid-2010s, in the face
of Russian revanchism and Chinese ambition—both emerging from authoritarian political models of one type or another—that argument was
discredited. It is important not to make similar Pollyannaish mistakes
today, lest we lower our guard and assume that the stability of today's
global order can somehow be put on autopilot.

Yet it would be almost as wrong to go to the other extreme. Depict-
ing today's world as comparably dangerous to that of the Cold War, for
example, is a serious intellectual and policy mistake. It may make American citizens wonder why it is worth the bother to sustain a system of
alliances and international economic relationships that is apparently so

brittle after so many decades of effort. That could breed cynicism and fatalism—and then isolationism. Or we could overreact, forcing a major great power showdown over a relatively minor crisis the next time Russia or China flexes its muscles. We might fear that to do otherwise would be akin to Neville Chamberlain's appeasement of Hitler at Munich or to Americans' indifference as Hitler took the Sudetenland and Austria and prepared his assaults on Poland and France.

In my view, however, the more trenchant and foreboding historical analogy could be the outbreak of World War I. In that conflict, hyper-competitive great powers overreacted to small problems. A minor crisis quickly escalated into catastrophic large-scale combat. Today, we may (or may not) be slightly wiser, but our weapons are even more potent and even more rapidly deployable. Outcomes in war can occur quickly and overwhelmingly.[2] Therefore, the premium on early and decisive action is high. Huge mistakes can happen very fast. We need a grand strategy of resoluteness—but also of patience and restraint that seeks to avoid firing the first shot, because we must do everything possible to avoid the great uncertainty and huge danger of great power war.

Moreover, while a healthy defense budget and strong military are important, exaggerating the immediate dangers of today's world could lead to a preoccupation with the hard-power tools of statecraft at the expense of other instruments. We could shortchange diplomacy and foreign assistance. Assistance has contributed importantly to impressive strides in human well-being and economic advancement by many countries around the world in recent decades, as noted in chapter 1.[3] But needs, as well as opportunities for further progress, remain significant. Covid-19 intensifies the challenges, as will the effects of climate change in the years ahead. To underfund diplomacy and assistance and related efforts would forget Jim Mattis's admonition that if you don't fund such things, "you need to buy me more ammunition." Overspending on defense could also weaken America's foundations of internal strength including in education, infrastructure, and scientific research and development. That would also ignore the simple and unalterable fact that the United States military is built on the nation's economic, scientific, and human foundations. It would forget Richard Haass's memorable admonition that "foreign policy begins at home."[4]

I might also call this last point about the domestic roots of foreign policy "Rivlin's Reminder," after my long-standing friend and colleague, the great Alice Rivlin, who died in 2019 at age eighty-eight after a remarkable career of public service. She always valued U.S. military strength but had an integrated view of national power that encompassed the underlying strength of our economy and the political cohesion of our people. We would be wise to remember, and heed, her counsel.

It is the global rules-based order, more than anyone's possible definition of a *liberal* order, we must preserve. The latter term is popular these days, but it is confusing, meaning one thing in American domestic politics and quite another in international relations. Worse, even when used in the international context, it lends itself to multiple interpretations in multiple domains—military, developmental, financial, trade-related, environmental, ideational, and so on.[5] Not all are equally attractive to American security partners or countries trying to find their peace, if possible, with both China and the United States.[6] Worst of all, the term "liberal order" is too ambitious as a near-term guide for policy making. It implies that we must keep progressing, steadily and fairly rapidly, toward a global environment that assertively promotes democracy, Western definitions of human rights, and other desirable yet often controversial and difficult goals. Supporters of a rules-based order, by contrast, can be more patient, slightly less ambitious, and more apt to roll with the punches—taking the occasional setback tactically as long as the fundamentals of the international environment remain solid.

The United States should of course promote democracy. Democracies are much better than any alternative for their citizens, and democracies tend not to fight each other, either.[7] The United States has a long tradition of supporting and attempting its best to exemplify democracy, as it is right to do. This has produced considerable success; despite the setbacks, there has never been a time when a higher fraction of humankind lived in free or partly free societies. Sometimes, however, the pursuit of an increasingly liberal order is seen to necessitate the application of military power. Elements of the neoconservatism tradition have advocated this in the past—for example, in regard to the 2003 Iraq war.[8] Promotion of democracy can also be dangerous if it leads, for instance, to instinctive expansion of a military alliance that was never designed for the democracy-promotion purpose. Generally, democracy promotion is not a domain of endeavor where military force should be invoked, except to protect existing democratic allies from threats when they need the help.[9]

For this complex and scary, yet also prosperous and reasonably peaceful, world of today, the United States needs to stay resolute in defense of existing allies and obligations. American engagement and leadership have been the central characteristic of a rules-based global order that has kept the great power peace for seventy-five years—after decades and centuries of spectacular failures when international anarchy reigned among states. The world's best chance for peace requires such a strong and purposeful America.

The United States should be restrained, however, in any ambitions to expand alliances further, to use force quickly and overwhelmingly in crises, or to stubbornly pursue maximal goals in difficult diplomatic endeavors over crucial matters including nuclear technology. If crises do occur, America should seek to use asymmetric and integrated defense methods that highlight the role of economics as much as any lethal application of military power, being especially reluctant to fire the first shot and draw first blood in any confrontation with other nuclear-armed states. The American people and their leaders should remember how World War I began—through hypercompetitive great powers who overreacted to crises and were blind to the dangers of doing so—as much as they remember how strength and power won World War II and the Cold War. Washington should also broaden its concept of threat beyond the Pentagon's 4+1 framework of past years, which remains useful but is incomplete. It should add a second dimension of threats to its national security and grand strategy calculus. The new 4+1 encompasses biological, nuclear, climatic, digital, and internal dangers. They are just as important as the old set.

As a matter of not just domestic economics and politics but foreign policy, too, the United States needs a big vision and well-resourced action plan for renewal at home. In this book about grand strategy, with primary emphasis on military power, diplomacy, foreign assistance, trade, and other tools of international statecraft, I have arrived at the conclu-

sion that the area of American governance in greatest need of more resources is in domestic and economic policy. It is in that realm where we
are, today, building the foundations for the national security policies, and
successes or failures, of years and decades to come.

Notes

Preface: The Education of a Defense Analyst

1. Congressional Budget Office, "Costs of Operation Desert Shield," Washington, D.C., January 1991, https://www.cbo.gov/sites/default/files/102nd-congress-1991-1992/reports/199101costofoperation.pdf. The study was published before the war was fought—and thus before the name changed to Desert Storm.

2. Alain C. Enthoven and K. Wayne Smith, *How Much Is Enough? Shaping the Defense Program, 1961–1969* (Santa Monica, Calif.: RAND, 1971), 1–90.

3. Michael E. O'Hanlon and Philip H. Gordon, "A Tougher Target: The Afghanistan Model of Warfare May Not Apply Very Well to Iraq," *Washington Post*, December 26, 2001; Ken Adelman, "Cakewalk in Iraq," *Washington Post*, February 13, 2002.

4. Philip H. Gordon, *Losing the Long Game: The False Promise of Regime Change in the Middle East* (New York: St. Martin's, 2020).

5. Tom Ricks recounts one panel in which I made this argument in the fall of 2002 at the American Enterprise Institute, seated next to the Iraqi dissident leader Ahmed Chalabi, who clearly did not agree with me. See Thomas E. Ricks, *Fiasco: The American Military Adventure in Iraq* (New York: Penguin, 2007).

6. Kenneth M. Pollack, *The Threatening Storm: The Case for Invading Iraq* (New York: Random House, 2002); Richard Butler, *The Greatest Threat: Iraq, Weapons of Mass Destruction, and the Growing Crisis of Global Security* (New York: Public Affairs, 2000); Hans Blix, *Disarming Iraq* (New York: Pantheon Books, 2004).

7. Kenneth M. Pollack, "Spies, Lies, and Weapons: What Went Wrong?" *Atlantic*, January–February 2004.

8. Michael E. O'Hanlon, "Should Serbia Be Scared?," *New York Times*, March 23, 1999.

9. Michael E. O'Hanlon and Kenneth M. Pollack, "A War We Just Might Win,"

New York Times, July 30, 2007. Bear in mind that op-ed writers generally do not choose their headlines and, as in this case, have no forewarning of what their essay will be titled! Ken and I were privileged to travel to Iraq with CSIS's Anthony Cordesman, one of America's great national security minds. My other frequent companions on trips to the Iraq and Afghanistan battlefields over the years include the brilliant Ron Neumann and Steve Biddle.

10. The surge was not simply an increase in U.S. forces, as well as the ongoing growth of Iraqi forces, but also a fundamental change in their tactics, a new emphasis on population protection rather than annihilation of the enemy, and the integration of military with political aspects of strategy. See, e.g., Peter Mansour, *Surge: My Journey with General David Petraeus and the Remaking of the Iraq War* (New Haven: Yale University Press, 2013).

11. Steven Pinker, *Enlightenment Now: The Case for Reason, Science, Humanism, and Progress* (New York: Penguin, 2018), 453.

12. John Keegan, *A History of Warfare* (New York: Vintage, 1993).

ONE   An Age of Fragile Peace and an Unsure America

1. There is no clear documentation of this line attributed to Churchill, but he is still widely credited with the sardonic remark. See "The Churchill Project," Hillsdale College, Hillsdale, Mich., 2016, https://winstonchurchill.hillsdale.edu/americans-will-always-right-thing.

2. See, e.g., Kenneth N. Waltz, *Theory of International Politics* (New York: Random House, 1979), 161–93.

3. Steven Pinker, *The Better Angels of Our Nature: Why Violence Has Declined* (New York: Penguin, 2015); see also Michael A. Cohen and Micah Zenko, *Clear and Present Safety: The World Has Never Been Better and Why That Matters to Americans* (New Haven: Yale University Press, 2019); and Steven Pinker, *Enlightenment Now: The Case for Reason, Science, Humanism, and Progress* (New York: Penguin, 2018), 159.

4. "JFK on Nuclear Weapons and Nonproliferation," Carnegie Endowment for International Peace, Washington, D.C., 2003, https://carnegieendowment.org/2003/11/17/jfk-on-nuclear-weapons-and-non-proliferation-pub-14652; "Press Conference by President John F. Kennedy," March 21, 1963, John F. Kennedy Presidential Library and Museum, https://www.jfklibrary.org/archives/other-resources/john-f-kennedy-press-conferences/news-conference-52.

5. Samuel P. Huntington, "The U.S.—Decline or Renewal?" *Foreign Affairs* 67, no. 2 (Winter 1988/1989): 76–96.

6. Bruce D. Jones, *Still Ours to Lead: America, Rising Powers, and the Tension between Rivalry and Restraint* (Washington, D.C.: Brookings Institution Press, 2014); Michael Beckley, *Unrivaled: Why America Will Remain the World's Sole Superpower* (Ithaca, N.Y.: Cornell University Press, 2018).

7. For a similar assessment, see Ashley Tellis, "Covid-19 Knocks on American Hegemony," National Bureau of Asian Research, Seattle, Wash., May 2020, https://www

.nbr.org/wp-content/uploads/pdfs/publications/new-normal-tellis-050420.pdf; on polling data, see James Dobbins, Gabrielle Tarini, and Ali Wyne, "The Lost Generation in American Foreign Policy," RAND Corporation, Santa Monica, Calif., September 2020, https://www.rand.org/pubs/perspectives/PEA232-1.html.

8. Tellis, "Covid-19 Knocks on American Hegemony."

9. Samuel P. Huntington, "Democracy's Third Wave," *Journal of Democracy* 2, no. 2 (Spring 1991): 12–34.

10. See, e.g., Greg Mills and Jeffrey Herbst, *Africa's Third Liberation* (New York: Penguin, 2012); and Steven Radelet, *The Great Surge: The Ascent of the Developing World* (New York: Simon and Schuster, 2015).

11. Bruce Jones and Michael O'Hanlon, "Democracy Is Far from Dead," *Wall Street Journal*, December 10, 2017.

12. See, e.g., David H. Petraeus, Robert B. Zoellick, and Shannon K. O'Neil, *North America: Time for a New Focus*, Task Force Report No. 71 (New York: Council on Foreign Relations, 2014).

13. On the first point, see Charles Kupchan, *No One's World: The West, the Rising Rest, and the Coming Global Turn* (Oxford: Oxford University Press, 2012); on the second, see G. John Ikenberry, *Liberal Leviathan: The Origins, Crisis, and Transformation of the American World Order* (Princeton, N.J.: Princeton University Press, 2011).

14. On al Qaeda, see Daniel Byman, "Does al Qaeda Have a Future?" *Washington Quarterly* 42, no. 3 (Fall 2019): 65–75.

15. Siobhan O'Grady, "How Has the Coronavirus Pandemic Affected Global Poverty?" *Washington Post*, July 3, 2020; Betsy McKay, "Coronavirus Deals Setback to Global Vaccination Programs, Gates Report Finds," *Wall Street Journal*, September 14, 2020.

16. Homi Kharas and Kristofer Hamel, "A Global Tipping Point: Half the World Is Now Middle Class or Wealthier," Brookings blog, September 27, 2018, https://www.brookings.edu/blog/future-development/2018/09/27/a-global-tipping-point-half-the-world-is-now-middle-class-or-wealthier; Homi Kharas, "The Unprecedented Expansion of the Global Middle Class: An Update," Global Economy and Development Working Paper No. 100 (Washington, D.C.: Brookings Institution, 2017), 12.

17. Radelet, *Great Surge*, 74; UNICEF, "Under Five Mortality," New York, September 2019, https://data.unicef.org/topic/child-survival/under-five-mortality.

18. See, e.g., Jonah Goldberg, "We Just Had a Global Super-Decade! Why Doesn't It Feel Like It?" *Los Angeles Times*, December 27, 2019. Goldberg quotes Matt Ridley's book *The Rational Optimist* (New York: HarperCollins, 2010) and more recent statements by Ridley as well as his own analysis. See also Arthur C. Brooks, "The World Is Doing Much Better Than the Bad News Makes Us Think," *Washington Post*, December 2, 2019.

19. See Vincent Bevins, "The 'Liberal World Order' Was Built with Blood," *New York Times*, May 29, 2020.

20. Paul Kennedy, *The Rise and Fall of the Great Powers: Economic Change and Military Conflict from 1500 to 2000* (London: Unwin Hyman, 1988), 514–35.

21. Hal Brands, *American Grand Strategy in the Age of Trump* (Washington, D.C.: Brookings Institution Press, 2018).

22. See Larry Diamond, "Democracy Demotion: How the Freedom Agenda Fell Apart," *Foreign Affairs* 98, no. 4 (July/August 2019): 17–25.

23. See Vanda Felbab-Brown, *Shooting Up: Counterinsurgency and the War on Drugs* (Washington, D.C.: Brookings Institution Press, 2009); Sarah Chayes, *Thieves of State: Why Corruption Threatens Global Security* (New York: W. W. Norton, 2015); and Moises Naim, *Illicit: How Smugglers, Traffickers, and Copycats Are Hijacking the Global Economy* (New York: Doubleday, 2005).

24. Geoffrey Gertz and Homi Kharas, "Toward Strategies for Ending Rural Hunger," Ending Rural Hunger Project, Brookings Institution, Washington, D.C., December 2019, https://www.brookings.edu/research/toward-strategies-for-ending-rural-hunger.

25. Maggie Tennis, "An Illiberal Plague," Foreign Policy Research Institute, Philadelphia, May 5, 2020, https://www.fpri.org/article/2020/05/an-illiberal-plague.

26. Richard K. Betts, *American Force: Dangers, Delusions, and Dilemmas in National Security* (New York: Columbia University Press, 2012), 177.

27. See Elbridge A. Colby and A. Wess Mitchell, "The Age of Great-Power Competition," *Foreign Affairs* 99, no. 1 (January/February 2020): 129; and Alexander Korolev, "On the Verge of an Alliance: Contemporary China-Russia Military Cooperation," *Asian Security* 15, no. 3 (2019): 233–52.

28. John Mecklin, ed., "Closer Than Ever: It Is 100 Seconds to Midnight," Bulletin of the Atomic Scientists, Chicago, 2020, https://thebulletin.org/doomsday-clock/current-time.

29. Chester A. Crocker, Fen Osler Hampson, and Pamela Aall, "The Center Cannot Hold: Conflict Management in an Era of Diffusion," in Chester A. Crocker, Fen Osler Hampson, and Pamela Aall, eds., *Managing Conflict in a World Adrift* (Washington, D.C.: U.S. Institute of Peace, 2015), 3–22; Sean McFate, *The New Rules of War: Victory in the Age of Durable Disorder* (New York: HarperCollins, 2019), 25–42.

30. See, e.g., Graham K. Brown and Frances Stewart, "Economic and Political Causes of Conflict: An Overview and Some Policy Implications," in Crocker, Hampson, and Aall, *Managing Conflict in a World Adrift*, 200–201.

31. Lotta Themnér and Erik Melander, "Patterns of Armed Conflict, 2006–2015," in *SIPRI Yearbook, 2016* (Oxford: Oxford University Press, 2016), https://www.sipri.org/sites/default/files/SIPRIYB16c06sII.pdf.

32. Lotta Themnar and Peter Wallensteen, "Armed Conflict, 1946–2013," *Journal of Peace Research* 51, no. 4 (2014), pcr.uu.se/research/ucdp/charts_and_graphs; Pinker, *Better Angels of Our Nature*, 303–4; Department of Peace and Conflict Research, Uppsala Conflict Data Program, "Number of Conflicts, 1975–2017," Uppsala University, Uppsala, Sweden, 2018, https://ucdp.uu.se/?id=1&id=1.

33. See "The Long and Short of the Problem," *Economist*, November 9, 2013; and Department of Peace and Conflict Research, Uppsala Conflict Data Program, "Number of Deaths, 1989–2017," Uppsala University, Uppsala, Sweden, 2018, https://ucdp.uu.se/#/exploratory.

34. Vanda Felbab-Brown and Paul Wise, "When Pandemics Come to Slums," *Order*

from Chaos (blog), April 6, 2020, https://www.brookings.edu/blog/order-from-chaos /2020/04/06/when-pandemics-come-to-slums.

35. Gen. Raymond Odierno (ret.) and Michael E. O'Hanlon, "Securing Global Cities," Brookings Institution, Washington, D.C., 2017, 8, https://www.brookings.edu /research/securing-global-cities-2.

36. Henry A. Kissinger, "The Coronavirus Pandemic Will Forever Alter the World Order," *Wall Street Journal*, April 3, 2020.

37. See, e.g., Dina Smeltz, Ivo H. Daalder, and Craig Kafura, "Foreign Policy in the Age of Retrenchment," Chicago Council on Global Affairs, September 2014, https:// www.thechicagocouncil.org/publication/foreign-policy-age-retrenchment; Chicago Council on Global Affairs, "Rejecting Retreat: Americans Support U.S. Engagement in Global Affairs," September 2019, https://digital.thechicagocouncil.org/lcc/rejecting-retreat; and Ruth Igielnik and Kim Parker, "Majorities of U.S. Veterans, Public Say the Wars in Iraq and Afghanistan Were Not Worth Fighting," Pew Research Center, Washington, D.C., July 10, 2019, https://www.pewresearch.org/fact-tank/2019/07/10/majorities-of-u-s-veterans -public-say-the-wars-in-iraq-and-afghanistan-were-not-worth-fighting.

38. See Michael J. Mazarr, "The World Has Passed the Old Grand Strategies By," *War on the Rocks*, October 5, 2016, https://warontherocks.com/2016/10/the-world-has -passed-the-old-grand-strategies-by.

39. Jim Golby and Peter Feaver, "Can Military Leaders Handle the Truth About Afghanistan?" *Defense One*, December 19, 2019, https://www.defenseone.com/ideas /2019/12/can-military-leaders-handle-truth-about-afghanistan/161986/.

40. See Robert Kagan, *Dangerous Nation II*, forthcoming; and Adam Tooze, *The Deluge: The Great War, America and the Remaking of the Global Order, 1916–1931* (New York: Penguin, 2014), 21–30.

41. Daniel W. Drezner, Ronald R. Krebs, and Randall Schweller, "The End of Grand Strategy: America Must Think Small," *Foreign Affairs* 99, no. 3 (May/June 2020): 107–8.

42. John Lewis Gaddis, *Strategies of Containment: A Critical Appraisal of American National Security Policy During the Cold War* (Oxford: Oxford University Press, 2005); William W. Kaufmann, *Planning Conventional Forces, 1950–1980* (Washington, D.C.: Brookings Institution Press, 1982); and Robert P. Haffa Jr., *The Half War: Planning U.S. Rapid Deployment Forces to Meet a Limited Contingency, 1960–1983* (Abingdon, U.K.: Taylor and Francis, 1984).

43. For similar views, see Francis J. Gavin and James B. Steinberg, "The Vision Thing," *Foreign Affairs* 99, no. 4 (July/August 2020): 187–91; and Andrew Ehrhardt and Maeve Ryan, "Grand Strategy Is No Silver Bullet, But It Is Indispensable," *War on the Rocks*, May 19, 2020, https://warontherocks.com/2020/05/grand-strategy-is-no-silver -bullet-but-it-is-indispensable.

44. See Travis Sharp, "Did Dollars Follow Strategy?" Center for Strategic and Budgetary Assessments, Washington, D.C., 2019, https://csbaonline.org/research/publications /did-dollars-follow-strategy-a-review-of-the-fy-2020-defense-budget.

45. The great theologian and writer Reinhold Niebuhr made similar arguments, too. For a thoughtful review, see Colin Dueck, "Reinhold Niebuhr and the Second World War," *Providence* (Spring 2020), https://www.aei.org/articles/reinhold-niebuhr-and-the -second-world-war/.

46. Anne-Marie Slaughter, *The Idea That Is America* (New York: Perseus, 2007).

47. Richard N. Haass, *The Reluctant Sheriff: The United States After the Cold War* (New York: Council on Foreign Relations, 1997); Robert Kagan, *Dangerous Nation: America's Foreign Policy from Its Earliest Days to the Dawn of the Twentieth Century* (New York: Alfred A. Knopf, 2006); and James Steinberg and Michael E. O'Hanlon, *Strategic Reassurance and Resolve: U.S.-China Relations in the 21st Century* (Princeton, N.J.: Princeton University Press, 2014).

48. See also Paul B. Stares, *Preventive Engagement: How America Can Avoid War, Stay Strong, and Keep the Peace* (New York: Columbia University Press, 2018), 118–20.

49. For a similar argument, see Mira Rapp-Hooper, *Shields of the Republic: The Triumph and Peril of America's Alliances* (Cambridge, Mass.: Harvard University Press, 2020).

50. As such, the long tradition of scathing criticism of American foreign policy by Americans, while often harsher in tone and substance in the modern era than I would prefer, often plays an essential role in improving U.S. foreign policy even when it goes too far to be fair or fully accurate. See, e.g., John Mearsheimer, "The Great Delusion," *National Interest,* October 2018, https://nationalinterest.org/feature/great-delusion-liberal -dreams-and-international-realities-32737; Clyde Prestowitz, *Rogue Nation: American Unilateralism and the Failure of Good Intentions* (New York: Perseus, 2003); Andrew Bacevich, *Washington Rules: America's Path to Permanent War* (New York: Metropolitan Books, 2010); and Christopher A. Preble, *The Power Problem: How American Military Dominance Makes Us Less Safe, Less Prosperous, and Less Free* (Ithaca, N.Y.: Cornell University Press, 2019).

51. Bruce D. Jones, *Still Ours to Lead: America, Rising Powers, and the Tension Between Rivalry and Restraint* (Washington, D.C.: Brookings Institution Press, 2014).

52. For the seminal discussion about the distinction between balancing against power and balancing against threat, see Stephen M. Walt, *The Origins of Alliances* (Ithaca, N.Y.: Cornell University Press, 1987).

53. Pew Research Center, "Public Trust in Government: 1958–2019," Washington, D.C., 2019, https://www.people-press.org/2019/04/11/public-trust-in-government-1958 -2019.

54. See Isabel Sawhill, *The Forgotten Americans: An Economic Agenda for a Divided Nation* (New Haven: Yale University Press, 2018).

55. See Salman Ahmed et al., "U.S. Foreign Policy for the Middle Class: Perspectives from Nebraska," Carnegie Endowment for International Peace, Washington, D.C., May 2020, https://carnegieendowment.org/2020/05/21/u.s.-foreign-policy-for-middle -class-perspectives-from-nebraska-pub-81767.

56. For a similar view, see Brands, *American Grand Strategy in the Age of Trump,* 1–23.

TWO A Grand Strategy of Resolute Restraint

1. Dale C. Copeland, *Economic Interdependence and War* (Princeton, N.J.: Princeton University Press, 2015).

2. Michael W. Doyle, *Liberal Peace: Selected Essays* (New York: Routledge, 2012).

3. Richard Betts is compelling on this point, as on many others. See Richard K. Betts, *American Force: Dangers, Delusions, and Dilemmas in National Security* (New York: Columbia University Press, 2012), xi–18.

4. Thomas Wright, *All Measures Short of War: The Contest for the 21st Century and the Future of American Power* (New Haven: Yale University Press, 2018).

5. See Elbridge A. Colby and A. Wess Mitchell, "The Age of Great-Power Competition," *Foreign Affairs* 99, no. 1 (January/February 2020): 129; and Alexander Korolev, "On the Verge of an Alliance: Contemporary China-Russia Military Cooperation," *Asian Security* 15, no. 3 (2019): 233–52.

6. There are various ways to define grand strategy. Hal Brands describes it as "the integrated set of concepts that gives purpose and direction to a country's dealings with the world." See the preface to Hal Brands, *American Grand Strategy in the Age of Trump* (Washington, D.C.: Brookings Institution Press, 2018). Barry Posen and John Lewis Gaddis tend to place greater emphasis, as do I, on matters of war and peace. See John Lewis Gaddis, *On Grand Strategy* (New York: Penguin, 2019).

7. On these themes, see John J. Mearsheimer, *The Tragedy of Great Power Politics* (New York: W. W. Norton, 2001), as well as Mearsheimer's *Great Delusion: Liberal Dreams and International Realities* (New Haven: Yale University Press, 2018); Niccolò Machiavelli, *The Prince* (New York: Penguin, 1961); Paul Kennedy, *The Rise and Fall of the Great Powers: Economic Change and Military Conflict from 1500 to 2000* (New York: Vintage, 1987); Kenneth N. Waltz, *Man the State and War* (New York: Columbia University Press, 1954); and Graham Allison, *Destined for War: America, China, and Thucydides' Trap* (Boston: Houghton Mifflin Harcourt, 2017). I agree with Allison's analysis, which suggests that avoiding war with the United States and China in particular will be difficult, more than with his title, which suggests that it will be impossible.

8. On Kennan, see James M. Goldgeier, "A Complex Man with a Simple Idea," in Michael Kimmage and Matthew Rojansky, *A Kennan for Our Times: Revisiting America's Greatest 20th Century Diplomat in the 21st Century* (Washington, D.C.: Wilson Center, 2019), 25–35.

9. On the intellectual roots of such analysis, including the ideas of Walter Lippman and others, see David Callahan, *Between Two Worlds: Realism, Idealism, and American Foreign Policy After the Cold War* (New York: HarperCollins, 1994), 18–29.

10. For a brilliant treatment of Kennan's thinking, see Barton Gellman, *Contending with Kennan: Toward a Philosophy of American Power* (New York: Praeger, 1984). For a similar appreciation of the value of Kennan's advice for today's world, including in regard to China, see Odd Arne Westad, "The Sources of Chinese Conduct: Are Washington and Beijing Fighting a New Cold War?" *Foreign Affairs* 98, no. 5 (September/October 2019): 86–95.

11. See Elbridge A. Colby and A. Wess Mitchell, "The Age of Great-Power Competition," *Foreign Affairs* 99, no. 1 (January/February 2020): 129.

12. See James G. Roche and Thomas G. Mahnken, "What Is Net Assessment?" in Thomas G. Mahnken, ed., *Net Assessment and Military Strategy: Retrospective and Prospective Essays* (Amherst, N.Y.: Cambria, 2020), 11–26.

13. See Joshua M. Epstein, "Dynamic Analysis and the Conventional Balance in Europe," *International Security* 12, no. 4 (Spring 1988): 154–65; and Michael E. O'Hanlon, *The Science of War: Defense Budgeting, Military Technology, Logistics, and Combat Outcomes* (Princeton, N.J.: Princeton University Press, 2009), 63–140.

14. See Alan J. Vick et al., *Air Base Defense* (Santa Monica, Calif.: RAND, 2020), 5–53; Tom Karako and Wes Rumbaugh, "Inflection Point: Missile Defense and Defeat in the 2021 Budget," Center for Strategic and International Studies, Washington, D.C., March 2020, https://www.csis.org/analysis/inflection-point-missile-defense-and-defeat-2021-budget; and Joseph T. Buontempo and Joseph E. Ringer, "Airbase Defense Falls Between the Cracks," *Joint Forces Quarterly,* no. 97 (Spring 2020): 114–20.

15. Kurt M. Campbell and Jake Sullivan, "Competition Without Catastrophe: How America Can Both Challenge and Coexist with China," *Foreign Affairs* 98, no. 5 (September/October 2019): 96–110; Fareed Zakaria, "The New China Scare: Why America Shouldn't Panic About Its Latest Challenger," *Foreign Affairs* 99, no. 1 (January/February 2020): 68.

16. Mark Gunzinger et al., "Force Planning for the Era of Great Power Competition" (Washington, D.C.: Center for Strategic and Budgetary Assessments, 2017).

17. For a similar view, see Christian Brose, *The Kill Chain: Defending America in the Future of High-Tech Warfare* (New York: Hachette Books, 2020).

18. Robert D. Blackwill and Jennifer M. Harris, *War by Other Means: Geoeconomics and Statecraft* (Cambridge, Mass.: Harvard University Press, 2016).

19. Ely Ratner, "Blunting China's Economic Coercion," Statement before the Senate Foreign Relations Committee Subcommittee on East Asia, the Pacific, and International Cybersecurity Policy, July 24, 2018, 3, https://www.foreign.senate.gov/imo/media/doc/072418_Ratner_Testimony.pdf.

20. Emily de la Bruyere, "The New Metrics for Building Geopolitical Power in a New World," *National Interest,* April 12, 2020, https://nationalinterest.org/feature/new-metrics-building-geopolitical-power-new-world-143147.

21. Jonathan Kirshner, "The Microfoundations of Economic Sanctions," *Security Studies* 6, no. 3 (Spring 1997): 32–64.

22. See Daniel W. Drezner, "Economic Statecraft in the Age of Trump," *Washington Quarterly* 42, no. 3 (Fall 2019): 7–24.

23. See Julianne Smith and Torrey Taussig, "The Old World and the Middle Kingdom: Europe Wakes Up to China's Rise," *Foreign Affairs* 98, no. 5 (September/October 2019): 112–24.

24. See also Anthony Dunkin, "Where Rumsfeld Got It Right," *Joint Forces Quarterly* 86 (2017): 66–72.

25. Robert M. Gates, "The Overmilitarization of American Foreign Policy," *Foreign Affairs* 99, no. 4 (July/August 2020): 128–32.

26. Edward Fishman, "Even Smarter Sanctions," *Foreign Affairs* 96, no. 6 (November/December 2017): 104–9.

27. Blackwill and Harris, *War by Other Means,* 1.

28. On the utility of various types of sanctions in statecraft, see also Juan C. Zarate, *Treasury's War: The Unleashing of a New Era of Financial Warfare* (New York: Public Affairs, 2013); Richard Nephew, *The Art of Sanctions: A View from the Field* (New York: Columbia University Press, 2017); Richard N. Haass and Meghan L. O'Sullivan, eds., *Honey and Vinegar: Incentives, Sanctions, and Foreign Policy* (Washington, D.C.: Brookings Institution Press, 2000); Eugene Gholz and Llewelyn Hughes, "Market Structure and Economic Sanctions: The 2010 Rare Earth Metals Episode as a Pathway Case of Market Adjustment," *Review of International Political Economy,* November 25, 2019; Thijs Van de Graaf and Jeff Colgan, "Russian Gas Games or Well-Oiled Conflict? Energy Security and the 2014 Ukraine Crisis," *Energy Research and Social Science,* December 23, 2016; and Gary Clyde Hufbauer et al., *Economic Sanctions Reconsidered,* 3rd ed. (Washington, D.C.: Peterson Institute for International Economics, 2009).

29. Robert A. Pape, "Why Economic Sanctions Do Not Work," *International Security* 22, no. 2 (Fall 1997): 90–136.

30. See Thomas C. Schelling, *Arms and Influence* (New Haven: Yale University Press, 1966); and Thomas C. Schelling, *The Strategy of Conflict* (Cambridge, Mass.: Harvard University Press, 1960).

31. Keith B. Payne, *The Great American Gamble: Deterrence Theory and Practice from the Cold War to the 21st Century* (Fairfax, Va.: National Institute Press, 2008).

32. Katie Simmons, Bruce Stokes, and Jacob Poushter, "NATO Publics Blame Russia for Ukrainian Crisis, but Reluctant to Provide Military Aid," Pew Charitable Trusts, Washington, D.C., June 2015.

33. See also Mira Rapp-Hooper, "Saving America's Alliances: The United States Still Needs the System That Put It on Top," *Foreign Affairs* 99, no. 2 (March/April 2020): 127–40.

34. A good explanation of some of the key interrelationships and dynamics can be found in Henry Farrell and Abraham L. Newman, "Weaponized Interdependence: How Global Economic Networks Shape State Coercion," *International Security* 44, no. 1 (Summer 2019): 42–79.

35. To quote the National Defense Strategy of 2018: "The Global Operating Model describes how the Joint Force will be postured and employed to achieve its competition and wartime missions. Foundational capabilities include: nuclear; cyber; space; C4ISR; strategic mobility; and counter WMD proliferation. It comprises four layers: contact, blunt, surge, and homeland. These are, respectively, designed to help us compete more effectively below the level of armed conflict; delay, degrade, or deny adversary aggression; surge war-winning forces and manage conflict escalation; and defend the U.S. homeland." See Secretary of Defense Jim Mattis, "Summary of the 2018 National Defense Strategy of the United States of America: Sharpening the American Military's Competitive Edge," Department of Defense, Washington, D.C., January 2018, 7, https://dod.defense.gov/Portals/1/Documents/pubs/2018-National-Defense-Strategy-Summary.pdf.

36. See Ash Carter, *Inside the Five-Sided Box: Lessons from a Lifetime of Leadership in the Pentagon* (New York: Dutton, 2019), 261–62.

37. It has similarities with what Andrew Ross and Barry Posen once described as "selective engagement," though of course I am writing in a different time, and any grand strategy only takes on real meaning when applied in detail to the specific problems of the day. See Barry R. Posen and Andrew L. Ross, "Competing Visions for U.S. Grand Strategy," *International Security* 21, no. 3 (Winter 1996/1997): 5–53.

38. For an outstanding explanation and defense of deep engagement, including the benefits for basic war-and-peace issues, protection of the commons, and nonproliferation policy, and the relatively limited dangers of U.S. entrapment in allies' excessive ambitions or uses of force, see Stephen G. Brooks, G. John Ikenberry, and William C. Wohlforth, "Don't Come Home, America: The Case Against Retrenchment," *International Security* 37, no. 3 (Winter 2012/2013). It was written partly in response to the provocative essay written during the period of America's "unipolar moment," as Charles Krauthammer called it; see Eugene Gholz, Daryl G. Press, and Harvey M. Sapolsky, "Come Home, America: The Strategy of Restraint in the Face of Temptation," *International Security* 21, no. 4 (Spring 1997): 5–48.

39. Several books that have considerable overlap with mine, and from which I have benefited intellectually, are Robert J. Art, *A Grand Strategy for America* (Ithaca, N.Y.: Cornell University Press, 2004); Seyom Brown, *Higher Realism: A New Foreign Policy for the United States* (Boulder, Colo.: Paradigm, 2009); Paul B. Stares, *Preventive Engagement: How America Can Avoid War, Stay Strong, and Keep the Peace* (New York: Columbia University Press, 2017); and Hal Brands, *American Grand Strategy in the Age of Trump* (Washington, D.C.: Brookings Institution Press, 2018).

40. See, e.g., Christopher Layne, *The Peace of Illusions: American Grand Strategy from 1940 to the Present* (Ithaca, N.Y.: Cornell University Press, 2007).

41. Barry R. Posen, *Restraint: A New Foundation for U.S. Grand Strategy* (Ithaca, N.Y.: Cornell University Press, 2014), 140–63.

42. See Robert Kagan, *Dangerous Nation II,* forthcoming.

43. Thomas Wright, "The Folly of Retrenchment: Why America Can't Withdraw from the World," *Foreign Affairs* 99, no. 2 (March/April 2020): 10.

44. See Richard C. Bush, *The Perils of Proximity: China-Japan Security Relations* (Washington, D.C.: Brookings Institution Press, 2013).

45. North Atlantic Treaty Organization, "Lord Ismay," Brussels, 2020, https://www.nato.int/cps/en/natohq/declassified_137930.htm.

46. Geoffrey Blainey, *The Causes of War* (New York: Free Press, 1973). I am indebted to Steve Walt for introducing me to this masterful book at the Woodrow Wilson School in the late 1980s.

47. See Michael J. Green, *Japan's Reluctant Realism: Foreign Policy Challenges in an Era of Uncertain Power* (New York: Palgrave-Macmillan, 2001); and H. D. P. Envall, "What Kind of Japan? Tokyo's Strategic Options in a Contested Asia," *Survival* 61, no. 4 (August–September 2019): 117–30. On Russia and China, see Jeffrey Feltman, "China's Expanding Influence at the United Nations—and How the United States Should React,"

Brookings Institution, Washington, D.C., September 2020, https://www.brookings.edu /wp-content/uploads/2020/09/FP_20200914_china_united_nations_feltman.pdf; and Andrea Kendall-Taylor, David Shullman, and Dan McCormick, "Navigating Sino-Russian Defense Cooperation," Center for a New American Security, Washington, D.C., August 4, 2020, https://www.cnas.org/publications/commentary/navigating-sino-russian -defense-cooperation.

48. Even President Obama's loyal and thoughtful first secretary of defense, Robert Gates, said as much about Libya in particular, and Obama himself acknowledged his administration's serious failure in planning for post-Qaddafi Libya. See Robert M. Gates, "The Overmilitarization of American Foreign Policy," *Foreign Affairs* 99, no. 4 (July/ August 2020): 124–25.

49. Carter, *Inside the Five-Sided Box*, 268–69.

50. See Derek Chollet, *The Long Game: How Obama Defied Washington and Redefined America's Role in the World* (New York: Public Affairs, 2016); for a much more critical treatment, from a cerebral scholar who also served in the Obama administration, see Vali Nasr, *The Dispensable Nation: American Foreign Policy in Retreat* (New York: Doubleday, 2013). See also Dana H. Allin and Erik Jones, *Weary Policeman: American Power in an Age of Austerity* (New York: Routledge for IISS, 2012), 183–90; Jonathan Tepperman, *The Fix: How Nations Survive and Thrive in a World in Decline* (New York: Tim Duggan Books, 2016), 227; Juliet Eilperin, "Obama Lays Out His Foreign Policy Doctrine: Singles, Doubles, and the Occasional Home Run," *Washington Post*, April 28, 2014; Jeffrey Goldberg, "The Obama Doctrine," *Atlantic,* April 2016; and William J. Burns, "A New U.S. Foreign Policy for the Post-Pandemic Landscape," Carnegie Endowment for International Peace, Washington, D.C., September 9, 2020, https://carnegieendowment .org/2020/09/09/new-u.s.-foreign-policy-for-post-pandemic-landscape-pub-82498.

51. Richard N. Haass, *War of Necessity, War of Choice: A Memoir of Two Iraq Wars* (New York: Simon and Schuster, 2009).

52. Eliot A. Cohen, *The Big Stick: The Limits of Soft Power and the Necessity of Military Force* (New York: Basic Books, 2016), 214–16.

53. See Ivo H. Daalder and Michael E. O'Hanlon, *Winning Ugly: NATO's War to Save Kosovo* (Washington, D.C.: Brookings Institution Press, 2000), 212–15.

54. Paul Huth and Bruce Russett, "Deterrence Failure and Crisis Escalation," *International Studies Quarterly* 32, no. 1 (March 1988): 29–45.

55. Frederick Kempe, *Berlin, 1961: Kennedy, Khrushchev, and the Most Dangerous Place on Earth* (New York: G. P. Putnam's Sons, 2011).

56. John Lewis Gaddis, *Strategies of Containment: A Critical Appraisal of Postwar American National Security Policy* (Oxford: Oxford University Press, 1982), 109–20; Dong-gil Kim and William Stueck, "Did Stalin Lure the United States into the Korean War? New Evidence on the Origins of the Korean War," Woodrow Wilson Center, Washington, D.C., July 2011, https://www.wilsoncenter.org/publication/did-stalin-lure-the-united-states -the-korean-war-new-evidence-the-origins-the-korean-war; Michael R. Gordon and General (ret.) Bernard E. Trainor, *The Generals' War: The Inside Story of the Conflict in the Gulf* (Boston: Little, Brown, 1995), 20–22.

57. Raymond L. Garthoff, *Détente and Confrontation: American-Soviet Relations from Nixon to Reagan*, rev. ed. (Washington, D.C.: Brookings Institution Press, 1994), 1023–46.

58. See, e.g., Angela Stent, *Putin's World: Russia Against the West and with the Rest* (New York: Twelve, 2019), 131, 270.

59. Speech of Secretary of Defense Robert M. Gates at the U.S. Military Academy, West Point, New York, February 25, 2011, https://archive.defense.gov/Speeches/Speech .aspx?SpeechID=1539.

60. Thomas Wright, "Trump's NATO Article Five Problem," *Order from Chaos* (blog), May 17, 2017, https://www.brookings.edu/blog/order-from-chaos/2017/05/17 /trumps-nato-article-5-problem.

61. See Robert Kagan, *Dangerous Nation: America's Foreign Policy from Its Earliest Days to the Dawn of the Twentieth Century* (New York: Vintage, 2006).

62. "The World; Osama bin Laden, in His Own Words," *New York Times*, August 23, 1998.

63. See Jonathan Mercer, *Reputation and International Politics* (Ithaca, N.Y.: Cornell University Press, 1996), 1–43; and Daryl G. Press, *Calculating Credibility: How Leaders Assess Military Threats* (Ithaca, N.Y.: Cornell University Press, 2005), 1–7. I thank Jeremy Shapiro for underscoring to me the importance of Press's and Mercer's excellent research. See also Keren Yarhi-Milo, *Who Fights for Reputation? The Psychology of Leaders in International Conflict* (Princeton, N.J.: Princeton University Press, 2018).

64. Alexander L. George and Richard Smoke, *Deterrence in American Foreign Policy: Theory and Practice* (New York: Columbia University Press, 1974).

65. Fred Charles Ikle, *Every War Must End* (New York: Columbia University Press, 1971), 107.

66. See, e.g., Richard Ned Lebow, *Between Peace and War: The Nature of International Crises* (Baltimore: Johns Hopkins University Press, 1981), 335; and Tony Zinni and Tony Koltz, *Before the First Shots Are Fired: How America Can Win or Lose Off the Battlefield* (New York: Palgrave MacMillan, 2014).

67. On the outbreak of World War I, see Christopher Clark, *The Sleepwalkers: How Europe Went to War in 1914* (New York: HarperCollins, 2012); John Keegan, *The First World War* (New York: Alfred A. Knopf, 1999); Margaret MacMillan, *The War That Ended Peace: The Road to 1914* (Toronto: AllenLane, 2013); and of course Barbara W. Tuchman, *The Guns of August* (New York: Macmillan, 1962).

68. See Tooze, *Deluge*, 33–251.

69. Stephen Sestanovich, *Maximalist: America in the World from Truman to Obama* (New York: Vintage, 2014); James Steinberg and Michael E. O'Hanlon, *Strategic Reassurance and Resolve: U.S.-China Relations in the 21st Century* (Princeton, N.J.: Princeton University Press, 2014).

70. See Scott D. Sagan and Kenneth N. Waltz, *The Spread of Nuclear Weapons: A Debate* (New York: W. W. Norton, 1995). My money is squarely in Sagan's camp on this one.

71. See Kurt M. Campbell and James B. Steinberg, *Difficult Transitions: Foreign*

Policy Troubles at the Outset of Presidential Power (Washington, D.C.: Brookings Institu-
tion Press, 2008), 137; Stephen M. Walt, *The Hell of Good Intentions: America's Foreign
Policy Elite and the Decline of U.S. Primacy* (New York: Farrar, Straus and Giroux, 2018);
Fareed Zakaria, "The New China Scare: Why America Shouldn't Panic About Its Latest
Challenger," *Foreign Affairs* 99, no. 1 (January/February 2020): 52–69; and Robert Jervis,
"Liberalism, the Blob, and American Foreign Policy: Evidence and Methodology," *Secu-
rity Studies* 29, no. 3 (May 2020): 434–56.

72. See Barry R. Posen, *Inadvertent Escalation: Conventional War and Nuclear
Risks* (Ithaca, N.Y.: Cornell University Press, 1991); and Caitlin Talmadge, "Would China
Go Nuclear? Assessing the Risk of Chinese Nuclear Escalation in a Conventional War
with the United States," *International Security* 41, no. 4 (Spring 2017): 50–92.

73. Bruce G. Blair, *Strategic Command and Control: Redefining the Nuclear Threat*
(Washington, D.C.: Brookings Institution Press, 1985). See also Defense Science Board,
"Task Force on Cyber Deterrence," Department of Defense, Washington, D.C., February
2017; and Frank Rose, "Russian and Chinese Nuclear Arsenals: Posture, Proliferation,
and the Future of Arms Control," Testimony before the House Committee on Foreign
Affairs, June 21, 2018, https://www.brookings.edu/testimonies/russian-and-chinese
-nuclear-arsenals-posture-proliferation-and-the-future-of-arms-control/.

74. See Scott D. Sagan, *The Limits of Safety: Organizations, Accidents, and Nuclear
Weapons* (Princeton, N.J.: Princeton University Press, 1993), 6.

75. On these debates, see esp. McGeorge Bundy, *Danger and Survival: Choices
About the Bomb in the First Fifty Years* (New York: Vintage, 1988), 453–58, 586–87; Michael Dobbs, *One Minute to Midnight* (New York: Alfred A. Knopf, 2008), 108–11, 170–82,
205–6, 350–53; and Frederick Kempe, *Berlin 1961: Kennedy, Khrushchev, and the Most
Dangerous Place on Earth* (New York: G. P. Putnam's Sons, 2011).

76. On nuclear escalation dynamics, see Herman Kahn, *On Thermonuclear War,*
2nd ed. (Princeton, N.J.: Princeton University Press, 1961); and Janne E. Nolan, *Guardians of the Arsenal: The Politics of Nuclear Strategy* (New York: Basic Books, 1989).

77. I am a great fan of former chairman of the joint chiefs of staff General Martin
Dempsey, but when he told *Foreign Affairs* magazine in 2016, shortly after his retirement
the year before, that the world of the mid-2016s was "the most dangerous period in my
lifetime," he exaggerated. Dempsey, after all, was born in 1952. See "A Conversation with
Martin Dempsey," *Foreign Affairs* 95, no. 5 (September/October 2016): 2. Another comment in this vein is that of Vayl Oxford of the Defense Threat Reduction Agency, who
wrote in 2019 that "the current geopolitical environment is the most complex, dynamic,
and dangerous the United States has ever faced." Complex and dynamic, yes; most dangerous, most assuredly not. See Vayl S. Oxford, "Countering Threat Networks to Deter,
Compete, and Win," *Joint Forces Quarterly* 95, no. 4 (2019): 78.

78. See Seyom Brown, "The New Nuclear MADness," *Survival* 62, no. 1 (February–
March 2020): 63–88.

79. See North Atlantic Treaty Organization, "The North Atlantic Treaty," Washington, D.C., 1949, https://www.nato.int/cps/ie/natohq/official_texts_17120.htm.

80. "Treaty of Mutual Cooperation and Security between Japan and the United

States of America," Washington, D.C., 1960, https://www.mofa.go.jp/region/n-america
/us/q&a/ref/1.html.

81. "Mutual Defense Treaty between the United States and the Republic of the
Philippines," *Avalon Project,* Lillian Goldman Law Library at Yale Law School, http://
avalon.law.yale.edu/20th_century/phil001.asp.

82. Secretary of Defense Jim Mattis, "Summary of the 2018 National Defense
Strategy of the United States of America: Sharpening the American Military's Competitive Edge," Department of Defense, Washington, D.C., January 2018, 5, https://dod
.defense.gov/Portals/1/Documents/pubs/2018-National-Defense-Strategy-Summary
.pdf.

83. Mattis, 4.

84. See "Southeast Asia Collective Defense Treaty," Manila, the Philippines, 1954,
https://avalon.law.yale.edu/20th_century/usmu003.asp; "Johnson Warns Inonu on Cyprus," *New York Times,* June 6, 1964; and Turgut Akgul, "An Analysis of the 1964 Johnson
Letter," Naval Postgraduate School, Monterey, Calif., December 2004, https://apps.dtic
.mil/dtic/tr/fulltext/u2/a429671.pdf.

85. See "Joint Chiefs Chairman Dunford on the '4+1 Framework' and Meeting
Transnational Threats," Brookings blog, February 24, 2017, https://www.brookings.edu
/blog/brookings-now/2017/02/24/joint-chiefs-chairman-dunford-transnational-threats.

86. On the way American internal politics intersect with grand strategy, see, e.g.,
Robert Kagan, *The Jungle Grows Back: America and Our Imperiled World* (New York:
Alfred A. Knopf, 2018).

THREE Europe and Russia

1. See John F. Helliwell et al., eds., *World Happiness Report, 2020,* 20–21, https://
worldhappiness.report/ed/2020/.

2. Ben S. Bernanke and Peter Olson, "Are Americans Better Off Than They Were
a Decade or Two Ago?" Brookings blog, October 2016, https://www.brookings.edu/blog
/ben-bernanke/2016/10/19/are-americans-better-off-than-they-were-a-decade-or
-two-ago.

3. For historical perspective it is informative to reread Richard H. Ullman, *Securing Europe* (Princeton, N.J.: Princeton University Press, 1991).

4. Henry A. Kissinger, *Diplomacy* (New York: Simon and Schuster, 1994), 804–
85; see also Kori N. Schake, *Managing American Hegemony: Essays on Power in a Time of
Dominance* (Stanford, Calif.: Hoover Institution Press, 2009), 146–54.

5. See Amanda Sloat, "The West's Turkey Conundrum," Brookings Institution,
Washington, D.C., February 2018, https://www.brookings.edu/research/the-wests-turkey
-conundrum; and Kemal Kirisci, *Turkey and the West: Fault Lines in a Troubled Alliance*
(Washington, D.C.: Brookings Institution Press, 2017).

6. For a brilliant article, see Constanze Stelzenmuller, "German Lessons," Brookings essay, Brookings Institution, Washington, D.C., November 2019, https://www
.brookings.edu/essay/german-lessons.

7. North Atlantic Treaty Organization, "Funding NATO," Brussels, March 2020, https://www.nato.int/cps/en/natohq/topics_67655.htm.

8. Steven Erlanger, "European Defense and 'Strategic Autonomy' Are Also Coronavirus Victims," *New York Times,* May 24, 2020.

9. European Defence Agency, "PESCO," European Union, Brussels, 2019, https://pesco.europa.eu.

10. See, e.g., Lawrence D. Freeman, "Britain Adrift: The United Kingdom's Search for a Post-Brexit Role," *Foreign Affairs* 99, no. 3 (May/June 2020): 118–30.

11. Leon Aron, "The Coronavirus Could Imperil Putin's Presidency," *Wall Street Journal,* April 23, 2020.

12. William C. Potter and Sarah Bidgood, eds., *Once and Future Partners: The United States, Russia and Nuclear Non-Proliferation* (New York: Routledge for IISS, 2018).

13. Fiona Hill and Clifford G. Gaddy, *Mr. Putin: Operative in the Kremlin* (Washington, D.C.: Brookings Institution Press, 2013). On Russia's role in the 2016 elections, as documented by the U.S. Intelligence Community and the U.S. Senate, see Joseph Marks, "The Cybersecurity 202: Senate Russia Report May Inspire Last Push for Election Security Changes Before November," *Washington Post,* April 22, 2020.

14. See, e.g., "Panama Papers Q&A: What Is the Scandal About?" *BBC News,* April 6, 2016, https://www.bbc.com/news/world-35954224.

15. Angela Stent, *Putin's World: Russia Against the West and with the Rest* (New York: Hachette, 2019).

16. On the prospects for longer-term Russian democracy, see Kirill Rogov and Maxim Ananyev, "Public Opinion and Russian Politics," in Daniel Treisman, ed., *The New Autocracy: Information, Politics, and Policy in Putin's Russia* (Washington, D.C.: Brookings Institution Press, 2018), 191–216.

17. Tony Judt, *Postwar: A History of Europe Since 1945* (New York: Penguin, 2005), 824–25; Hill and Gaddy, *Mr. Putin;* Strobe Talbott, *The Russia Hand: A Memoir of Presidential Diplomacy* (New York: Random House, 2002), 366–67.

18. Betts, *American Force,* 189–90. See also Bill Bradley, *We Can All Do Better* (New York: Vanguard, 2012), 112–15; and James Goldgeier, *Not Whether but When: The U.S. Decision to Enlarge NATO* (Washington, D.C.: Brookings Institution Press, 1999).

19. Thomas Graham, "Let Russia Be Russia: The Case for a More Pragmatic Approach to Moscow," *Foreign Affairs* 98, no. 6 (November/December 2019): 134–46.

20. See Hans Binnendijk and David Gompert, "Decisive Response: A New Nuclear Strategy for NATO," *Survival* 61, no. 5 (October/November 2019): 113–28; Vladimir Isachenkov, "Russia Warns It Will See Any Incoming Missile as Nuclear," *Washington Post,* August 7, 2020; and Dean Wilkening, "Hypersonic Weapons and Strategic Stability," *Survival* 61, no. 5 (October/November 2019): 129–48.

21. Johan Norberg and Martin Goliath, "The Fighting Power of Russia's Armed Forces in 2019," in Fredrik Westerlund and Susanne Oxenstierna, eds., "Russian Military Capability in a Ten-Year Perspective—2019," FOI Report R-4758-SE, Stockholm, December 2019, 59–78.

22. For a discussion of some of these tactics, see James Kirchick, *The End of Eu-*

rope: Dictators, Demagogues, and the Coming Dark Age (New Haven: Yale University Press, 2017), 215–23; and J. B. Vowell, "Maskirovka: From Russia, with Deception," *Real Clear Defense,* October 30, 2016, https://www.realcleardefense.com/articles/2016/10/31/maskirovka_from_russia_with_deception_110282.html.

23. Andrew Higgins, "Russia's War Games with Fake Enemies Cause Real Alarm," *New York Times,* September 13, 2017.

24. For an excellent treatment, see Sir Richard Shirreff, *War with Russia: An Urgent Warning from Senior Military Command* (New York: Quercus, 2016).

25. George Friedman, *The Next 100 Years: A Forecast for the 21st Century* (New York: Doubleday/Anchor, 2009), 102–4.

26. David A. Shlapak and Michael W. Johnson, "Reinforcing Deterrence on NATO's Eastern Flank: Wargaming the Defense of the Baltics," RAND, Santa Monica, Calif., 2016.

27. For one estimate, see Michael E. O'Hanlon, *The Future of Land Warfare* (Washington, D.C.: Brookings Institution Press, 2015), 82–90. In these calculations, using a modified Trevor Dupuy method, I assign NATO forces a 50 percent advantage over Russian personnel in quality and give NATO a further 25 percent advantage for its likely ability to choose the time and place of attack in a way that confers ambush advantages. If these assumptions are too generous to NATO, then larger forces might be needed. See also Trevor N. Dupuy, *Attrition: Forecasting Battle Casualties and Equipment Losses in Modern Warfare* (Fairfax, Va.: Hero Books, 1990); John J. Mearsheimer, Barry R. Posen, and Eliot A. Cohen, "Correspondence: Reassessing Net Assessment," *International Security* 13, no. 4 (Spring 1989): 128–79 (separate letters); and Joshua M. Epstein, "Dynamic Analysis and the Conventional Balance in Europe," *International Security* 12, no. 4 (Spring 1988): 155–58.

28. Steven Erlanger, Julie Hirschfeld Davis, and Stephen Castle, "NATO Plans a Special Force to Reassure Eastern Europe and Deter Russia," *New York Times,* September 5, 2014.

29. Brooks Tignor, "NATO Works to Flesh Out Readiness Action Plan," *Jane's Defence Weekly,* September 17, 2014, 5.

30. Michael Shurkin, "The Abilities of the British, French, and German Armies to Generate and Sustain Armored Brigades in the Baltics," RAND, Santa Monica, Calif., 2017.

31. North Atlantic Treaty Organization, "Enhanced Forward Presence (EFP)," Izmir, Turkey, 2020, https://lc.nato.int/operations/enhanced-forward-presence-efp.

32. John R. Deni, *NATO and Article V: The Transatlantic Alliance and the Twenty-First-Century Challenges of Collective Defense* (Lanham, Md.: Rowman and Littlefield, 2017), 1–3.

33. Julian E. Barnes, "NATO Fears Its Forces Not Ready to Confront Russian Threat," *Wall Street Journal,* March 28, 2018.

34. Helene Cooper and Julian E. Barnes, "U.S. Officials Scrambled Behind the Scenes to Shield NATO Deal from Trump," *New York Times,* August 9, 2018.

35. See Ambassador Alexander R. Vershbow (ret.) et al., "Permanent Deterrence:

Enhancements to the U.S. Military Presence in North Central Europe," Atlantic Council, Washington, D.C., February 2019, https://www.atlanticcouncil.org/in-depth-research -reports/report/permanent-deterrence/; and Eva Hagstrom Frisell et al., "Deterrence by Reinforcement: The Strengths and Weaknesses of NATO's Evolving Defence Strategy," FOI Report R-4843-SE, Stockholm, November 2019, https://www.foi.se/rapportsam manfattning?reportNo=FOI-R--4843--SE.

36. General Curtis M. Scaparrotti (ret.), Ambassador Colleen B. Bell (ret.), and Wayne Schroeder, "Moving Out: A Comprehensive Assessment of European Military Mobility," Atlantic Council, Washington, D.C., April 2020, https://www.atlanticcouncil. org/in-depth-research-reports/report/moving-out-a-comprehensive-assessment-of -european-military-mobility/.

37. Michael E. O'Hanlon, *The Senkaku Paradox: Risking Great Power War over Small Stakes* (Washington, D.C.: Brookings Institution Press, 2019).

38. North Atlantic Treaty Organization, "The North Atlantic Treaty," Washington, D.C., April 4, 1949, http://www.nato.int/cps/en/natolive/official_texts_17120.htm.

39. Ivo H. Daalder, "Responding to Russia's Resurgence: Not Quiet on the Eastern Front," *Foreign Affairs* 96, no. 6 (November/December 2017): 33; Robert Coalson, "Putin Pledges to Protect All Ethnic Russians Anywhere; So, Where Are They?" Radio Free Europe/Radio Liberty, April 10, 2014, https://www.rferl.org/a/russia-ethnic-russification -baltics-kazakhstan-soviet/25328281.html; David M. Herszenhorn, "Putin Warns Again of Force as Ukraine Fighting Spreads," *New York Times,* July 2, 2014; and Anna Dolgov, "Russia Sees Need to Protect Russian Speakers in NATO Baltic States," *Moscow Times,* September 16, 2014.

40. Maj. Anthony Mercado, "The Evolution of Russian Nonlinear Warfare," in Matthew R. Slater, Michael Purcell, and Andrew M. Del Gaudio, eds., *Considering Russia: Emergence of a Near Peer Competitor* (Quantico, Va.: Marine Corps University, 2017), 54–71.

41. For a similar view based on detailed assessment of the Russian military posture in the region, which could sustain a major invasion of Ukraine but seems more consistent with a limited, hybrid threat to the Baltics, see Catherine Harris and Frederick W. Kagan, "Russian Military Posture: Ground Forces Order of Battle," Institute for the Study of War, Washington, D.C., March 2018.

42. Gudrun Persson, ed., *Russian Military Capability in a Ten-Year Perspective— 2016* (Stockholm: FOI [Swedish Defense Research Agency], 2016), 92–94.

43. Tim Boersma and Michael E. O'Hanlon, "Why Europe's Energy Policy Has Been a Strategic Success Story," *Order from Chaos* (blog), May 2, 2016, https://www .brookings.edu/blog/order-from-chaos/2016/05/02/why-europes-energy-policy-has -been-a-strategic-success-story/.

44. Victoria Nuland, "Pinning Down Putin: How a Confident America Should Deal with Russia," *Foreign Affairs* (July/August 2020): 93–106.

45. Nigel Gould-Davies, "Russia, the West and Sanctions," *Survival* 62, no. 1 (February–March 2020): 7–28.

46. Kimberly Marten, "NATO Enlargement: Evaluating Its Consequences in Russia," in *International Politics* 57, no. 3 (June 2020): 401–26.

47. On the decision-making process, see Goldgeier, *Not Whether but When.*

48. Steven Pifer, *The Eagle and the Trident: U.S.-Ukraine Relations in Turbulent Times* (Washington, D.C.: Brookings Institution Press, 2017). See also Daniel Treisman, "Crimea: Anatomy of a Decision," in Daniel Treisman, ed., *The New Autocracy: Information, Politics, and Policy in Putin's Russia* (Washington, D.C.: Brookings Institution Press, 2018), 277–95.

49. M. E. Sarotte, "How to Enlarge NATO: The Debate Inside the Clinton Administration, 1993–1995," *International Security* 44, no. 1 (Summer 2019): 39.

50. See Donald Kagan, *On the Origins of War and the Preservation of Peace* (New York: Anchor, 1995), 8, referencing Thucydides, *History of the Peloponnesian War* 1.76.

51. See Gary J. Schmitt, ed., *A Hard Look at Hard Power: Assessing the Defense Capabilities of Key U.S. Allies and Security Partners* (Carlisle, Pa.: U.S. Army War College Press, 2015).

52. See North Atlantic Treaty Organization, "North Atlantic Treaty."

53. Pifer, *Eagle and Trident,* 309; see also Yevhen Mahda, *Russia's Hybrid Aggression: Lessons for the World* (Kyiv, Ukraine: Kalamar, 2018).

54. Pifer, *Eagle and Trident,* 37–76.

55. See Timothy Snyder, *The Road to Unfreedom: Russia, Europe, America* (New York: Tim Duggan Books, 2018); James Kirchick, *The End of Europe: Dictators, Demagogues, and the Coming Dark Age* (New Haven: Yale University Press, 2017), 11–39; and Chris Meserole and Alina Polyakova, "Disinformation Wars," *Foreign Policy,* May 25, 2018, https://foreignpolicy.com/2018/05/25/disinformation-wars/.

56. See Samuel Charap and Timothy J. Colton, *Everyone Loses: The Ukraine Crisis and the Ruinous Contest for Post-Soviet Eurasia* (New York: Routledge for IISS, 2017), 151–84.

57. Pifer, *Eagle and Trident,* 324–35; see also Ivo Daalder et al., "Preserving Ukraine's Independence, Resisting Russian Aggression: What the United States and NATO Must Do," Atlantic Council, Brookings Institution, and Chicago Council on Global Affairs, February 2015, https://www.brookings.edu/research/preserving-ukraines-independence -resisting-russian-aggression-what-the-united-states-and-nato-must-do.

58. Samuel Charap et al., *A Consensus Proposal for a Revised Regional Order in Post-Soviet Europe and Eurasia* (Santa Monica, Calif.: RAND, 2019).

59. Eileen Sullivan, "Trump Questions the Core of NATO: Mutual Defense, Including Montenegro," *New York Times,* July 18, 2018.

60. Alexander D. Chekov et al., "War of the Future: A View from Russia," *Survival* 61, no. 6 (December 2019–January 2020): 25–48.

61. Sen. Jack Reed, "Floor Statement on Deterring and Countering the Russian Information Warfare Playbook for 2020," October 22, 2019, https://www.reed.senate .gov/news/speeches/floor-speech_-deterring-and-countering-the-russian-information -warfare-playbook-for-2020.

62. Joseph Marks, "The Cybersecurity 202: Senate Russia Report May Inspire Last Push for Election Security Changes Before November," *Washington Post,* April 22, 2020.

63. Daniel Fried and Alina Polyakova, "Democratic Defense Against Disinforma-

tion 2.0," Atlantic Council, Washington, D.C., June 2019, https://www.atlanticcouncil
.org/in-depth-research-reports/report/democratic-defense-against-disinformation-2-0;
see also Laura Rosenberger, "Making Cyberspace Safe for Democracy," *Foreign Affairs*
99, no. 3 (May/June 2020): 146–59.

64. See, e.g., Hadley Hitson, "Just How Regulated Are Our Nation's Elections?"
Fortune, December 4, 2019, https://fortune.com/2019/12/04/election-security-regulations
-united-states.

FOUR The Pacific and China

1. Evan Osnos, *Age of Ambition: Chasing Fortune, Truth, and Faith in the New
China* (New York: Farrar, Straus and Giroux, 2014). See also Melvyn P. Leffler, "China
Isn't the Soviet Union; Confusing the Two Is Dangerous," *Atlantic*, December 2, 2019,
https://www.theatlantic.com/ideas/archive/2019/12/cold-war-china-purely-optional
/601969.

2. On Chinese military concepts, including in regard to nuclear forces, see
M. Taylor Fravel, *Active Defense: China's Military Strategy Since 1949* (Princeton, N.J.:
Princeton University Press, 2019).

3. H. R. McMaster, "How China Sees the World, and How We Should See
China," *Atlantic*, May 2020.

4. Ash Carter, *Inside the Five-Sided Box: Lessons from a Lifetime of Leadership in
the Pentagon* (New York: Dutton, 2019), 261–89.

5. See, e.g., Mitt Romney, "America Is Awakening to China; This Is a Clarion
Call to Seize the Moment," *Washington Post*, April 23, 2020.

6. In this regard, the Trump administration's National Security Strategy and National Defense Strategy have it about right, given that they prioritize both countries as a
matter of national security policy. See President Donald J. Trump, "National Security
Strategy of the United States of America," The White House, Washington, D.C., December 2017, *National Interest* (blog), https://nationalinterest.org/blog/buzz/pandemics-can
-fast-forward-rise-and-fall-great-powers-136417; and Secretary of Defense Jim Mattis,
"Summary of the 2018 National Defense Strategy of the United States of America: Sharpening the American Military's Competitive Edge," Department of Defense, Washington,
D.C., January 2018, https://dod.defense.gov/Portals/1/Documents/pubs/2018-National
-Defense-Strategy-Summary.pdf.

7. Graham Allison, *Destined for War: America, China, and Thucydides' Trap* (Boston: Houghton Mifflin Harcourt, 2017).

8. Michael J. Green, *By More Than Providence: Grand Strategy and American
Power in the Asia Pacific Since 1783* (New York: Columbia University Press, 2017).

9. Barton Gellman, *Contending with Kennan: Toward a Philosophy of American
Power* (New York: Praeger, 1984), 40.

10. See James Steinberg and Michael E. O'Hanlon, *Strategic Reassurance and Resolve: U.S.-China Relations in the 21st Century* (Princeton, N.J.: Princeton University
Press, 2014).

11. See Henry Kissinger, *On China* (New York: Penguin, 2011).

12. See Paul Kennedy, *The Rise and Fall of the Great Powers: Economic Change and Military Conflict from 1500 to 2000* (New York: Random House, 1987); and Allison, *Destined for War*.

13. For a fascinating analysis of this problem, see Jennifer Lind, *Sorry States: Apologies in International Politics* (Ithaca, N.Y.: Cornell University Press, 2008).

14. Evan S. Medeiros, "The Changing Fundamentals of U.S.-China Relations," *Washington Quarterly* 42, no. 3 (Fall 2019): 111–12; Jacob M. Schlesinger, "What's Biden's New China Policy? It Looks a Lot Like Trump's," *Wall Street Journal*, September 10, 2020.

15. For a good capturing of the evolution of this debate, see Kurt M. Campbell and Ely Ratner, "The China Reckoning," *Foreign Affairs* 97, no. 2 (March/April 2018): 60–70; and responses to Ratner and Campbell, *Foreign Affairs* 97, no. 4 (July/August 2018): 183–95. For a good review of events in the early Trump years, see National Institute for Defense Studies, *East Asian Strategic Review, 2019* (Tokyo, 2019), 52–57.

16. Mira Rapp-Hooper, "Parting the South China Sea: How to Uphold the Rule of Law," *Foreign Affairs* 95, no. 5 (September/October 2016): 76–78.

17. For a balanced take on China's rise and how the United States can find a new consensus on China policy going forward, see Ryan Hass, *Stronger: Updating American Strategy to Outpace an Ambitious and Ascendant China* (New Haven: Yale University Press, 2021).

18. See Kurt M. Campbell, *The Pivot: The Future of American Statecraft in Asia* (New York: Twelve, 2016).

19. See, e.g., Mackenzie Eaglen, "What Is the Third Offset Strategy?" *Real Clear Defense*, February 15, 2016, https://www.realcleardefense.com/articles/2016/02/16/what_is_the_third_offset_strategy_109034.html.

20. Kurt M. Campbell and Rush Doshi, "The Coronavirus Could Reshape Global Order: China Is Maneuvering for International Leadership as the United States Falters," *Foreign Affairs*, March 18, 2020, https://www.foreignaffairs.com/articles/china/2020-03-18/coronavirus-could-reshape-global-order.

21. See Alessandra Bocchi, "China's Coronavirus Diplomacy," *Wall Street Journal*, March 20, 2020; Jeremy Page, "China's Progress Against Coronavirus Used Draconian Tactics Not Deployed in the West," *Wall Street Journal*, March 24, 2020; Jeremy Page, Wenxin Fan, and Natasha Khan, "How It All Started: China's Early Coronavirus Missteps," *Wall Street Journal*, March 6, 2020; James Jay Carafano, "Great Power Competition After the Coronavirus Crisis: What Should America Do?" *National Interest*, March 24, 2020, https://nationalinterest.org/feature/great-power-competition-after-coronavirus-crisis-what-should-america-do-136967.

22. Steinberg and O'Hanlon, *Strategic Reassurance and Resolve*.

23. Frank A. Rose, "Managing China's Rise in Outer Space," Brookings Institution, Washington, D.C., April 2020, https://www.brookings.edu/wp-content/uploads/2020/04/FP_20200427_china_outer_space_rose_v3.pdf.

24. Michael E. O'Hanlon and James Steinberg, *A Glass Half Full? Rebalance, Reas-

surance, and Resolve in the U.S.-China Strategic Relationship (Washington, D.C.: Brookings Institution Press, 2017).

25. McMaster, "How China Sees the World"; "Remarks by Vice President Mike Pence at the Frederick V. Malek Memorial Lecture," The White House, Washington, D.C., October 24, 2019, https://www.whitehouse.gov/briefings-statements/remarks-vice-president-pence-frederic-v-malek-memorial-lecture/.

26. See Clifford Gaddy, *The Price of the Past: Russia's Struggle with the Legacy of a Militarized Economy* (Washington, D.C.: Brookings Institution Press, 2001); and Directorate of Intelligence, "A Comparison of Soviet and U.S. Gross National Products, 1960–1983," Central Intelligence Agency, Washington, D.C., 1984, https://www.cia.gov/library/readingroom/docs/DOC_0000498181.pdf. The Soviet GDP was perhaps half of America's in the latter Cold War decades, plus or minus.

27. On the nature of net assessment, see James G. Roche and Thomas G. Mahnken, "What Is Net Assessment?" in Thomas G. Mahnken, ed., *Net Assessment and Military Strategy: Retrospective and Prospective Essays* (Amherst, N.Y.: Cambria Press, 2020), 11–26.

28. See Office of the Under Secretary of Defense (Comptroller), "Defense Budget Overview: United States Department of Defense Fiscal Year 2021 Budget Request," Department of Defense, Washington, D.C., February 2020, 1–4, https://comptroller.defense.gov/Portals/45/Documents/defbudget/fy2021/fy2021_Budget_Request_Overview_Book.pdf; Department of Defense, "Annual Report to Congress: Military and Security Developments Involving the People's Republic of China, 2019," Washington, D.C., May 2019, 95, https://media.defense.gov/2019/May/02/2002127082/-1/-1/1/2019_CHINA_MILITARY_POWER_REPORT.pdf; and Michael E. O'Hanlon and James Steinberg, *A Glass Half Full? Rebalance, Reassurance, and Resolve in the U.S.-China Strategic Relationship* (Brookings Institution, Washington, D.C., 2017), 25–32.

29. Steinberg and O'Hanlon, *Strategic Reassurance and Resolve,* 104–5.

30. Dennis J. Blasko, *The Chinese Army Today: Tradition and Transformation for the 21st Century,* 2nd ed. (New York: Routledge, 2012), 116–38.

31. See Department of Defense, "Annual Report to Congress," 31–67, 116–17; Eric Heginbotham et al., *The U.S.-China Military Scorecard: Forces, Geography, and the Evolving Balance of Power, 1996–2017* (Santa Monica, Calif.: RAND, 2015); and O'Hanlon and Steinberg, *A Glass Half Full?* 25–42.

32. Gregory C. Allen, "Understanding China's AI Strategy: Clues to Chinese Strategic Thinking on Artificial Intelligence and National Security," Center for a New American Security, Washington, D.C., February 6, 2019.

33. "US Aerospace and Defense Export Competitiveness Study," Deloitte, April 2016, 1–10, https://www2.deloitte.com/content/dam/Deloitte/us/Documents/manufacturing/us-manufacturing-ad-export-competitiveness.pdf.

34. See Shipbuilders' Association of Japan, "Shipbuilding Statistics," Tokyo, 2017.

35. Organisation for Economic Co-Operation and Development, *Main Science and Technology Indicators, Volume 2017 Issue 2* (Paris: OECD Publishing, 2018).

36. Bruce Jones, *Still Ours to Lead: America, Rising Powers, and the Tension between Rivalry and Restraint* (Washington, D.C.: Brookings Institution Press, 2014), 11–36; Robert Kagan, *The World America Made* (New York: Alfred A. Knopf, 2012); Times Higher Education, "World University Rankings 2018," https://www.timeshighereducation.com/world-university-rankings/2018/world-ranking.

37. Klaus Schwab, ed., *The Global Competitiveness Report, 2019* (Davos: World Economic Forum, 2019), xiii.

38. Peter Grier, "Rare-Earth Uncertainty," *Air Force Magazine,* February 2018, 52–55.

39. Spencer Jakab, "Will Tesla Die for Lack of Cobalt?" *Wall Street Journal,* November 29, 2017.

40. U.S. Geological Survey, "Risk and Reliance: The U.S. Economy and Mineral Resources," Reston, Va., April 2017.

41. Timothy Puko, "U.S. Is Vulnerable to China's Dominance in Rare Earths, Report Finds," *Wall Street Journal,* June 29, 2020.

42. U.S. Energy Information Administration, "U.S. Energy Facts Explained," May 2017, https://www.eia.gov/energyexplained/us-energy-facts/.

43. U.S. Energy Information Administration, "International," May 2017, https://www.eia.gov/international/overview/world.

44. Benoit Faucon and Timothy Puko, "U.S. and Allies Consider Possible Oil-Reserve Release," *Wall Street Journal,* July 13, 2018.

45. U.S. Energy Information Administration, "Frequently Asked Questions," April 2018, https://www.eia.gov/tools/faqs/faq.php?id=74&t=11.

46. U.S. Energy Information Administration, "Petroleum and Other Liquids: U.S. Imports by Country of Origin," April 2018, https://www.eia.gov/petroleum/data.php.

47. Masayuki Masuda, Hiroshi Yamazoe, and Shigeki Akimoto, "NIDS China Security Report 2020: China Goes to Eurasia," National Institute for Defense Studies, Tokyo, 2019, 49–52.

48. Organization of the Petroleum Exporting Countries, "OPEC Share of World Crude Oil Reserves, 2016," Vienna, 2018; Russell Gold, "Global Investment in Wind and Solar Energy Is Outshining Fossil Fuels," *Wall Street Journal,* June 11, 2018.

49. "Oil and Petroleum Products: A Statistical Overview," *Eurostat,* June 2020, https://ec.europa.eu/eurostat/statistics-explained/index.php?title=Oil_and_petroleum_products_-_a_statistical_overview "Energy Production and Imports," *Eurostat,* June 2020, https://ec.europa.eu/eurostat/statistics-explained/index.php?title=Energy_production_and_imports; John Barrasso, "Europe's Addiction to Russian Energy Is Dangerous," *Washington Post,* July 27, 2018.

50. International Energy Agency, *Key World Energy Statistics 2017* (2017), 15.

51. Japanese Ministry of Economy, Trade, and Industry, "Japan's Energy: 20 Questions," Tokyo, December 2016.

52. Jacky Wong, "When the Chips Are Down, China's Tech Giants Will Step Up," *Wall Street Journal,* May 28, 2018.

53. Morrison, "China-U.S. Trade Issues," 9.

54. Chuin-Wei Yap, "Taiwan's Technology Secrets Come Under Assault from China," *Wall Street Journal,* July 1, 2018.

55. Michaela D. Platzer and John F. Sargent Jr., "U.S. Semiconductor Manufacturing: Industry Trends, Global Competition, Federal Policy," Congressional Research Service, CRS Report R44544, June 27, 2016, 1–14; Raman Chitkara and Jianbin Gao, "China's Impact on the Semiconductor Industry: 2016 Update," PricewaterhouseCoopers, 2017.

56. Jeanne Whalen, "Lawmakers Propose Billions to Boost U.S. Semiconductor Manufacturing and Research," *Washington Post,* June 10, 2020.

57. Department of the Treasury, "Major Foreign Holders of Treasury Securities," Washington, D.C., https://ticdata.treasury.gov/Publish/mfh.txt; Morrison, "China-U.S. Trade Issues," 19; Thomas J. Christensen, *The China Challenge: Shaping the Choices of a Rising Power* (New York: W. W. Norton, 2015), 56–62. For general principles of how the Federal Reserve can respond to a crisis, see Ben Bernanke, *The Courage to Act: A Memoir of a Crisis and Its Aftermath* (New York: W. W. Norton, 2015).

58. See Michael Brown, Eric Chewning, and Pavneet Singh, "Preparing the United States for the Superpower Marathon with China," Brookings Institution, Washington, D.C., April 2020, https://www.brookings.edu/wp-content/uploads/2020/04/FP_20200427_superpower_marathon_brown_chewning_singh.pdf; and Elsa B. Kania, "'AI Weapons' in China's Military Innovation," Brookings Institution, Washington, D.C., April 2020, https://www.brookings.edu/wp-content/uploads/2020/04/FP_20200427_ai _weapons_kania_v2.pdf.

59. Jeanne Whalen and John Hudson, "Too Big to Sanction? U.S. Struggles with Punishing Large Russian Businesses," *Washington Post,* August 26, 2018; Chuin-Wei Yap, "U.S. Reliance on Obscure Imports from China Points to Strategic Vulnerability," *Wall Street Journal,* September 24, 2018.

60. Ely Ratner, "Blunting China's Economic Coercion," Statement before the Senate Foreign Relations Committee Subcommittee on East Asia, the Pacific, and International Cybersecurity Policy, July 24, 2018, 8, https://www.foreign.senate.gov/imo/media /doc/072418_Ratner_Testimony.pdf.

61. See David Dollar, "The Future of U.S.-China Economic Ties," Brookings Institution, Washington, D.C., October 2016, https://www.brookings.edu/research/the -future-of-u-s-china-trade-ties.

62. Ian Talley, "U.S. to Block Potential Russian Move into American Energy," *Wall Street Journal,* August 31, 2017.

63. Ned Mamula and Catrina Rorke, "America's Untapped Riches," *U.S. News and World Report,* July 11, 2017; U.S. Geological Survey, *Mineral Commodity Summaries 2017* (Reston, Va.: U.S. Geological Survey, 2017), 7; Murray Hitzman, "Foreign Minerals Dependency," Statement before the Energy and Mineral Resources Subcommittee, House Committee on Natural Resources, December 12, 2017, https://www.doi.gov/ocl/foreign -minerals-dependency; Kent Hughes Butts, Brent Bankus, and Adam Norris, "Strategic Minerals: Is China's Consumption a Threat to United States Security?" (Carlisle, Pa.: U.S. Army War College, July 2011).

64. U.S. Geological Survey, *Mineral Commodity Summaries 2017,* 5.

65. U.S. Geological Survey, 135.

66. Andrew Imbrie and Ryan Fedasiuk, "Untangling the Web: Why the U.S. Needs Allies to Defend Against Chinese Technology Transfer," Brookings Institution, Washington, D.C., April 2020, https://www.brookings.edu/wp-content/uploads/2020/04/FP_20200427_chinese_technology_transfer_imbrie_fedasiuk.pdf.

67. See Michael Green et al., "Counter-Coercion Series: East China Sea Air Defense Identification Zone," Center for Strategic and International Studies, Washington, D.C., 2017, https://amti.csis.org/counter-co-east-china-sea-adiz.

68. Jon Harper, "Top Marine in Japan: If Tasked, We Could Retake the Senkakus from China," *Stars and Stripes,* April 11, 2014; Jeffrey A. Bader, *Obama and China's Rise: An Insider's Account of America's Strategy* (Washington, D.C.: Brookings Institution Press, 2013), 107–8.

69. "Treaty of Mutual Cooperation and Security between Japan and the United States of America," January 19, 1960, Ministry of Foreign Affairs of Japan, http://www.mofa.go.jp/region/n-america/us/q&a/ref/1.html.

70. Ankit Panda, "Mattis: Senkakus Covered Under U.S.-Japan Security Treaty," *Diplomat,* February 6, 2017, https://thediplomat.com/2017/02/mattis-senkakus-covered-under-us-japan-security-treaty/. For background, see Richard C. Bush, *The Perils of Proximity: China-Japan Security Relations* (Washington, D.C.: Brookings Institution Press, 2010), 259–60.

71. Christian Brose, *The Kill Chain: Defending America in the Future of High-Tech Warfare* (New York: Hachette, 2020), x–xii.

72. For example, see Tanya Ogilvie-White, *On Nuclear Deterrence: The Correspondence of Sir Michael Quinlan* (New York: Routledge, 2011), 63–81; on China, see Fiona S. Cunningham and M. Taylor Fravel, "Dangerous Confidence: Chinese Views on Nuclear Escalation," *International Security* 44, no. 2 (Fall 2019): 61–109.

73. Michael R. Gordon, "Possible Chinese Nuclear Testing Stirs U.S. Concern," *Wall Street Journal,* April 15, 2002.

74. On this question, in addition to classics like Bernard Brodie's *Strategy in the Missile Age* (Princeton, N.J.: Princeton University Press, 1959); and Thomas Schelling's *Arms and Influence* (New Haven: Yale University Press, 1966) and *Strategy of Conflict* (Cambridge, Mass.: Harvard University Press, 1960); see Robert Jervis, *The Illogic of American Nuclear Strategy* (Ithaca, N.Y.: Cornell University Press, 1984); Richard K. Betts, *Nuclear Blackmail and Nuclear Balance* (Washington, D.C.: Brookings Institution Press, 1987), 213–14; Matthew Kroenig, "Nuclear Superiority and the Balance of Resolve: Explaining Nuclear Crisis Outcomes," *International Organizations* 67, no. 1 (2013): 141–71; Francis J. Gavin, *Nuclear Weapons and American Grand Strategy* (Washington, D.C.: Brookings Institution Press, 2020), 52–58; and Daniel Kahneman, *Thinking, Fast and Slow* (New York: Farrar, Straus and Giroux, 2011).

75. Regine Cabato and Shibani Mahtani, "Pompeo Promises Intervention if Philippines Is Attacked in South China Sea Amid Rising Chinese Militarization," *Washington Post,* February 28, 2019.

76. See Bruce D. Jones, *To Rule the Waves: How Control of the World's Oceans Determines the Fate of the Superpowers* (New York: Scribner, 2021).

77. Michael O'Hanlon and Gregory Poling, "Rocks, Reefs, and Nuclear War," Asia Maritime Transparency Initiative, Center for Strategic and International Studies, Washington, D.C., January 14, 2020, https://amti.csis.org/rocks-reefs-and-nuclear-war/.

78. Beckley, *Unrivaled*, 84.

79. Bernard D. Cole, "Right-Sizing the Navy: How Much Naval Force Will Beijing Deploy?" in Roy Kamphausen and Andrew Scobell, eds., *Right-Sizing the People's Liberation Army: Exploring the Contours of China's Military* (Carlisle, Pa.: Strategic Studies Institute, Army War College, 2007), 541–42.

80. Mark A. Stokes, "Employment of National-Level PLA Assets in a Contingency: A Cross-Strait Conflict as Case Study," in Andrew Scobell et al., *The People's Liberation Army and Contingency Planning in China* (Washington, D.C.: National Defense University Press, 2015), 135–46.

81. For a discussion of Chinese writings that seem to take a similar tack, see Roger Cliff et al., *Entering the Dragon's Lair: Chinese Antiaccess Strategies and Their Implications for the United States* (Santa Monica, Calif.: RAND, 2007), 66–73. Among other naval force modernizations, China now has about thirty-five or more modern attack submarines in its fleet, and it is also expected to acquire ocean reconnaissance satellites (early versions of which it already reportedly possesses) as well as communications systems capable of reaching deployed forces in the field in the next five to ten years.

82. Eric Heginbotham and others, *The U.S.-China Military Scorecard: Forces, Geography, and the Evolving Balance of Power, 1996–2017* (Santa Monica, Calif.: RAND, 2015), 185.

83. See, e.g., David A. Shlapak et al., *A Question of Balance: Political Context and Military Aspects of the China-Taiwan Dispute* (Santa Monica, Calif.: RAND, 2009), 31–90.

84. Heginbotham et al., *U.S.-China Military Scorecard*, 248–55; Todd Harrison, Kaitlyn Johnson, and Thomas G. Roberts, "Space Threat Assessment 2018," Center for Strategic and International Studies, Washington, D.C., April 2018, 6–11, https://www.csis.org/analysis/space-threat-assessment-2018.

85. Christensen, *China Challenge*, 85–104.

86. Heginbotham et al., *U.S.-China Military Scorecard*, 75–84, 149–50; Roger Cliff et al., *Shaking the Heavens and Splitting the Earth: Chinese Air Force Employment Concepts in the 21st Century* (Santa Monica, Calif.: RAND, 2011), xxiii, 209–15.

87. See Congressional Budget Office, *U.S. Naval Forces: The Sea Control Mission* (Washington, D.C.: CBO, 1978).

88. Capt. Wayne P. Hughes Jr. (U.S. Navy, ret.), *Fleet Tactics and Coastal Combat*, 2nd ed. (Annapolis, Md.: Naval Institute Press, 2000), 172–73; Heginbotham et al., *U.S.-China Military Scorecard*, 184–99. See also Owen R. Cote Jr., "Assessing the Undersea Balance between the U.S. and China," SSP Working Paper WP11–1, Security Studies Program, MIT, Cambridge, Mass., February 2011.

89. Timothy W. Crawford, *Pivotal Deterrence: Third-Party Statecraft and the Pursuit of Peace* (Ithaca, N.Y.: Cornell University Press, 2003), 1–24, 187–201.

90. Chen Aizhu and Florence Tan, "BP Holds Millions of Barrels of Oil off China as Demand Falters," Reuters, June 29, 2018, https://www.reuters.com/article/us-china -bp-oil-independents/bp-holds-millions-of-barrels-of-oil-off-china-as-demand-falters -idUSKBN1JP1DN.

91. "Strait of Hormuz: Frequently Asked Questions," Robert Strauss Center for International Security and Law, University of Texas at Austin, https://www.strausscenter .org/strait-of-hormuz-faq/.

92. Dan Blumenthal, "China's Worldwide Military Expansion," Statement before the House Permanent Select Committee on Intelligence, U.S. Congress, Washington, D.C., May 17, 2018, https://docs.house.gov/meetings/IG/IG00/20180517/108298/HHRG -115-IG00-Wstate-BlumenthalD-20180517.pdf; Joel Wuthnow, "The PLA Beyond Asia: China's Growing Military Presence in the Red Sea Region," *Strategic Forum No. 303,* Institute for National Strategic Studies, National Defense University, Washington, D.C., January 2020.

93. David H. Petraeus and Philip Caruso, "Coherence and Comprehensiveness: An American Foreign Policy Imperative," Belfer Center for Science and International Affairs, Harvard Kennedy School, Cambridge, Mass., March 2019, https://www.belfer center.org/publication/coherence-and-comprehensiveness-american-foreign-policy -imperative.

94. On unmanned ships, see Bryan Clark and Bryan McGrath, "A Guide to the Fleet the United States Needs," *War on the Rocks,* February 10, 2017, https://warontherocks .com/2017/02/a-guide-to-the-fleet-the-united-states-needs/.

95. See Tanvi Madan, *Fateful Triangle: How China Shaped U.S.-India Relations During the Cold War* (Washington, D.C.: Brookings Institution Press, 2020); and Bruce Riedel, *JFK's Forgotten Crisis: Tibet, the CIA, and the Sino-Indian War* (Washington, D.C.: Brookings Institution Press, 2015).

96. See Strobe Talbott, *Engaging India: Diplomacy, Democracy, and the Bomb* (Washington, D.C.: Brookings Institution Press, 2004).

97. See Stephen P. Cohen and Sunil Dasgupta, *Arming Without Aiming: India's Military Modernization* (Washington, D.C.: Brookings Institution Press, 2012); and Ivo H. Daalder and James M. Lindsay, *The Empty Throne: America's Abdication of Global Leadership* (New York: Public Affairs, 2018), 176.

98. See Alyssa Ayres, *Our Time Has Come: How India Is Making Its Place in the World* (Oxford: Oxford University Press, 2018), 207–46; and William J. Burns, *The Back Channel: A Memoir of American Diplomacy and the Case for Its Revival* (New York: Random House, 2019), 256–65.

99. Krishna Pokharel and Bill Spindle, "After China Border Fight, India Likely Weighs Closer U.S. Military Ties," *Wall Street Journal,* June 21, 2020.

FIVE Korea

1. See Barbara Demick, *Nothing to Envy: Ordinary Lives in North Korea* (New York: Spiegel and Grau, 2010).

2. Eleanor Albert, "North Korea's Military Capabilities," Council on Foreign Relations, New York, December 2019, https://www.cfr.org/backgrounder/north-koreas -military-capabilities.

3. "North Korea's Missile and Nuclear Programme," *BBC,* October 9, 2019, https://www.bbc.com/news/world-asia-41174689.

4. The missile tests demonstrated an ICBM capability to reach North America, based on analysis by David Wright of the Union of Concerned Scientists. See Mark Landler, Choe Sang-Hun, and Helene Cooper, "North Korea Fires a Ballistic Missile, in a Further Challenge to Trump," *New York Times,* November 28, 2017; and David E. Sanger and Choe Sang-Hun, "North Korea Links 2nd 'Crucial' Test to Nuclear Weapons Program," *New York Times,* December 14, 2019.

5. Jung H. Pak, *Becoming Kim Jong Un: A Former CIA Officer's Insights into North Korea's Enigmatic Young Dictator* (New York: Ballantine, 2020), 104 (on byungjin).

6. Jonathan D. Pollack, *No Exit: North Korea, Nuclear Weapons, and International Security* (New York: Routledge for IISS, 2011); Victor Cha, *The Impossible State: North Korea, Past and Future* (New York: HarperCollins, 2012).

7. Evans J. R. Revere, "Kim's 'New Path' and the Failure of Trump's North Korea Policy," *East Asia Forum,* Canberra, Australia, January 26, 2020, https://www.eastasia forum.org/2020/01/26/kims-new-path-and-the-failure-of-trumps-north-korea-policy; National Institute for Defense Studies, *East Asian Strategic Review, 2019* (Tokyo, 2019), 2–3.

8. Jung H. Pak, "The Education of Kim Jong Un," Brookings Institution, Washington, D.C., February 2018, https://www.brookings.edu/essay/the-education-of-kim -jong-un.

9. United Nations Security Council Subsidiary Organs, "Resolutions Pursuant to UNSCR 1718," New York, December 2017, https://www.un.org/sc/suborg/en/sanctions /1718/resolutions; Dianne Rennack, "North Korea: Legislative Basis for U.S. Economic Sanctions," Congressional Research Service, CRS Report R41438, January 14, 2016.

10. Benjamin Katzeff Silberstein, "North Korea's Economic Contraction in 2018: What the Numbers Tell Us," *38 North,* Washington, D.C., July 26, 2019, https://www .nkeconwatch.com/category/organizations/bank-of-korea.

11. Ryan Kilpatrick, "The Evacuation of Americans from South Korea Is Going to Be Rehearsed in June," *Time,* April 24, 2017.

12. David Brunnstrom, "North Korea May Have Made More Nuclear Bombs, but Threat Reduced: Study," *Reuters,* February 12, 2019, https://www.reuters.com/article/us -northkorea-usa-nuclear-study/north-korea-may-have-made-more-nuclear-bombs-but -threat-reduced-study-idUSKCN1Q10EL; Siegfried S. Hecker, Robert Carlin, and Elliot Serbin, "The More We Wait, the Worse It Will Get," *38 North,* Washington, D.C., September 4, 2019, https://www.38north.org/2019/09/sheckerrcarlineserbin090419.

13. Kim Min-Seok, "The State of the North Korean Military," in Chung Min Lee and Kathryn Botto, eds., *Korea Net Assessment: Politicized Security and Unchanging Strategic Realities* (Washington, D.C.: Carnegie Endowment for International Peace, 2020), 19–30.

14. See Don Oberdorfer and Robert Carlin, *The Two Koreas: A Contemporary History,* rev. ed. (New York: Basic Books, 2013).

15. For other recent writings that do not envision North Korean near-term denuclearization, see Jina Kim and John K. Warden, "Limiting North Korea's Coercive Nuclear Leverage," *Survival* 62, no. 1 (February/March 2020): 31–38; Adam Mount and Mira Rapp-Hooper, "Nuclear Stability on the Korean Peninsula," *Survival* 62, no. 1 (February/ March 2020): 39–46; Vipin Narang and Ankit Panda, "North Korea: Risks of Escalation," *Survival* 62, no. 1 (February/March 2020): 47–54; and Edward Ifft, "Lessons for Negotiating with North Korea," *Survival* 62, no. 1 (February/March 2020): 89–106.

16. Pak, *Becoming Kim Jong Un.*

17. On the basic logic of this, which builds in part on the Vietnam experience in modern times, see John Delury, "Trump and North Korea: Reviving the Art of the Deal," *Foreign Affairs* 96, no. 2 (March/April 2017): 2–7; and Michael E. O'Hanlon and Mike M. Mochizuki, *Crisis on the Korean Peninsula: How to Deal with a Nuclear North Korea* (New York: McGraw-Hill, 2003).

18. Ashton B. Carter and William J. Perry, "If Necessary, Strike and Destroy: North Korea Cannot Be Allowed to Test this Missile," *Washington Post,* June 22, 2006.

19. Tom Karako, Ian Williams, and Wes Rumbaugh, "Missile Defense 2020: Next Steps for Defending the Homeland," Center for Strategic and International Studies, Washington, D.C., April 2017, 65–75, https://www.csis.org/analysis/missile-defense-2020.

20. Joby Warrick, "North Korea Never Halted Efforts to Build Powerful New Weapons, Experts Say," *Washington Post,* December 24, 2019.

21. On this, see Bruce E. Bechtol Jr., *North Korean Military Proliferation in the Middle East and Africa: Enabling Violence and Instability* (Lexington: University Press of Kentucky, 2018).

22. Choe Sang-Hun, "South Korea Plans 'Decapitation Unit' to Try to Scare North's Leaders," *New York Times,* September 12, 2017.

23. Elizabeth N. Saunders, "The Domestic Politics of Nuclear Choices—A Review Essay," *International Security* 44, no. 2 (Fall 2019): 180–82; and Vipin Narang and Ankit Panda, "Command and Control in North Korea: What a Nuclear Launch Might Look Like," *War on the Rocks,* September 15, 2017, https://warontherocks.com/2017/09/command-and-control-in-north-korea-what-a-nuclear-launch-might-look-like.

24. For a similar view, see James Dobbins, "War with China," *Survival* 54, no. 4 (August–September 2012): 9.

25. Larry M. Wortzel, "PLA 'Joint' Operational Contingencies in South Asia, Central Asia, and Korea," in Roy Kamphausen, David Lai, and Andrew Scobell, eds., *Beyond the Strait: PLA Missions Other Than Taiwan* (Carlisle, Pa.: Strategic Studies Institute, U.S. Army War College, 2008), 360.

26. See Zbigniew Brzezinski, *Strategic Vision: America and the Crisis of Global Power* (New York: Perseus, 2012), 85; and Robert Kagan, *The World America Made* (New York: Alfred A. Knopf, 2012), 126.

27. See Henry Kissinger, *On China* (New York: Penguin, 2011), 80–82; and Aaron L. Friedberg, *A Contest for Supremacy: China, America, and the Struggle for Mastery in Asia* (New York: W. W. Norton, 2011), 176.

28. Yong-Sup Han, "The ROK-US Cooperation for Dealing with Political Crises in North Korea," *International Journal of Korean Studies* 16, no. 1 (Spring/Summer 2012): 70–73.

29. Comments by Professor Andrew Erickson of the Naval War College, Henry L. Stimson Center, Washington, D.C., July 30, 2012, used with Erickson's permission.

30. Geoffrey Blainey, *The Causes of War* (New York: Free Press, 1973), 245–49.

31. Gen. David H. Petraeus and Lt. Gen. James F. Amos, *The U.S. Army/Marine Corps Counterinsurgency Field Manual* (Chicago: University of Chicago Press, 2007), 23; James Dobbins et al., *America's Role in Nation-Building: From Germany to Iraq* (Santa Monica, Calif.: RAND, 2003), 150–51.

32. Jee Abbey Lee, "North Korea's 'Apology' over Land Mine Attack Criticized," *VoA News,* August 26, 2015, https://www.voanews.com/east-asia/north-koreas-apology -over-land-mine-attack-criticized.

33. The higher number would come from assuming that, per soldier and airman, the roughly thirty thousand U.S. forces stationed in Korea are somewhat more expensive than the average GI—and also that their costs should be attributed primarily to the Korea mission since they are not easily rotated from that location for other purposes, given the importance of sustaining a strong deterrent in place. To the extent that much of the U.S. military force structure *not* routinely stationed or deployed in Korea is considered a cost of the alliance, the price tag could go much higher, of course—into the many tens of billions. But that argument has receded somewhat as the two-regional war construct for sizing U.S. combat forces has receded in importance in American defense planning. See Michael E. O'Hanlon, *The Science of War: Defense Budgeting, Military Technology, Logistics, and Combat Outcomes* (Princeton, N.J.: Princeton University Press, 2009), 18–52.

34. David Maxwell, "U.S.-ROK Relations: An Ironclad Alliance or a Transactional House of Cards?" *National Bureau of Asian Research,* Seattle, Wash., November 15, 2019, https://www.nbr.org/publication/u-s-rok-relations-an-ironclad-alliance-or-a-transactional -house-of-cards.

35. For a similar view, see Paul B. Stares, *Preventive Engagement: How America Can Avoid War, Stay Strong, and Keep the Peace* (New York: Columbia University Press, 2018), 186.

36. See, e.g., Robert Einhorn and Michael E. O'Hanlon, "Walking Back from the Brink with North Korea," *Order from Chaos* (blog), September 27, 2017, https://www .brookings.edu/blog/order-from-chaos/2017/09/27/walking-back-from-the-brink-with -north-korea; for a related Chinese view, see Sun Xiaokun, "A Chinese Perspective on U.S. Alliances," *Survival* 61, no. 6 (December 2019–January 2020): 75–76.

37. Jung H. Pak, *Becoming Kim Jong Un: A Former CIA Officer's Insights into North Korea's Enigmatic Young Dictator* (New York: Ballantine, 2020); Pollack, *No Exit;* Victor Cha, *The Impossible State: North Korea, Past and Future* (New York: HarperCollins, 2012).

38. See Ryan Hass and Michael O'Hanlon, "On North Korea, Don't Get Distracted by the Hydrogen Bomb Test, We Can Still Negotiate," *USA Today,* September 4, 2017.

39. Scott Snyder, "Can South Korea Save Itself?: Using an Olympic Peace to Avert

Nuclear Confrontation," *Foreign Affairs,* February 23, 2018, https://www.foreignaffairs
.com/articles/north-korea/2018-02-23/can-south-korea-save-itself.

40. See Kurt M. Campbell, *The Pivot: The Future of American Statecraft in Asia*
(New York: Twelve, 2016); and Michael J. Green, *By More Than Providence: Grand Strat-
egy and American Power in the Asia Pacific Since 1783* (New York: Columbia University
Press, 2017), 518–40.

41. Scott Snyder, "American Attitudes Toward Korea: Growing Support for a Solid
Relationship," Chicago Council on Global Affairs, October 2014, https://www.the
chicagocouncil.org/sites/default/files/USSouthKorea_Snyder.pdf.

42. For an elegant articulation of these views, see comments of Michael J. Green,
"Reimagining the U.S.-South Korea Alliance," Brookings Institution, Washington, D.C.,
August 22, 2018, https://www.brookings.edu/events/reimagining-the-u-s-south-korea
-alliance.

43. Andrew Jeong, "Defense Scale-Down on Korean DMZ Raises Security Risks,
U.S. General Says," *Wall Street Journal,* August 22, 2018.

44. International Institute for Strategic Studies, *The Military Balance, 2017* (New
York: Routledge for IISS, 2017), 309; Ian Livingston and Michael O'Hanlon, "The Afghanistan Index," Washington, D.C., Brookings Institution, January 30, 2012, https://
www.brookings.edu/wp-content/uploads/2016/07/index20120130.pdf; Oberdorfer, *Two
Koreas,* 64.

45. Michael J. Green, "Constructing a Successful China Strategy," Brookings Institution, Washington, D.C., 2008, available at https://www.brookings.edu/wp-content
/uploads/2016/07/PB_China_Green-1.pdf.

46. Pew Research Center, "South Korea Opinion of China," Washington, D.C.,
2018, http://www.pewglobal.org/database/indicator/24/country/116.

47. Aaron L. Friedberg, *A Contest for Supremacy: China, America, and the Struggle for Mastery in Asia* (New York: W. W. Norton, 2011), 175–76; Henry Kissinger, *On
China* (New York: Penguin, 2011), 80–82.

48. Briefing to author, "8th Army Command Brief," Camp Humphries, Republic
of Korea, May 1, 2018; International Institute for Strategic Studies, *The Military Balance,
2017* (New York: Routledge for IISS, 2017), 59.

49. Oberdorfer, *Two Koreas,* 86, 311.

50. See James Steinberg and Michael O'Hanlon, *Strategic Reassurance and Resolve:
U.S.-China Relations in the 21st Century* (Princeton, N.J.: Princeton University Press,
2014), 124–30; Scott Snyder, "Expanding the U.S.-South Korea Alliance," in Scott Snyder,
ed., *The U.S.-South Korea Alliance: Meeting New Security Challenges* (Boulder, Colo.:
Lynne Rienner, 2012), 1–20; and Michael O'Hanlon and Mike Mochizuki, *Crisis on the
Korean Peninsula* (New York: McGraw-Hill, 2003), 145–65.

SIX   The Middle East and Central Command Theater

1. Mara Karlin and Tamara Cofman Wittes, "America's Middle East Purgatory:
The Case for Doing Less," *Foreign Affairs* 8, no. 1 (January/February 2019): 88–100; Mar-

tin Indyk, "The Middle East Isn't Worth It Anymore," *Wall Street Journal,* January 17, 2002.

2. Such a policy was effectively where the nation moved in the second Obama term. See "A Conversation with Martin Dempsey," *Foreign Affairs* 95, no. 5 (September/October 2016): 5–6.

3. Ben Hubbard, "Little Outrage in Arab World over Netanyahu's Vow to Annex West Bank," *New York Times,* September 10, 2019.

4. Khaled Elgindy, *Blind Spot: America and the Palestinians, from Balfour to Trump* (Washington, D.C.: Brookings Institution Press, 2019); Shibley Telhami, *The World Through Arab Eyes: Arab Public Opinion and the Reshaping of the Middle East* (New York: Basic Books, 2013); Martin Indyk, *Innocent Abroad: An Intimate Account of American Peace Diplomacy in the Middle East* (New York: Simon and Schuster, 2009).

5. Daniel Yergin, *The Quest: Energy, Security, and the Remaking of the Modern World* (New York: Penguin, 2011), 284–341.

6. The six, working from west to east, are in Libya, Israel, Syria, Iraq, Iran, and Pakistan. Even more countries in the region have at least considered pursuing the bomb.

7. On this, see Omer Taspinar, *What the West Is Getting Wrong About the Middle East: Why Islam Is Not the Problem* (New York: I. B. Tauris, 2020), 218–23.

8. See Kenneth M. Pollack, *Armies of Sand: The Past, Present, and Future of Arab Military Effectiveness* (Oxford: Oxford University Press, 2019); and Caitlin Talmadge, *The Dictator's Army: Battlefield Effectiveness in Authoritarian Regimes* (Ithaca, N.Y.: Cornell University Press, 2015).

9. See Paul R. Pillar, *Terrorism and U.S. Foreign Policy* (Washington, D.C.: Brookings Institution Press, 2001). See also Marc Sageman, *Understanding Terror Networks* (Philadelphia: University of Pennsylvania Press, 2004); Daniel Byman, *Road Warriors: Foreign Fighters in the Armies of Jihad* (Oxford: Oxford University Press, 2019); and Steve Coll, *Ghost Wars: The Secret History of the CIA, Afghanistan, and Bin Laden, from the Soviet Invasion to September 10, 2001* (New York: Penguin, 2004), among others in the rich literature on what "causes" terrorism. For a very good if somewhat dated case study on the difficult path to reform in the broader Middle East, see William B. Quandt, *Between Ballots and Bullets: Algeria's Transition from Authoritarianism* (Washington, D.C.: Brookings Institution Press, 1998).

10. Bruce Riedel, *Kings and Presidents: Saudi Arabia and the United States Since FDR* (Washington, D.C.: Brookings Institution Press, 2018); see also Rachel Bronson, *Thicker Than Oil: America's Uneasy Relationship with Saudi Arabia* (Oxford: Oxford University Press, 2006).

11. See International Institute for Strategic Studies, *The Military Balance, 2019* (New York: Routledge for IISS, 2019), 59–61.

12. For one important aspect of this, see Christopher M. Schroeder, *Startup Rising: The Entrepreneurial Revolution Remaking the Middle East* (New York: Palgrave Macmillan, 2013).

13. See, e.g., Katherine Zimmerman, "Congratulations, Baghdadi Is Dead; But We're No Closer to Victory in the 'Forever War,'" Critical Threats Project, American

Enterprise Institute, Washington, D.C., October 29, 2019, https://www.aei.org/foreign-and-defense-policy/congratulations-baghdadi-is-dead-but-were-no-closer-to-victory-in-the-forever-war/; Kenneth M. Pollack, *A Path Out of the Desert: A Grand Strategy for America in the Middle East* (New York: Random House, 2009); and Tamara Wittes, *Freedom's Unsteady March: America's Role in Building Arab Democracy* (Washington, D.C.: Brookings Institution Press, 2008).

14. See Thomas Barfield, *Afghanistan: A Cultural and Political History* (Princeton, N.J.: Princeton University Press, 2010); Seth G. Jones, *In the Graveyard of Empires: America's War in Afghanistan* (New York: W. W. Norton, 2009); and Ronald E. Neumann, *The Other War: Winning and Losing in Afghanistan* (Dulles, Va.: Potomac Books, 2009).

15. See Vanda Felbab-Brown, *Aspiration and Ambivalence: Strategies and Realities of Counterinsurgency and State-Building in Afghanistan* (Washington, D.C.: Brookings Institution Press, 2012).

16. Rod Nordland, "Afghan Government Control over Country Falters, U.S. Report Says," *New York Times,* January 31, 2019.

17. John R. Allen, Saad Mohseni, and Michael E. O'Hanlon, "Good Deals—and Bad Ones—with the Taliban," *Order from Chaos* (blog), February 25, 2020, https://www.brookings.edu/blog/order-from-chaos/2020/02/25/good-deals-and-bad-ones-with-the-taliban; David H. Petraeus and Vance Serchuk, "Can America Trust the Taliban to Prevent Another 9/11? A Dangerous Asymmetry Lies at the Heart of the Afghan Peace Deal," *Foreign Affairs,* April 1, 2020, https://www.foreignaffairs.com/articles/afghanistan/2020-04-01/can-america-trust-taliban-prevent-another-911.

18. Laurel E. Miller and Jonathan S. Blake, *Envisioning a Comprehensive Peace Agreement for Afghanistan* (Santa Monica, Calif.: RAND, 2019); Vanda Felbab-Brown, "After the U.S.-Taliban Deal, What Might Negotiations Between the Taliban and the Afghan Side Look Like?" *Order from Chaos* (blog), February 19, 2020, https://www.brookings.edu/blog/order-from-chaos/2020/02/19/after-the-us-taliban-deal-what-might-negotiations-between-the-taliban-and-afghan-side-look-like; Christopher Kolenda and Michael O'Hanlon, "The New Afghanistan Will Be Built on Ceasefire Solutions and Taliban Tradeoffs," *National Interest,* February 25, 2019, https://nationalinterest.org/feature/new-afghanistan-will-be-built-ceasefire-solutions-and-taliban-tradeoffs-45537.

19. See Madiha Afzal, *Pakistan Under Siege: Extremism, Society, and the State* (Washington, D.C.: Brookings Institution Press, 2018); and Bruce Riedel, *Deadly Embrace: Pakistan, America, and the Future of the Global Jihad* (Washington, D.C.: Brookings Institution Press, 2011).

20. Ambassador James B. Cunningham et al., "Forging an Enduring Partnership with Afghanistan," *National Interest,* September 14, 2016, http://nationalinterest.org/feature/forging-enduring-partnership-afghanistan-17708.

21. Madiha Afzal, "An Inflection Point for Pakistan's Democracy," Brookings Institution, Washington, D.C., February 2020, https://www.brookings.edu/wp-content/uploads/2019/02/FP_20190226_pakistan_afzal.pdf.

22. Joshua T. White, "The Other Nuclear Threat: America Can't Escape Its Role in

the Conflict Between India and Pakistan," *Atlantic*, March 5, 2019, https://www.theatlantic
.com/ideas/archive/2019/03/americas-role-india-pakistan-nuclear-flashpoint/584113;
Madiha Afzal, "Why Is Pakistan's Military Repressing a Huge, Nonviolent Pashtun Protest Movement?" Brookings blog, February 2020, https://www.brookings.edu/blog/order
-from-chaos/2020/02/07/why-is-pakistans-military-repressing-a-huge-nonviolent
-pashtun-protest-movement.

23. I am indebted to Steve Heydeman in particular for help on Syria matters; to
Fred Kagan and colleagues at the American Enterprise Institute's Critical Threats Project
and to Kimberly Kagan and colleagues at the Institute for the Study of War.

24. For an excellent if sad read on the first five years of U.S. policy towards the
Syrian civil war, see Charles Lister, *The Syrian Jihad: Al Qaeda, the Islamic State, and the
Evolution of an Insurgency* (Oxford: Oxford University Press, 2016); see also Will Mc-
Cants, *The ISIS Apocalypse: The History, Strategy, and Doomsday Vision of the Islamic
State* (New York: St. Martin's, 2015).

25. See Michael Land, "Syria Situation Report: February 19–March 3, 2020," Institute for the Study of War, Washington, D.C., March 2020, http://www.understandingwar
.org/backgrounder/syria-situation-report-february-19-march-3-2020; Jennifer Cafarella
et al., "Turkey Commits to Idlib," Institute for the Study of War, Washington, D.C.,
March 18, 2020, http://www.understandingwar.org/backgrounder/turkey-commits-idlib;
and Ranj Alaaldin et al., "A Ten-Degree Shift in Syria Strategy," Brookings Institution,
Washington, D.C., September 2018, https://www.brookings.edu/wp-content/uploads/2018
/09/FP_20180907_syria_strategy.pdf.

26. Michael O'Hanlon and Steven Heydemann, "Syria Is Not a Lost Cause for the
United States—But It Is Getting Close," *The Hill*, February 13, 2020, https://thehill.com
/opinion/international/482942-syria-is-not-a-lost-cause-for-the-us-but-it-is-getting-close.

27. See, e.g., Joseph Felter and Brian Fishman, "Al-Qaida's Foreign Fighters in Iraq:
A First Look at the Sinjar Records," Harmony Center: Combating Terrorism Center at
West Point, December 2007, 19, http://www.ctc.usma.edu/harmony/pdf/CTCForeign
Fighter.19.Dec07.pdf; and Jason H. Campbell and Michael E. O'Hanlon, "Iraq Index,"
Brookings Institution, Washington, D.C., March 31, 2008, 26, https://www.brookings
.edu/wp-content/uploads/2016/07/index20080331.pdf.

28. Frederic Wehrey, *The Burning Shores: Inside the Battle for the New Libya* (New
York: Farrar, Straus and Giroux, 2018).

29. John R. Allen and Others, "Empowered Decentralization: A City-Based Strategy for Rebuilding Libya," Brookings Institution, Washington, D.C., February 2019,
https://www.brookings.edu/research/empowered-decentralization-a-city-based-strategy
-for-rebuilding-libya/; see also Wehrey, *Burning Shores*.

30. On some of the rivalrous dynamics between various foreign leaders and nations involved in the Libyan war, see Gönül Tol, "Is Erdogan Misreading Putin on
Libya?" Middle East Institute, Washington, D.C., March 12, 2020, https://www.mei.edu
/publications/erdogan-misreading-putin-libya.

31. See Hafed al-Ghwell and Karim Mezran, "A Way Forward in Libya," *The Hill*,
June 1, 2019, https://thehill.com/opinion/international/446455-a-way-forward-in-libya.

32. Karim Mezran and Federica Saini Fasanotti, "Another Conference, Another Incomplete Solution for Libya," Atlantic Council blog, November 21, 2019, https://www .atlanticcouncil.org/blogs/menasource/another-conference-another-incomplete -solution-for-libya-2.

33. For a passionate defense of the operation, see Michael Doran, "Trump's Ground Game Against Iran," *New York Times,* January 3, 2020; see also Karim Sadjadpour, "The Sinister Genius of Qassem Soleimani," *Wall Street Journal,* January 10, 2020.

34. Suzanne Maloney, "Iran Knows How to Bide Its Time; Don't Expect Immediate Retaliation for Soleimani," *Washington Post,* January 3, 2020; Sara Allawi and Michael O'Hanlon, "The Relationship Between Iraq and the U.S. Is in Danger of Collapse; That Can't Happen," *USA Today,* March 19, 2020.

35. See Linda Robinson, "Winning the Peace in Iraq: Don't Give Up on Baghdad's Fragile Democracy," *Foreign Affairs* 98, no. 5 (September/October 2019): 162–72; and Allawi and O'Hanlon, "Relationship Between Iraq and the U.S."

36. Kenneth M. Pollack, "Pushing Back on Iran, Part 2: An Overview of the Strategy," American Enterprise Institute blog, February 13, 2018, https://www.aei.org/foreign -and-defense-policy/middle-east/pushing-back-on-iran-part-2-an-overview-of-the -strategy.

37. See Dexter Filkins, "The Twilight of the Iranian Revolution," *New Yorker,* May 25, 2020.

38. See, e.g., Stephen J. Solarz, *Journeys to War and Peace: A Congressional Memoir* (Waltham, Mass.: Brandeis University Press, 2011); Linda L. Fowler, *Watchdogs on the Hill: The Decline of Congressional Oversight of U.S. Foreign Relations* (Princeton, N.J.: Princeton University Press, 2015); Brian Finlay, "John D. Steinbruner, 1941–2015," Stimson Center, Washington, D.C., April 2015, https://www.stimson.org/2015/john-d-steinbruner -1941-2015; Ivo H. Daalder and James M. Lindsay, *The Empty Throne: America's Abdication of Global Leadership* (New York: Public Affairs, 2018), 106–7, 124–29; and Thomas E. Mann and Norman J. Ornstein, *The Broken Branch: How Congress Is Failing America and How to Get It Back on Track* (New York: Oxford University Press, 2006), 220–24.

39. Congress declared war against Great Britain in 1812, against Mexico in 1846, against Spain in 1898, against Germany and Austria-Hungary in 1917, and against Germany, Italy, Japan, Bulgaria, Hungary, and Romania in 1941–42. It authorized the use of force eleven other times, including seven since World War II: in regard to Formosa/ Taiwan (1955), the Middle East (1957), Vietnam through the Gulf of Tonkin Resolution (1964), Lebanon (1983), Iraq (1991), global extremist/terrorist movements (2001), and Iraq again (2002). See Garance Franke-Ruta, "All the Previous Declarations of War," *Atlantic,* August 31, 2013, https://www.theatlantic.com/politics/archive/2013/08/all-the -previous-declarations-of-war/279246; and Jennifer K. Elsea and Matthew C. Reed, "Declarations of War and Authorizations for the Use of Military Force," Congressional Research Service, CRS Report RL31133, April 18, 2014.

40. See, e.g., David J. Barron, *Waging War: The Clash Between Presidents and Congress, 1776 to ISIS* (New York: Simon and Schuster, 2016), 289–427; United States Constitution, Articles I & II, *Avalon Project,* Lillian Goldman Law Library at Yale Law

School, http://avalon.law.yale.edu/18th_century/usconst.asp; Robert Dallek, "Power and the Presidency, From Kennedy to Obama," *Smithsonian Magazine,* January 2011; Jack Goldsmith and Matthew C. Waxman, "The Legal Legacy of Light-Footprint Warfare," *Washington Quarterly,* Summer 2016, 7–21; and Dawn Johnsen, "The Lawyers' War: Counterterrorism from Bush to Obama to Trump," *Foreign Affairs* 96, no. 1 (January/February 2017): 148–55.

41. Jonathan Masters, "U.S. Foreign Policy Powers: Congress and the President," Council on Foreign Relations, March 2017, https://www.cfr.org/backgrounder/us-foreign-policy-powers-congress-and-president; Council on Foreign Relations, "Backgrounder: Balance of U.S. War Powers," New York, 2013, https://www.cfr.org/backgrounder/balance-us-war-powers; Micah Zenko, *Between Threats and War: U.S. Discrete Military Operations in the Post-Cold-War World* (Stanford, Calif.: Stanford University Press, 2010), 163.

42. See, e.g., Amy McGrath, "It's Time to Rethink the Congressional Authorization for Use of Military Force," *USA Today,* January 21, 2020; and Robert Chesney, "A Primer on the Corker-Kaine Draft AUMF," *Lawfare* (blog), April 17, 2018, https://www.lawfareblog.com/primer-corker-kaine-draft-aumf.

43. Michael Beschloss, *Presidents of War: The Epic Story, from 1807 to Modern Times* (New York: Crown, 2018).

44. Richard K. Betts and Matthew C. Waxman, "The President and the Bomb: Reforming the Nuclear Launch Process," *Foreign Affairs* 97, no. 2 (March/April 2018): 119–28.

SEVEN   The Other 4+1

1. Anthony Cilluffo and Neil G. Ruiz, "World's Population Is Projected to Nearly Stop Growing by the End of the Century," Pew Research Center, Washington, D.C., June 17, 2019, https://www.pewresearch.org/fact-tank/2019/06/17/worlds-population-is-projected-to-nearly-stop-growing-by-the-end-of-the-century.

2. See Bryan Walsh, *End Times: A Brief Guide to the End of the World* (New York: Hachette, 2019), 15–85.

3. See Matthew Kroenig, "Pandemics Can Fast Forward the Rise and Fall of Great Powers," *National Interest* (blog), March 23, 2020, https://nationalinterest.org/blog/buzz/pandemics-can-fast-forward-rise-and-fall-great-powers-136417; and Jared Diamond, *Guns, Germs, and Steel: The Fates of Human Societies* (New York: W. W. Norton, 1999).

4. Vanda Felbab-Brown, *The Extinction Market: Wildlife Trafficking and How to Counter It* (Oxford: Oxford University Press, 2017).

5. Erik Frinking et al., "The Increasing Threat of Biological Weapons," Hague Center for Strategic Studies, The Hague, 2016, https://hcss.nl/report/increasing-threat-biological-weapons.

6. See Anthony Lake, *Six Nightmares: Real Threats in a Dangerous World and How America Can Meet Them* (Boston: Little, Brown, 2000), 1–32; and John D. Steinbruner, *Principles of Global Security* (Washington, D.C.: Brookings Institution Press, 2000).

7. Steinbruner, *Principles of Global Security,* 179–93.

8. Karl Rove, "Clinton and Bush Prepared for Pandemics," *Wall Street Journal,* April 8, 2020.

9. John B. Foley, "A Nation Unprepared: Bioterrorism and Pandemic Response," *Interagency Journal* 11, no. 1 (2020): 33–41.

10. See Department of Health and Human Services, "National Strategic Stockpile," Washington, D.C., 2020, https://chemm.nlm.nih.gov/sns.htm#authorize.

11. Bill Gates, "Here's How to Make Up for Lost Time on Covid-19," *Washington Post,* April 1, 2020; Scott Gottlieb and Lauren Silvis, "The Road Back to Normal: More, Better Testing," *Wall Street Journal,* March 29, 2020; Tom Inglesby and Anita Cicero, "How to Confront the Coronavirus at Every Level," *New York Times,* March 2, 2020.

12. Gottlieb and Silvis, "Road Back to Normal."

13. Lena H. Sun, William Wan, and Yasmeen Abutaleb, "A Plan to Defeat Coronavirus Finally Emerges, But It's Not from the White House," *Washington Post,* April 10, 2020.

14. James Ruvalcaba and Joe Plenzler, "As Military Planners, We Strategized for a Pandemic; Here's What We Learned," *Military.com,* April 10, 2020, https://www.military.com/daily-news/2020/04/10/military-planners-we-strategized-pandemic-heres-what-we-learned.html.

15. Gottlieb and Silvis, "Road Back to Normal."

16. See Scott Gottlieb et al., "National Coronavirus Response: A Road Map to Reopening," American Enterprise Institute, Washington, D.C., March 28, 2020, https://www.aei.org/wp-content/uploads/2020/03/National-Coronavirus-Response-a-Road-Map-to-Recovering-2.pdf.

17. Susan Athey et al., "In the Race for a Coronavirus Vaccine, We Must Go Big; Really, Really Big," *New York Times,* May 4, 2020.

18. Elizabeth Warren, "Congress Needs a Plan to Confront the Coronavirus; I Have One," *New York Times,* April 8, 2020; and Scott Gottlieb, "America Needs to Win the Coronavirus Vaccine Race," *Wall Street Journal,* April 26, 2020.

19. Bill Gates, "Here's How to Make Up for Lost Time on Covid-19," *Washington Post,* April 1, 2020.

20. Felbab-Brown, *Extinction Market.*

21. Stewart Patrick, "When the System Fails: Covid-19 and the Costs of Global Dysfunction," *Foreign Affairs* 99, no. 4 (July/August 2020): 50.

22. See Laura Winig, Margaret Bourdeaux, and Juliette Kayyam, "Managing a Security Response to the Ebola Epidemic in Liberia," John F. Kennedy School of Government, Harvard University, Cambridge, Mass., April 1, 2020, https://case.hks.harvard.edu/managing-a-security-response-to-the-ebola-epidemic-in-liberia-a/; and Michael E. O'Hanlon, *The Future of Land Warfare* (Washington, D.C.: Brookings Institution Press, 2015).

23. On this important topic, a timeless study is Dana Priest, *The Mission: Waging War and Keeping Peace with America's Military* (New York: W. W. Norton, 2003). On peace operations and the responsibility to protect, see Stares, *Preventive Engagement,*

223–44; Victoria K. Holt and Tobias C. Berkman, *The Impossible Mandate? Military Preparedness, the Responsibility to Protect and Modern Peace Operations* (Washington, D.C.: Stimson Center, 2006); Gareth Evans, *The Responsibility to Protect: Ending Mass Atrocity Crimes Once and for All* (Washington, D.C.: Brookings Institution Press, 2008); Madeleine K. Albright, William S. Cohen, and the Genocide Prevention Task Force, *Preventing Genocide: A Blueprint for U.S. Policymakers* (Washington, D.C.: Holocaust Memorial Museum, 2008); Jean-Marie Guehenno, *The Fog of Peace: A Memoir of International Peacekeeping in the 21st Century* (Washington, D.C.: Brookings Institution Press, 2015); and Adekeye Adebajo, *U.N. Peacekeeping in Africa: From the Suez Crisis to the Sudan Conflicts* (Boulder, Colo.: Lynne Rienner, 2011). There are also more technical and specific keys to greater success, such as greater attention to building a professional criminal justice system early in any peacemaking effort. See Seth G. Jones et al., *Establishing Law and Order After Conflict* (Santa Monica, Calif.: RAND, 2005), 27–60.

24. Center on International Cooperation, *Annual Review of Global Peace Operations, 2013* (Boulder, Colo.: Lynne Rienner, 2013), 9; United Nations Peacekeeping, "Data," February 2019, https://peacekeeping.un.org/en/data.

25. Stephen John Stedman, "Spoiler Problems in Peace Processes," *International Security* 22, no. 2 (Fall 1997): 5–53.

26. See Bruce Jones, "Testimony: United Nations Peacekeeping and Opportunities for Reform," December 9, 2015, http://www.brookings.edu/research/testimony/2015/12/09-un-peacekeeping-opportunities-jones.

27. Lise Morje Howard, *Power in Peacekeeping* (Cambridge: Cambridge University Press, 2019), 8. See also Michael W. Doyle, "Postbellum Peacebuilding: Law, Justice, and Democratic Peacebuilding," in Chester A. Crocker, Fen Osler Hampson, and Pamela Aall, eds., *Managing Conflict in a World Adrift* (Washington, D.C.: U.S. Institute of Peace, 2015), 535–53.

28. See, e.g., Michael O'Hanlon, "Strengthen Stability in Africa," Brookings Institution, Washington, D.C., January 23, 2014, https://www.brookings.edu/research/strengthen-stability-in-africa.

29. Thomas Burke et al., "Covid-19 and Military Readiness: Preparing for the Long Game," Brookings blog, April 22, 2020, https://www.brookings.edu/blog/order-from-chaos/2020/04/22/covid-19-and-military-readiness-preparing-for-the-long-game.

30. William J. Perry, *My Journey at the Nuclear Brink* (Stanford, Calif.: Stanford University Press, 2015); George P. Shultz et al., "A World Free of Nuclear Weapons," *Wall Street Journal*, January 4, 2007.

31. Walsh, *End Times*, 105–25; Eric Schlosser, *Command and Control: Nuclear Weapons, the Damascus Accident, and the Illusion of Safety* (New York: Penguin, 2013).

32. Kurt M. Campbell, Robert J. Einhorn, and Mitchell B. Reiss, eds., *The Nuclear Tipping Point: Why States Reconsider Their Nuclear Choices* (Washington, D.C.: Brookings Institution Press, 2004).

33. David Albright, *Peddling Peril: How the Secret Nuclear Trade Arms America's Enemies* (New York: Free Press, 2010), 246.

34. Bruce Riedel, *Deadly Embrace: Pakistan, America, and the Future of the Global Jihad* (Washington, D.C.: Brookings Institution Press, 2011).

35. It is not clear to what extent Cold Start is a formal doctrine—but Pakistanis are surely aware of the concept. See Jaganath Sankaran, "The Enduring Power of Bad Ideas: 'Cold Start' and Battlefield Nuclear Weapons in South Asia," *Arms Control Today* 44, no. 9 (November 2014): 16–21.

36. On Pakistani, and Indian, nuclear doctrine, see Daniel Hooey, "Pakistan's Low Yield in the Field: Diligent Deterrence or De-Escalation Debacle?" *Joint Forces Quarterly* 95, no. 4 (2019): 34–45; Gurmeet Kanwal, *Sharpening the Arsenal: India's Evolving Nuclear Deterrence Policy* (New York: HarperCollins, 2017); Mark Fitzpatrick, *Overcoming Pakistan's Nuclear Dangers* (New York: Routledge for IISS, 2014); and Inderjit Panjrath, *Pakistan's Tactical Nuclear Weapons: Giving the Devil More Than His Due* (New Delhi: Vij Books, 2018).

37. Samuel Glasstone, ed., *The Effects of Nuclear Weapons,* rev. ed. (Washington, D.C: United States Atomic Energy Commission, 1962), 40.

38. See Barry R. Posen, *Inadvertent Escalation: Conventional War and Nuclear Risks* (Ithaca, N.Y.: Cornell University Press, 1991); and Bruce G. Blair, *The Logic of Accidental Nuclear War* (Washington, D.C.: Brookings Institution Press, 1993).

39. Ron Suskind, *The One Percent Doctrine* (New York: Simon and Schuster, 2006).

40. On some of these matters, see Michael Levi, *On Nuclear Terrorism* (Cambridge, Mass.: Harvard University Press, 2007). See also George Tenet, *At the Center of the Storm: My Years at the CIA* (New York: HarperCollins, 2007); and Steve Manning, "Loose Nukes: Black Market Sales of Nuclear Weapons and Materials in Russia," Nuclear Threat Initiative, Washington, D.C., 1997, https://www.nti.org/analysis/articles/loose-nukes-black-market-sales-nuclear-weapons-and-material-russia.

41. Steven Pifer and Michael E. O'Hanlon, *The Opportunity: Next Steps in Reducing Nuclear Arms* (Washington, D.C.: Brookings Institution Press, 2012).

42. See the work of Bruce Blair and others in Harold A. Feiveson, ed., *The Nuclear Turning Point: A Blueprint for Deep Cuts and De-Alerting of Nuclear Weapons* (Washington, D.C.: Brookings Institution Press, 1999).

43. Matthew Bunn, Nickolas Roth, and William H. Tobey, "A Vision for Nuclear Security," Belfer Center, Harvard University, Cambridge, Mass., January 2019, https://www.belfercenter.org/sites/default/files/2019-01/NuclearSecurityPolicyBrief_1.pdf.

44. See William C. Potter and Sarah Bidgood, "Lessons for the Future," in William C. Potter and Sarah Bidgood, eds., *Once and Future Partners: The United States, Russia and Nuclear Non-Proliferation* (New York: Routledge for IISS, 2018), 217–43; and Albright, *Peddling Peril*, 1–69, 227–54.

45. Robert R. Holt, "Meeting Einstein's Challenge: New Thinking About Nuclear Weapons," *Bulletin of the Atomic Scientists,* April 3, 2015, https://thebulletin.org/2015/04/meeting-einsteins-challenge-new-thinking-about-nuclear-weapons.

46. Andrew Freedman and Jason Samenow, "The Strongest, Most Dangerous Hurricanes Are Now Far More Likely Because of Climate Change, Study Shows," *Washington Post,* May 18, 2020.

47. Madhuri Karak, "Climate Change and Syria's Civil War," *JSTOR Daily,* September 12, 2019, https://daily.jstor.org/climate-change-and-syrias-civil-war.

48. On the stronger storms in the United States, already roughly 25 to 55 percent more potent than back in the 1950s, see Ellen Gray and Jessica Merzdorf, "Earth's Freshwater Future: Extremes of Flood and Drought," NASA Global Climate Change, Jet Propulsion Laboratory, Pasadena, Calif., June 13, 2019, https://climate.nasa.gov/news/2881/earths-freshwater-future-extremes-of-flood-and-drought. On drought, and the uncertainties associating with measuring and projecting its future course, see Kevin E. Trenberth et al., "Global Warming and Changes in Drought," *Nature Climate Change* 4 (January 2014): 17–22; and J. Lehmann, F. Mempel, and D. Coumou, "Increased Occurrence of Record-Wet and Record-Dry Months Reflect Changes in Mean Rainfall," *Geophysical Research Letters* 45, no. 24 (December 2018), https://doi.org/10.1029/2018GL079439. See also Joshua Busby, "Warming World," *Foreign Affairs* 97, no. 4 (July/August 2018): 70–81.

49. Earth Science Communications Team, "The Effects of Climate Change," NASA Global Climate Change, Jet Propulsion Laboratory, Pasadena, Calif., April 6, 2020, https://climate.nasa.gov/effects.

50. Intergovernmental Panel on Climate Change, "Report 2018," http://report.ipcc.ch/sr15/pdf/sr15_spm_final.pdf; Kevin J. Noone, "Sea-Level Rise," in Kevin J. Noone, Ussif Rashid Sumaila, and Robert J. Diaz, eds., *Managing Ocean Environments in a Changing Climate: Sustainability and Economic Perspectives* (Amsterdam: Elsevier, 2013), 97–126; Charles Geisler and Ben Currens, "Impediments to Inland Resettlement Under Conditions of Accelerated Sea Level Rise," *Land Use Policy* 66 (July 2017): 322–30.

51. Boris Worm, "Avoiding a Global Fisheries Disaster," *Proceedings of the National Academy of Sciences* 113, no. 18 (2016): 4895–97.

52. Katharine J. Mach et al., "Climate as a Risk Factor for Armed Conflict," *Nature* 571 (2019): 193–97.

53. Bill Spindle, "'We Can't Waste a Drop': India Is Running Out of Water," *Wall Street Journal,* August 23, 2019; Rutger Willem Hofste, Paul Reig, and Leah Schleifer, "17 Countries, Home to One-Quarter of the World's Population, Face Extremely High Water Stress," World Resources Institute blog, August 2019, https://www.wri.org/blog/2019/08/17-countries-home-one-quarter-world-population-face-extremely-high-water-stress.

54. See William Antholis and Strobe Talbott, *Fast Forward: Ethics and Politics in the Age of Global Warming* (Washington, D.C.: Brookings Institution Press, 2010); and Pat Mulroy, ed., *The Water Problem: Climate Change and Water Policy in the United States* (Washington, D.C.: Brookings Institution Press, 2017).

55. Daniel Yergin, *The Quest: Energy, Security, and the Remaking of the Modern World* (New York: Penguin, 2011), 711–17; "International Energy Outlook 2018," U.S. Energy Information Administration, Washington, D.C., 2018, https://www.eia.gov/pressroom/presentations/capuano_07242018.pdf.

56. M. Mitchell Waldrop, "The Chips Are Down for Moore's Law," *Nature* 530 (2016): 144–47. See also Rose Hansen, "A Center of Excellence Prepares for Sierra," *Science and Technology Review* (Lawrence Livermore National Laboratory), March 2017, 5–11.

57. Joseph S. Nye Jr., "Deterrence and Dissuasion in Cyberspace," *International Security* 41, no. 3 (Winter 2016/17): 44–71.

58. Nigel Inkster, "Measuring Military Cyber Power," *Survival* 59, no. 4 (August–September 2017): 32; Damien Dodge, "We Need Cyberspace Damage Control," *Proceedings* (U.S. Naval Institute), November 2017, 61–65.

59. David C. Gompert and Martin Libicki, "Cyber War and Nuclear Peace," *Survival* 61, no. 4 (August–September 2019): 45–62.

60. Tunku Varadarajan, "Report from the Cyberwar Front Lines," *Wall Street Journal*, December 29, 2017.

61. Erica D. Borghard and Shawn W. Lonergan, "The Logic of Coercion in Cyberspace," *Security Studies* 26, no. 3 (2017): 452–81; Travis Sharp, "Theorizing Cyber Coercion: The 2014 North Korean Operation against Sony," *Journal of Strategic Studies,* April 11, 2017; David D. Kirkpatrick, "British Cybersecurity Chief Warns of Russian Hacking," *New York Times,* November 14, 2017; Nicole Perlroth, "Hackers Are Targeting Nuclear Facilities, Homeland Security Department and FBI Say," *New York Times,* July 6, 2017.

62. Michael Frankel, James Scouras, and Antonio De Simone, "Assessing the Risk of Catastrophic Cyber Attack: Lessons from the Electromagnetic Pulse Commission" (Laurel, Md.: Johns Hopkins University Applied Physics Laboratory, 2015); Robert McMillan, "Cyber Experts Identify Malware That Could Disrupt U.S. Power Grid," *Wall Street Journal,* June 12, 2017.

63. Defense Science Board, "Task Force on Cyber Deterrence," Department of Defense, Washington, D.C., February 2017.

64. Richard A. Clarke and Robert K. Knake, *The Fifth Domain: Defending Our Country, Our Companies, and Ourselves in the Age of Cyber Threats* (New York: Penguin, 2019), 85–203.

65. Yoshihiro Yamaguchi, "Strengthening Public-Private Partnership in Cyber Defense: A Comparison with the Republic of Estonia," *NIDS Journal of Defense and Security,* no. 20 (December 2019): 67–111.

66. Duncan Brown, "Joint Staff J-7 Sponsored Science, Technology, and Engineering Futures Seminar," (Laurel, Md.: Johns Hopkins University Applied Physics Laboratory, July 2014), 17–24. For a good overview, see Sukeyuki Ichimasa, "Threat of Cascading 'Permanent Blackout' Effects and High Altitude Electromagnetic Pulse (HEMP)," *NIDS Journal of Defense and Security* 17 (December 2016): 3–20.

67. See Charles Murray, *Coming Apart: The State of White America, 1960–2010* (New York: Crown Forum, 2012); and Célia Belin, "Democracy in America 2020: A French Perspective on the Battle for the Democratic Nomination," Brookings blog, February 11, 2020, https://www.brookings.edu/blog/fixgov/2020/02/11/democracy-in-america-2020-a-french-perspective-on-the-battle-for-the-democratic-nomination/.

68. Darrell M. West, *The Future of Work: Robots, AI, and Automation* (Washington, D.C.: Brookings Institution Press, 2018).

69. Robert D. Reischauer, "Budgeting for Tomorrow's Workforce and Economy," in *Today's Children, Tomorrow's America: Six Experts Face the Facts* (Washington, D.C.: Urban Institute, 2011), 7.

70. Gareth Cook, "The Economist Who Would Fix the American Dream," *Atlantic*, August 2019.

71. Michael R. Strain, "The American Dream Is Alive and Well," *New York Times*, May 18, 2020.

72. Anne Case and Angus Deaton, *Deaths of Despair and the Future of Capitalism* (Princeton, N.J.: Princeton University Press, 2020).

73. See J. D. Vance, *Hillbilly Elegy: A Memoir of a Family and Culture in Crisis* (New York: HarperCollins, 2016); and Katherine J. Cramer, *The Politics of Resentment: Rural Consciousness in Wisconsin and the Rise of Scott Walker* (Chicago: University of Chicago Press, 2016).

74. See Joseph E. Stiglitz, *Globalization and Its Discontents* (New York: W. W. Norton, 2002).

75. Mireya Solis, *Dilemmas of a Trading Nation: Japan and the United States in the Evolving Asia-Pacific Order* (Washington, D.C.: Brookings Institution Press, 2017), 11–35.

76. Bill Bradley, *The New American Story* (New York: Random House, 2008).

77. STEM refers, of course, to science, technology, engineering, and math. See James Manyika, William H. McRaven, and Adam Segal, *Innovation and National Security: Keeping Our Edge,* Independent Task Force Report No. 77 (New York: Council on Foreign Relations, 2019); and National Science Board, "Science and Engineering Indicators 2020: The State of U.S. Science and Engineering," National Science Foundation, Alexandria, Va., 2020, 2–5.

78. William G. Gale, *Fiscal Therapy: Curing American's Debt Addiction and Investing in the Future* (Oxford: Oxford University Press, 2019), 116–18, 167–206. For additional thoughtful comments on infrastructure, see John K. Delaney, *The Right Answer: How We Can Unify Our Divided Nation* (New York: Henry Holt, 2018), 24–38.

79. Douglas W. Elmendorf and Louise Sheiner, "Persistently Low Interest Rates Argue for Delayed Budget Belt-Tightening Even in an Aging America," Brookings Institution, Washington, D.C., October 2016, https://www.brookings.edu/research/persistently -low-interest-rates-argue-for-delayed-budget-belt-tightening-even-in-an-aging-america.

80. Maya MacGuineas, "Trump-Xi Trade Talks at G20: America's Biggest Weakness Is No Big Secret," *Fox Business News,* June 25, 2019, https://www.foxbusiness.com /markets/trump-xi-trade-war-summit-g20-us-china.

81. As Ben Bernanke, Tim Geithner, and Hank Paulson put it in 2019, "In short, the U.S. economy and financial system today may be less prone to modest brush fires but more vulnerable to a major inferno if, despite updated and improved fire codes, a conflagration were to begin." See Ben S. Bernanke, Timothy F. Geithner, and Henry M. Paulson Jr., *Firefighting: The Financial Crisis and Its Lessons* (New York: Penguin, 2019).

82. Daniel Egel et al., "Defense Budget Implications of the Covid-19 Pandemic," RAND blog, April 7, 2020, https://www.rand.org/blog/2020/04/defense-budget-impli cations-of-the-covid-19-pandemic.html.

83. Gene Sperling, *The Pro-Growth Progressive: An Economic Strategy for Shared Prosperity* (New York: Simon and Schuster, 2005); Gene Sperling, *Economic Dignity* (New York: Penguin, 2020); Richard V. Reeves, "Realism Trumps Purism: Ideas from Brook-

ings and AEI to Cut Poverty and Promote Opportunity," Brookings blog, December 3, 2015, https://www.brookings.edu/blog/social-mobility-memos/2015/12/03/realism-trumps -purism-ideas-from-brookings-and-aei-to-cut-poverty-and-promote-opportunity. For the original study, see AEI-Brookings Task Force on Poverty and Opportunity, "Opportunity, Responsibility, and Security: A Consensus Plan for Reducing Poverty and Restoring the American Dream," Brookings Institution, Washington, D.C., 2015, https://www .brookings.edu/wp-content/uploads/2016/07/Full-Report.pdf. See also Isabel Sawhill, *The Forgotten Americans: An Economic Agenda for a Divided Nation* (New Haven: Yale University Press, 2018).

84. See Century Foundation Working Group on Community College Financial Resources, *Restoring the American Dream: Providing Community Colleges with the Resources They Need* (New York: Century Foundation Press, 2019).

85. Sperling, *Economic Dignity*, 172–89.

86. Marc M. Howard, "What Serena Williams' Defeat Tells Us About the Criminal Justice System," *Washington Post*, September 11, 2018.

87. Andre M. Perry et al., "To Add Value to Black Communities, We Must Defund the Police and Prison Systems," Brookings blog, June 11, 2020, https://www.brookings .edu/blog/how-we-rise/2020/06/11/to-add-value-to-black-communities-we-must -defund-the-police-and-prison-systems.

88. National Science Board, "Science and Engineering Indicators 2020: The State of U.S. Science and Engineering," National Science Foundation, Alexandria, Va., 2020, 5.

89. See Jeb Bush and Clint Bolick, *Immigration Wars: Forging an American Solution* (New York: Threshold Editions, 2013); and Darrell M. West, *Brain Gain: Rethinking U.S. Immigration Policy* (Washington, D.C.: Brookings Institution Press, 2010), 126–54.

90. This trend was recognized by Alice Rivlin and Gary Burtless at least three decades ago and has, of course, only intensified since then. See Alice Rivlin, *Reviving the American Dream: The Economy, the States, and the Federal Government* (Washington, D.C.: Brookings Institution Press, 1992), 47; Gale, *Fiscal Therapy*, 1–15, 92; and Richard V. Reeves, *Dream Hoarders: How the American Upper Middle Class Is Leaving Everyone Else in the Dust, Why That Is a Problem, and What to Do About It* (Washington, D.C.: Brookings Institution Press, 2017).

91. Reeves, *Dream Hoarders*.

92. John E. Schwarz et al., "Please Talk Wages," *Democracy: A Journal of Ideas*, no. 56 (Spring 2020): 62–72.

EIGHT   The American Armed Forces

1. See "A Conversation with Secretary of Defense Mark T. Esper," Brookings Institution, Washington, D.C., May 4, 2020, https://www.brookings.edu/events/webinar -a-conversation-with-secretary-of-defense-mark-t-esper.

2. See James M. Dubik, *Just War Reconsidered: Strategy, Ethics, and Theory* (Lexington: University of Kentucky Press, 2016), 173–77.

3. See Samuel P. Huntington, *The Soldier and the State: The Theory and Politics of*

Civil-Military Relations (Cambridge, Mass.: Harvard University Press, 1957); Morris Janowitz, *The Professional Soldier: A Social and Political Portrait* (New York: Free Press, 1960); and Samuel E. Finer, *The Man on Horseback: The Role of the Military in Politics* (New Brunswick, N.J.: Transaction, 2002).

4. David Halberstam, *War in a Time of Peace: Bush, Clinton, and the Generals* (New York: Scribner, 2001), 378–86.

5. Michael R. Gordon and Bernard E. Trainor, *Endgame: The Inside Story of the Struggle for Iraq, from George W. Bush to Barack Obama* (New York: Vintage, 2013); Ivo H. Daalder and I. M. Destler, *In the Shadow of the Oval Office: Profiles of the National Security Advisers and the Presidents They Served—From JFK to George W. Bush* (New York: Simon and Schuster, 2011).

6. Vanda Felbab-Brown, *Aspiration and Ambivalence: Strategies and Realities of Counterinsurgency and State-Building in Afghanistan* (Washington, D.C.: Brookings Institution Press, 2012); Martin S. Indyk, Kenneth G. Lieberthal, and Michael E. O'Hanlon, *Bending History: Barack Obama's Foreign Policy* (Washington, D.C.: Brookings Institution Press, 2012).

7. Frederick W. Kagan, "Afghanistan Is Not Vietnam," *Real Clear Defense,* December 20, 2019, https://www.realcleardefense.com/articles/2019/12/20/afghanistan_is_not_vietnam_114942.html.

8. David Brunnstrom and Mike Stone, "U.S. Nuclear General Says Would Resist 'Illegal' Trump Strike Order," *Reuters,* November 18, 2017, https://www.reuters.com/article/us-usa-nuclear-commander/u-s-nuclear-general-says-would-resist-illegal-trump-strike-order-idUSKBN1DI0QV.

9. See "A Conversation with Martin Dempsey," *Foreign Affairs* 95, no. 5 (September/October 2016): 9.

10. PBS News Hour, "Read James Mattis' Full Resignation Letter," *PBS,* December 20, 2018, https://www.pbs.org/newshour/politics/read-james-mattis-full-resignation-letter.

11. Peter Feaver, "We Don't Need Generals to Become Cheerleaders at Political Conventions," *Foreign Policy,* July 29, 2016, https://foreignpolicy.com/2016/07/29/we-dont-need-generals-to-become-cheerleaders-at-political-conventions.

12. Leon E. Panetta et al., "89 Former Defense Officials: The Military Must Never Be Used to Violate Constitutional Rights," *Washington Post,* June 5, 2020.

13. Gordon Lubold and Nancy A. Youssef, "Top General Apologizes for Being at Trump Church Photo Shoot," *Wall Street Journal,* June 11, 2020.

14. See George Packer, *The Assassins' Gate: America in Iraq* (New York: Farrar, Straus and Giroux, 2006); and Kurt M. Campbell and Michael E. O'Hanlon, *Hard Power: The New Politics of National Security* (New York: Basic Books, 2006).

15. On these subjects, see H. R. McMaster, *Dereliction of Duty: Johnson, McNamara, the Joint Chiefs of Staff, and the Lies That Led to Vietnam* (New York: Harper Perennial, 1998); Andrew F. Krepinevich Jr., *The Army and Vietnam* (Baltimore: Johns Hopkins University Press, 1988); Ivo H. Daalder and Michael E. O'Hanlon, *Winning Ugly: NATO's War to Save Kosovo* (Washington, D.C.: Brookings Institution Press, 2000);

Janne E. Nolan, *Guardians of the Arsenal: The Politics of Nuclear Strategy* (New York: Basic Books, 1989); and Francis J. Gavin, *Nuclear Weapons and American Grand Strategy* (Washington, D.C.: Brookings Institution Press, 2020), 52–58, 153–54.

16. Kathy Roth-Douquet and Frank Schaeffer, *AWOL: The Unexcused Absence of America's Upper Classes from Military Service—and How It Hurts Our Country* (New York: HarperCollins, 2006); Jim Mattis and Kori N. Schake, *Warriors and Citizens: American Views of Our Military* (Stanford, Calif.: Hoover Institution Press, 2016).

17. David Barno and Nora Bensahel, "Can the U.S. Military Halt Its Brain Drain?" *Atlantic,* November 5, 2015, http://www.theatlantic.com/politics/archive/2015/11 /us-military-tries-halt-brain-drain/413965; Lori J. Robinson and Michael E. O'Hanlon, "Women Warriors: The Ongoing Story of Integrating and Diversifying the American Armed Forces," Brookings Institution, Washington, D.C., May 2020, https://www .brookings.edu/essay/women-warriors-the-ongoing-story-of-integrating-and -diversifying-the-armed-forces/.

18. Office of Management and Budget, *Historical Tables: Budget of the U.S. Government, Fiscal Year 2009* (Washington, D.C.: GPO, 2008), 137.

19. Taking the budget years 1951–90 as the duration of the Cold War, I used table 6–11 in the Comptroller's "Green Book" cited below to calculate the average (in 2020 dollars) of discretionary and mandatory outlays for the Department of Defense. The result was just under $500 billion ($497 billion, to be precise). Adding in Department of Energy nuclear-weapons costs and a few other small expenses yields the ballpark figure of $525 billion, for overall national defense outlays, defined formally as the 050 account. See Office of Management and Budget, *Historical Tables: Fiscal Year 2020,* https://www .whitehouse.gov/omb/historical-tables, 123–30; and Office of the Under Secretary of Defense (Comptroller), *Defense Budget Estimates for FY 2020* (Washington, D.C., April 2019), 100–160, 250–55, https://comptroller.defense.gov/Portals/45/Documents/defbud get/fy2020/FY20_Green_Book.pdf.

20. George Ingram, "What Every American Should Know About Foreign Aid," Brookings Institution, Washington, D.C., October 2, 2019, https://www.brookings.edu /opinions/what-every-american-should-know-about-u-s-foreign-aid.

21. Statement of Robert F. Hale, Under Secretary of Defense for Financial Management and Comptroller, Brookings Institution, Washington, D.C., January 7, 2013, https://www.c-span.org/video/?c4480536/user-clip-span-video-school.

22. Robert F. Hale, "Promoting Efficiency in the Department of Defense: Keep Trying, But Be Realistic," Center for Strategic and Budgetary Assessments, Washington, D.C., January 2002, https://csbaonline.org/uploads/documents/2002.01.25-DoD-Efficiency.pdf.

23. For a related view, see Kathleen Hicks, "Getting to Less: The Truth About Defense Spending," *Foreign Affairs* 99, no. 2 (March/April 2020): 57–58.

24. Peter Levine, *Defense Management Reform: How to Make the Pentagon Work Better and Cost Less* (Stanford, Calif.: Stanford University Press, 2020), 3–5.

25. See Mac Thornberry and Andrew F. Krepinevich Jr., "Preserving Primacy: A Defense Strategy for the New Administration," *Foreign Affairs* 95, no. 5 (September/ October 2016): 28–32.

26. For a good discussion of this issue, see Michael C. Horowitz et al., "Correspondence," *International Security* 44, no. 2 (Fall 2019): 185–92.

27. On this calculation, see Congressional Budget Office, "The U.S. Military's Force Structure: A Primer," Washington, D.C., July 2016, https://www.cbo.gov/publication/51535; and Michael E. O'Hanlon, *Defense 101* (Ithaca, N.Y.: Cornell University Press, 2021).

28. See, e.g., Michael E. O'Hanlon and James Steinberg, *A Glass Half Full? Rebalance, Reassurance, and Resolve in the U.S.-China Strategic Relationship* (Washington, D.C.: Brookings Institution Press, 2017), 27.

29. See Michael E. O'Hanlon, *The $650 Billion Bargain: The Case for Modest Growth in America's Defense Budget* (Washington, D.C.: Brookings Institution Press, 2016).

30. Webinar with Gen. David Goldfein, Chief of Staff, United States Air Force, Brookings Institution, Washington, D.C., July 1, 2020.

31. Webinar with Gen. Joseph Lengyel, Chief of National Guard Bureau, Brookings Institution, Washington, D.C., July 2, 2020.

32. See Office of the Under Secretary of Defense (Comptroller)/Chief Financial Officer, "Defense Budget Overview: United States Department of Defense Fiscal Year 2021 Budget Request," February 2020, 3–1 through 3–11, https://comptroller.defense.gov /Budget-Materials; Congressional Budget Office, "Trends in Selected Indicators of Military Readiness, 1980 through 1993," Washington, D.C., March 1994, 68–71, https://www .cbo.gov/sites/default/files/103rd-congress-1993-1994/reports/doc13.pdf; O'Hanlon, *$650 Billion Bargain;* An Interview with Secretary of the Army Ryan McCarthy, "The Army's Strategy in the Indo-Pacific," Brookings Institution, Washington, D.C., January 10, 2020, https://www.brookings.edu/wp-content/uploads/2020/01/fp_20200110_army_indo pacific_transcript.pdf; Brendan R. Stickles, "How the U.S. Military Became the Exception to America's Wage Stagnation Problem," Brookings blog, November 29, 2018, https:// www.brookings.edu/blog/order-from-chaos/2018/11/29/how-the-u-s-military-became -the-exception-to-americas-wage-stagnation-problem; Thomas Brading, "Army Retention Hits Goal Five Months Early," *Army News Service,* October 8, 2019, https://www .army.mil/article/223295/army_retention_hits_goal_five_months_early; and Claudia Grisales, "Military Recruitment, Retention Challenges Remain, Service Chiefs Say," *Stars and Stripes,* May 16, 2019.

33. See Gen. David H. Berger, "The Case for Change: Meeting the Principal Challenges Facing the Corps," *Marine Corps Gazette,* June 2020, 8–12.

34. See Matthew N. Metzel et al., "Failed Megacities and the Joint Force," *Joint Forces Quarterly,* no. 96 (2020): 109–14; Michael O'Hanlon and David Petraeus, "America's Awesome Military: And How to Make It Even Better," *Foreign Affairs* 95, no. 5 (September/October 2016): 10–17; and Michael E. O'Hanlon, *The Future of Land Warfare* (Washington, D.C.: Brookings Institution Press, 2015). On the challenges of building a competent stabilization force and conducting a viable stabilization strategy, see Brendan R. Gallagher, *The Day After: Why America Wins the War but Loses the Peace* (Ithaca, N.Y.: Cornell University Press, 2019); David E. Johnson et al., *The U.S. Army and the Battle for Baghdad: Lessons Learned—and Still to Be Learned* (Santa Monica, Calif.: RAND, 2019); Pat Proctor, *Lessons Unlearned: The U.S. Army's Role in Creating the For-*

ever Wars in Afghanistan and Iraq (Columbia: University of Missouri Press, 2020); and David Fitzgerald, *Learning to Forget: U.S. Army Counterinsurgency Doctrine and Practice from Vietnam to Iraq* (Stanford, Calif.: Stanford University Press, 2013).

35. See Michele Flournoy, "How to Prevent a War in Asia," *Foreign Affairs,* June 18, 2020, https://www.foreignaffairs.com/articles/united-states/2020-06-18/how-prevent-war-asia. For a related vivid, insightful, and provocative scenario, see P. W. Singer and August Cole, *Ghost Fleet: A Novel of the Next World War* (Boston: Mariner, 2015).

36. See P. W. Singer, *Wired for War: The Robotics Revolution and Conflict in the 21st Century* (New York: Penguin, 2009).

37. For more on the development of military technology over the past two decades, see Michael O'Hanlon, "A Retrospective on the So-Called Revolution in Military Affairs, 2000–2020," Brookings Institution, Washington, D.C., September 2018, https://www.brookings.edu/research/a-retrospective-on-the-so-called-revolution-in-military-affairs-2000-2020/. For more on likely future developments in military technology over the coming decades, see Michael O'Hanlon, "Forecasting Change in Military Technology, 2020–2040," Brookings Institution, Washington, D.C., September 2018, https://www.brookings.edu/research/forecasting-change-in-military-technology-2020-2040.

38. U.S. Army, "Techniques for Tactical Radio Operations," ATP 6-02.53, January 2016, http://www.apd.army.mil/epubs/DR_pubs/DR_a/pdf/ARN3871_ATP%206-02.53%20FINAL%20WEB.pdf; David Axe, "Failure to Communicate: Inside the Army's Doomed Quest for the 'Perfect' Radio," Center for Public Integrity, Washington, D.C., May 19, 2014, https://publicintegrity.org/national-security/failure-to-communicate-inside-the-armys-doomed-quest-for-the-perfect-radio/; James Hasik, "Avoiding Despair About Military Radio Communications Is the First Step Towards Robust Solutions," *Real Clear Defense,* July 24, 2017, https://www.realcleardefense.com/articles/2017/07/24/avoiding_despair_about_military_radio_communications_is_the_first_step_towards_robust_solutions_111884.html.

39. Briefing at the Army's Maneuver Warfare Center of Excellence, Fort Benning, Ga., December 13, 2017.

40. For a good general overview of this subject and related matters that goes beyond the military sphere, see Darrell M. West, *The Future of Work: Robots, AI, and Automation* (Washington, D.C.: Brookings Institution Press, 2018).

41. Thomas B. Udvare, "Wingman Is the First Step Toward Weaponized Robotics," *Army AT&L,* January–March 2018, 86–89; Hector Montes et al., "Energy Efficiency Hexapod Walking Robot for Humanitarian Demining," *Industrial Robot* 44, no. 4 (2016): 457–66; Robert Wall, "Armies Race to Deploy Drone, Self-Driving Tech on the Battlefield," *Wall Street Journal,* October 29, 2017; Scott Savitz, "Rethink Mine Countermeasures," *Proceedings* (U.S. Naval Institute) 143, no. 7 (July 2017), https://www.usni.org/magazines/proceedings/2017/july/rethink-mine-countermeasures.

42. Matthew Rosenberg and John Markoff, "The Pentagon's 'Terminator Conundrum': Robots That Could Kill on Their Own," *New York Times,* October 25, 2016.

43. Austin Long and Brendan Rittenhouse Green, "Stalking the Secure Second

Strike: Intelligence, Counterforce, and Nuclear Strategy," *Journal of Strategic Studies* 38, nos. 1–2 (2015): 38–73.

44. Paul Scharre, *Army of None: Autonomous Weapons and the Future of War* (New York: W. W. Norton, 2018); Anika Torruella, "USN Seeks to Fill SSN Shortfalls with Unmanned Capabilities," *Jane's Defence Weekly*, July 5, 2017, 11; Scott Savitz et al., *U.S. Navy Employment Options for Unmanned Surface Vehicles* (Santa Monica, Calif.: RAND, 2013), xiv–xxv.

45. Bryan Clark and Bryan McGrath, "A Guide to the Fleet the United States Needs," *War on the Rocks*, February 9, 2017, https://warontherocks.com/2017/02/a-guide -to-the-fleet-the-united-states-needs/.

46. Kris Osborn, "Navy Littoral Combat Ship to Operate Swarms of Attack Drone Ships," *Warrior Maven*, March 28, 2018, https://defensemaven.io/warriormaven/sea/navy -littoral-combat-ship-to-operate-swarms-of-attack-drone-ships-cSVfXZfBME2bm1 dTX1tsIw.

47. Shawn Brimley, "While We Can: Arresting the Erosion of America's Military Edge," Center for a New American Security, Washington, D.C., December 17, 2015, https://www.cnas.org/publications/reports/while-we-can-arresting-the-erosion -of-americas-military-edge.

48. T. X. Hammes, "The Future of Conflict," in R. D. Hooker Jr., ed., *Charting a Course: Strategic Choices for a New Administration* (Washington, D.C.: National Defense University Press, 2016), 25–27.

49. Rosenberg and Markoff, "Pentagon's 'Terminator Conundrum.'"

50. Patrick Tucker, "Russia to the United Nations: Don't Try to Stop Us from Building Killer Robots," *Defense One*, November 21, 2017, https://www.defenseone.com /technology/2017/11/russia-united-nations-dont-try-stop-us-building-killer-robots /142734/; "Special Report: The Future of War," *Economist*, January 27, 2018, 4.

51. Elsa B. Kania, "Battlefield Singularity: Artificial Intelligence, Military Revolu- tion, and China's Future Military Power," Center for a New American Security, Wash- ington, D.C., November 28, 2017, https://www.cnas.org/publications/reports/battlefield -singularity-artificial-intelligence-military-revolution-and-chinas-future-military-power.

52. See Permanent Court of Arbitration, "Press Release: The South China Sea Arbitration (The Republic of the Philippines v. the People's Republic of China)," The Hague, July 12, 2016, https://docs.pca-cpa.org/2016/07/PH-CN-20160712-Press-Release -No-11-English.pdf.

53. See Steven Pifer, "Don't Resume Nuclear Testing," Brookings blog, May 28, 2020, https://www.brookings.edu/blog/order-from-chaos/2020/05/28/dont-resume-nuclear -testing.

54. See Preparatory Commission of the Comprehensive Nuclear Test Ban Treaty, "Status of Signature and Ratification," Vienna, 2020, https://www.ctbto.org/the-treaty /status-of-signature-and-ratification; Lawrence Scheinman, "Comprehensive Test Ban Treaty," Nuclear Threat Initiative, Washington, D.C., April 2003, https://www.nti.org /analysis/articles/comprehensive-test-ban-treaty; Steve Fetter, *Toward a Comprehensive*

Test Ban (Pensacola, Fla.: Ballinger, 1988); and Michael A. Levi and Michael E. O'Hanlon, *The Future of Arms Control* (Washington, D.C.: Brookings Institution Press, 2004).

55. See, e.g., Robert Einhorn et al., "Experts Assess the Nuclear Non-Proliferation Treaty, 50 Years After It Went into Effect," Brookings blog, March 3, 2020, https://www .brookings.edu/blog/order-from-chaos/2020/03/03/experts-assess-the-nuclear-non -proliferation-treaty-50-years-after-it-went-into-effect.

56. See, e.g., David C. Gompert and Martin Libicki, "Cyber War and Nuclear Peace," *Survival* 61, no. 4 (August–September 2019): 45–62; Steven Pifer, "Don't Let New START Die," Brookings blog, February 6, 2020, https://www.brookings.edu/blog/order -from-chaos/2020/02/06/dont-let-new-start-die; Ernest J. Moniz and Sam Nunn, "The Return of Doomsday: The New Nuclear Arms Race—and How Washington and Moscow Can Stop It," *Foreign Affairs* 98, no. 5 (September/October 2019): 150–61; Frank A. Rose, "Deterrence, Modernization, and Alliance Cohesion: The Case for Extending New START with Russia," Brookings blog, January 16, 2020, https://www.brookings.edu/blog /order-from-chaos/2020/01/16/deterrence-modernization-and-alliance-cohesion-the -case-for-extending-new-start-with-russia; Michael Krepon, "Space Diplomacy," Stimson Center, Washington, D.C., February 25, 2020, https://www.armscontrolwonk.com /archive/1208971/space-diplomacy-2; and Frank A. Rose, "Safeguarding the Heavens: The United States and The Future of Norms of Behavior in Outer Space," Brookings Policy Brief, June 2018, https://www.brookings.edu/wp-content/uploads/2018/06/FP _20180614_safeguarding_the_heavens.pdf.

57. Christian Brose, *The Kill Chain: Defending America in the Future of High-Tech Warfare* (New York: Hachette, 2020), 232.

58. Brose, *Kill Chain,* 235; Hicks, "Getting to Less."

Conclusion

1. Francis Fukuyama, "The End of History?" *National Interest,* Summer 1989, 18.

2. Stephen Biddle, *Military Power: Explaining Victory and Defeat in Modern Battle* (Princeton, N.J.: Princeton University Press, 2004).

3. See Steve Radelet, "Once More Into the Breach: Does Foreign Aid Work?" Brookings blog, May 2017, https://www.brookings.edu/blog/future-development/2017 /05/08/once-more-into-the-breach-does-foreign-aid-work; and George Ingram, "Adjusting Assistance to the 21st Century: A Revised Agenda for Foreign Assistance Reform," Working Paper 75, Global Economy and Development Program, Brookings Institution, Washington, D.C., July 2014, https://www.brookings.edu/wp-content/uploads/2016/06 /Ingram-Aid-Reform-Final2.pdf.

4. Richard N. Haass, *Foreign Policy Begins at Home: The Case for Putting America's House in Order* (New York: Basic Books, 2013).

5. See Alastair Iain Johnston, "China in a World of Orders: Rethinking Compliance and Challenge in Beijing's International Relations," *International Security* 44, no. 2 (Fall 2019): 57.

6. See Jonathan Stromseth, "Beyond Binary Choices? Navigating Great Power

Competition in Southeast Asia," Brookings Report, Brookings Institution, Washington, D.C., April 2020, https://www.brookings.edu/research/beyond-binary-choices-navigating -great-power-competition-in-southeast-asia.

7. Condoleeza Rice, *Democracy: Stories from the Long Road to Freedom* (New York: Twelve, 2017).

8. Justin Vaisse, *Neoconservatism: The Biography of a Movement* (Cambridge, Mass.: Harvard University Press, 2010), 239–51; Walter Russell Mead, "The Jacksonian Tradition and American Foreign Policy," *National Interest,* no. 58 (Winter 1999/2000): 5–29; Walter Russell Mead, "The Jacksonian Revolt: American Populism and the Liberal Order," *Foreign Affairs* 96, no. 2 (January/February 2017): 2–7.

9. See Joshua Muravchik, *Exporting Democracy: Fulfilling America's Destiny* (Washington, D.C.: AEI Press, 1992), 117–18; and Stephen D. Krasner, "Learning to Live with Despots: The Limits of Democracy Promotion," *Foreign Affairs* 99, no. 2 (March/April 2020): 49–55.

Index

nonlethal weapons, 106
North Atlantic Council, 63
North Korea (Democratic People's
  Republic of Korea), xix, 7, 9, 19, 31,
  40–43, 49, 54, 111–33, 170
Norway, 29
nuclear arms control, 172
nuclear deterrence, 21, 171
nuclear escalation, 21, 101–2, 171
Nuclear Non-Proliferation Treaty (NPT),
  114, 154, 172, 204
nuclear proliferation, 2, 169–73
Nuclear Suppliers' Group, 172
nuclear taboo, 170
Nunn, Sam, 74, 155, 169, 172

Obama, Barack, 18, 41–42, 73, 100, 137,
  140, 141, 144, 146, 191
Obama doctrine, 41–42
offshore balancing, 37–38, 40
Okinawa, 34, 101
Oman, 140
opcon (operational control) transfer,
  Korea, 122
Operation Atlantic Resolve, 68–69
Operation Desert Storm, xiii–xv, 137
Operation Iraqi Freedom, 118
Osan Air Base, Korea, 132
Osnos, Evan, 83
Other Transaction Authority (OTA), 206
Outer Space Treaty, 204

Pak, Jung, 113, 154
Pakistan, 4, 7, 53, 109, 143–45, 170, 171, 175
Palestinians, 136
Panama Papers, 64
pandemic disease, 163–69
Peace Research Institute, Oslo, 8
Pence, Mike, 73
Permanent Court of Arbitration, 88, 204
Permanent Structured Cooperation
  (PESCO), EU, 61
Perry, Bill, 74, 117, 169

Pershing rule, 124
Persian Gulf, 106
Petraeus, David, 134, 137, 141, 190, 201
Pew Charitable Trusts, polls of, 34, 87
"phase 4," in U.S. military operations, xv
Philippines, 6, 29, 88, 107, 129, 155
Pifer, Steven, 75, 76
Pinker, Steven, xvii, xviii, 2
"pivot," 88
Poland, 40, 74, 76
Pollack, Kenneth, xvi, 134
Polyakova, Alina, 80
Pompeo, Mike, 102, 147, 153
population, global, 161
Posen, Barry, 25, 38–39, 50
Powell, Colin, 43, 190
Powell doctrine, 43
Press, Daryl, 46
primacy, U.S. 28
procurement policy, U.S. DoD, 205–7
Putin, Vladimir, 33, 49, 51, 62, 63–66,
  72–79, 155

Qaddafi, Muammar, 113, 125, 149
Quds force, Iranian, 150–52

Ramadi, Iraq, 134
RAND Corporation, 68, 202
rare Earth metals, 29, 94–95
Ratner, Ely, 97–98
Rawalpindi, 170, 171
readiness, U.S. military, 199–200
Reagan, Ronald, 18
reassurance of allies, 34
"rebalance," by U.S. to Asia-Pacific, 88
red line, Obama in Syria in 2013, 46
Reed, Jack, 80
Reeves, Richard, 184, 186
refugees, 147
Reischauer, Robert, xiii, 182
resilience, economic and strategic, 72
"resolute restraint," xii, xviii, 22–25, 32–38
restraint versus retrenchment, 38–39